PENGUIN BOOKS

WHY EMPATHY MATTERS

J. D. Trout is professor of philosophy and psychology at Loyola University in Chicago. His research has been featured in the The New York Times, The Wall Street Journal, and The Globe and Mail (Toronto). He has written for the Chicago Tribune and Psychology Today, and held fellowships from the National Science Foundation, Mellon Foundation, and National Endowment for the Humanities. His previous books include Epistemology and the Psychology of Human Judgment, Measuring the Intentional World, and The Theory of Knowledge. He lives in Evanston, Illinois, with his wife and two children.

Praise for *Why Empathy Matters*

"*Why Empathy Matters* is an important and engaging book, and Trout's ideas are eye-opening and fascinating. Trout explains a large set of new ideas about human rationality, emotion and well-being, and connects them to pressing social and political issues. This is an invaluable enrichment of public discourse, which could lead to new ways of framing our current dilemmas and to new solutions to them."
    —Steven Pinker, author of *The Blank Slate* and *The Stuff of Thought*

"Trout engagingly identifies the issues facing citizens who worry about others exploiting their natural imperfections as decision makers, but also worry about relying on paternalistic institutions to protect them. Recognizing that those institutions are similarly flawed, Trout calls for information sharing, public deliberation, and empirical evaluation of interventions."
    —Baruch Fischhoff, Howard Heinz University Professor, Social and Decision Sciences, Carnegie Mellon University, and past president of the Society for Judgment and Decision Making

"J. D. Trout's *Why Empathy Matters* provides insightful answers to explain how good people can look the other way and do so little to respond to massive problems affecting other human beings. He uses the latest findings in behavioral decision research, with his practical understanding of philosophy, to outline a better world. We would all be better off if the new administration in Washington read and understood the messages that are outlined in this. In fact, Trout's *Why Empathy Matters* explains so much of what has gone wrong for the last eight years. This work has the power to transform how we think about and act on challenges to improve society."
    —Max H. Bazerman, Straus Professor, Harvard Business School, and coauthor of *Negotiation Genius*

"In this dramatic challenge to cherished American concepts like individualism, free will and laissez-faire economics, Trout (*Epistemology and the Psychology of Human Judgment*) presents 'an alternative story grounded not in the abstractions of political theory or economics, but in the moisture and grit of human psychology.'"   —*Publishers Weekly*

Why
EMPATHY MATTERS

The Science and Psychology
of Better Judgment

J. D. TROUT

PENGUIN BOOKS

Previously published as *The Empathy Gap*

PENGUIN BOOKS

Published by the Penguin Group
Penguin Group (USA) Inc., 375 Hudson Street, New York, New York 10014, U.S.A.
Penguin Group (Canada), 90 Eglinton Avenue East, Suite 700, Toronto,
Ontario, Canada M4P 2Y3 (a division of Pearson Penguin Canada Inc.)
Penguin Books Ltd, 80 Strand, London WC2R 0RL, England
Penguin Ireland, 25 St Stephen's Green, Dublin 2, Ireland (a division of Penguin Books Ltd)
Penguin Group (Australia), 250 Camberwell Road, Camberwell,
Victoria 3124, Australia (a division of Pearson Australia Group Pty Ltd)
Penguin Books India Pvt Ltd, 11 Community Centre, Panchsheel Park, New Delhi – 110 017, India
Penguin Group (NZ), 67 Apollo Drive, Rosedale, North Shore 0632,
New Zealand (a division of Pearson New Zealand Ltd)
Penguin Books (South Africa) (Pty) Ltd, 24 Sturdee Avenue,
Rosebank, Johannesburg 2196, South Africa

Penguin Books Ltd, Registered Offices:
80 Strand, London WC2R 0RL, England

First published in the United States of America as *The Empathy Gap* by Viking Penguin,
a member of Penguin Group (USA) Inc. 2009
Published in Penguin Books 2010

1   3   5   7   9   10   8   6   4   2

THE LIBRARY OF CONGRESS HAS CATALOGED THE HARDCOVER EDITION AS FOLLOWS:
Trout, J. D.
The empathy gap : building bridges to the good life and the good society / J. D. Trout.
p. cm.
Includes bibliographical references and index.
ISBN 978-0-670-02044-7 (hc.)
ISBN 978-0-14-311661-5 (pbk.)
1. Social psychology.   2. Interpersonal relations.   3. Empathy.
4. Helping behavior—Social aspects.   I. Title.
HM1033.T77 2009
303.3'72—dc22   2008029333

Printed in the United States of America
Set in Berkeley Oldstyle Std • Designed by Sabrina Bowers

For Janice

Contents

Why
EMPATHY MATTERS

Introduction

Decency to Spare

S THE UNITED STATES OPENED THE WAR IN IRAQ IN 2003, another kind of news was spreading on the homefront: Military families across the United States were the uncomfortable neighbors of payday loan establishments. The high-interest, short-term loans offered by these lenders are designed to cover expenses till payday when the paycheck comes up short. The typical payday borrower eventually hands over $793 for a $325 loan.[1] Many lower-income families, who sacrifice 10 to 15 percent of their paychecks each month to paying off payday loans,[2] represent a consumer base trapped in a cycle of debt. With no place else to go for money or affordable housing, the military families stationed at places such as Camp Pendleton (whose zip code has more payday lenders than any other in California)[3] and Point Loma were by 2005 growing more dependent on, and dismayed by, these fast-cash storefronts clustering near military bases.

When we hear about such alarming and regrettable imbalances of opportunity, our tendency is to fight to a stalemate. We try to stop the offense, even if we cannot achieve a durable remedy. Americans appreciate the need sometimes to be protected from our own temptations and vulnerabilities, and yet we cherish the very freedom that allows a good to lure us to our ruin. The mythic American vision of self-determination might maintain that with better budgeting, and more careful shopping habits, some people could avoid payday loans. This is not to say that payday loans are never a good option. Taking out a payday loan may be a good decision only because all the other choices you might consider to relieve your financial duress, such as foreclosure, theft, or prostitution, are worse. After all, *good* is a relative term. Some good decisions are just the best among an undesirable lot, the consequence of making the most out of what we have. But when we face them, such choices are not free; they are forced. They may be rational, but they sure aren't voluntary. We might ask why the world's most affluent society forces its citizens—and especially its soldiers in uniform—to make such choices. A decent society avoids doing so.

These are demographic facts, but there are real people behind them. Payday loan scandals are a microcosm of failed policy wrapped around unconscious bias. Each example represents millions of personal tragedies. Bank lending regulations ensnare consumers who, stoked by desperation, borrow overconfidently and recklessly, and in doing so, irrationally discount their futures. Payday loans may even cause personal bankruptcy.[4] This should not be especially surprising. Predatory payday lending now costs American families $4.2 billion per year in excessive fees, and states that ban this form of lending save their citizens an estimated $1.4 billion in such fees every year.[5] But more can be done to free borrowers originally driven by poor options. After all, credit industry regulations allow payday loans to impose punishing rates without allowing people a way out of poor credit status. Paying off a payday loan cannot improve one's credit rating,[6] steering payday debtors inevitably toward further dead-end credit vehicles. The question remains whether those who rely on these loans can find suitable substitutes for meeting their monthly needs.

Overconfidence, and the tendency to discount the future, are far more likely to destroy fundamental hopes and prospects if a person is poor. But these cognitive frailties are not just a poor person's hubris. Wealthy investors, too, are dramatically overconfident in their beliefs that their intuition is reliable and their judgment correct. Indeed, the extent of the 2007–2008 subprime mortgage crisis owed much to the overconfidence of professionals. It was a punishing gamble.

Like a veteran gambler, every savvy investor has a system. Anyone who plays the market is sure that he possesses some unique insight that puts him out in front of the other guy. But just as a gambler always loses to the house in the long run, an overconfident investor will eventually get burned. Clever investors and fund managers characteristically pride themselves on anticipating the slightest uptick or downturn in their stocks, and in their ability to time their trades precisely. Ironically, the cleverer they think they are—the more actively they buy and sell—the more likely they are to lose. Data consistently show that overmanagement of one's stocks, with frequent and aggressive trading, will result directly in diminished returns. Conversely, a bundle of thoughtfully chosen stocks left untouched for a period of years—in an index fund, say—will steadily increase in value as the market's overall value increases.

Short-term, overconfident thinking causes the average family to lose roughly a quarter of a million dollars over a lifetime.[7] Why do so many millions of people continue to insist on trying to outsmart the markets? Quite simply because they believe they can, and they believe so in the face of overwhelming—albeit counterintuitive—evidence to the contrary.

A normal reaction to hearing about these all-too-human foibles—simple investment overconfidence and seduction by payday loans—is empathy. People's wills are powerless in the grip of overconfidence or in the face of desperation. We can hardly blame military families for choosing as best they can from a slate of terrible options. The natural thing to do is empathize with them, to feel their desperation and understand their position. And knowing that the world changes in ways that are harmful and surprising, an effective empathy must be vigilant; it must survey the social landscape for similar cases in which the market, together with existing laws, could crush the prospects of citizens burdened by their own decency, honor, or helplessness. In fact, at the first signs that military families were special targets of payday lenders, moral outrage animated the public outcry. Only empathy can explain this. Referring to the payday loan industry as "an open sore," one of the primary sponsors of the 2002 law that had made Virginia a payday-lending state eventually confessed, "I'm embarrassed I was ever affiliated with it at all."[8]

Because most American citizens treat military service as a cherished value, this publicity shamed government officials into reversing the permissive regulations offered to payday lenders in earlier legislation.[9] But it soon became clear that other victims of predatory lending were not so different from military families—for example, single mothers abandoned by their spouses but too noble to neglect their children, or middle-class families bravely trying to ride out periods of job loss and career change in a volatile employment atmosphere. Predatory lending affects all of these groups. Even in states where military bases don't predominate, the number of payday lending stores has grown rapidly. In Ohio, payday lending stores in the state have increased in number from 107 in 1996 to more than 1,500 in 2007. According to the Ohio Coalition for Responsible Lending, Ohio now has more payday lending stores than McDonald's, Burger King, and Wendy's restaurants combined.[10] The next step, now being taken, will protect middle-class people with uncertain credit from subprime credit card merchants.[11]

There are worse things in life than making poor decisions—such as living in a society where there are no good options. Fortunately, that's not our problem in the United States. Our problem is that the genuinely good options aren't available to everybody. People don't choose to ignore their health or to embrace predatory lending rates. The idea that people can choose what they want is an oversimplification, and a dangerous one. And when we choose poorly, these failures do not have a pure pedigree. They are part individual irrationality, part unconscious influence, and part lousy choices. Risks that appear to result from personal choice often have a political origin. Errors in reasoning at the individual level usually have a social or political component. A family living in a deteriorating public school district may pay for a private substitute, forcing them to run up credit debt on other expenses. This may be a choice of some sort, but not a happy or a frivolous one. Or consider the government's recent "war on obesity." Private and government media campaigns urge individuals to "eat well and exercise." But this makes obesity sound as if it is mainly a matter of self-control, an impression that is misleading. Those most prone to obesity live in neighborhoods where the public parks are unsafe and healthy food is not easily accessible.[12] These don't sound like exercise and diet *choices* that people make; they sound more like bad options that political decisions impose. As a result, it is no mystery why this book opts for a vocabulary of science over the rhetoric of personal responsibility.[13] It is just too easy to make people look personally responsible for bad outcomes when, in fact, all of their realistic options were bad ones. We are not alone in our choices, or unshaped by the opinions of others or the shortcomings of human judgment.

A cardinal value of American individualism holds individual freedom of choice and self-determination dear. But not at any cost. We also revere and demand an informed citizenry, as an acknowledged bulwark of democracy, and at least some decisions—about medications, risky medical procedures, and "guaranteed" investment returns, for example—are not ours to make. As good citizens, perhaps we have by now learned to put sufficient trust in science, and have finally begun to let go of those choices science tells us are based on unreliable intuition. In doing so, we can safely forego options in the short term to achieve greater and more far-reaching freedom and opportunity for ourselves later.

It isn't inevitable that our affluent democracy will improve. Its gains will depend on our ability to identify the risk and suffering of its citizens. Evolution has left us with two interacting systems—emotional and rational. Our emotional reactions to human suffering are momentary and provincial; they prize our selves, our kin, and our tribe. That is where empathy operates. Our rationality is deliberate and carries out long-term calculation and estimation. A successful response to human need will require both.[14]

Empathy often goes off the rails, leading people to value the suffering of others beyond all proportion, in turn prompting them to misdirect resources to causes they might not support in the harsh light of day. There was a tremendous and dramatic outpouring of sympathy following the death of Princess Diana—one person. Whether you pick a prioritizing standard based on number or severity, a surprising amount of attention is lavished on beached whales and puppies stuck in drainpipes. Empathy without reason is blind.

Indeed, we shouldn't expect too much intelligence from empathy. The pool of suffering is too deep to plumb using simple intuition. This pool contains everything from sick, uninsured children to wealthy but lonely retirees, healthy jobless adults in need of training for a new economy to youthful public servants unable to repay college debts. Better military pay is needed, and so are evening community sports programs, to keep teenagers out of jail. Which urgent need gets top billing? A long-term educational program that will improve the learning of millions of children in the United States, or an antimalarial program that will save hundreds of thousands of young lives in a country far away? This is no easy call. Empathy is inefficient, and it can also be fickle. We can see its unsystematic nature in our past acts. Americans felt terrible for the victims of the Indonesian tsunami in December 2004, and gave liberally to that cause. But we largely ignored the Kashmir earthquake that occurred just months later, despite very significant destruction and loss of life there.

Empathy is central to our humanity.[15] But rather than elevating empathy, public dialogue has marginalized it, giving way to authoritative and sober pronouncements that we can't help everyone. But the truth is, government efforts have flagged. No doubt, closing the empathy gap is a difficult task. We must balance the forces of emotion and rationality. And in order to do that, we have to know a lot about how both operate. But thanks to progress in psychology, behavioral economics, and neuroscience, we now have much of that knowledge. Together with empathy, our system of rational and deliberate thought can now extend our moral concern to people further from our private lives, but equally deserving.[16] This would constitute moral progress, if only we could find our place in this network, and trace our connections to the others who experience joy and suffering.

Serious social proposals for pursuing the good life and the good society are complex, and require the mastery of findings in several distinct fields, drawing on psychology, economics, neuroscience, and politics. Many of those findings pertain to the difference between happiness and mere contentment; to the role of money, freedom, and fortune in a good life; and to the importance of truth and intellectual virtue—and these new findings punctuate a long philosophical tradition. But philosophical analysis is often short on advice. It ignores the counterintuitive findings of psychological research demonstrating that we can't spontaneously control our biases. This neglect leaves us powerless to answer a practical question: How can we defeat cognitive and empathic biases if they are unconscious and automatic—if experience and nature have seated them deeply in our brains? Overconfident investment behavior, for example, appears to feed a reward cycle in the brain that explains at once the addictiveness of day trading, the tendency to chase top-performing stocks and funds, and the impulse to overtrade—all financially destructive investment habits.[17]

Even when we have the willpower, humans fall far short of rational decision making. But our shortcomings haven't always been apparent. Many of the Enlightenment philosophers rhapsodized about the boundless nature of human reason. Condorcet, the great French polymath, personifies this hopeful attitude: "[N]o bounds have been fixed to the improvement of the human faculties; that the perfectibility of man is absolutely indefinite. . . ."[18] Sadly, the Enlightenment philosophes were wrong. We do not have unlimited mental powers, let alone time and stamina. Worse yet, evolution left us with cognitive and emotional limitations that have conspired to sabotage our policy efforts. Fortunately, new research on judgment and decision-making helps reveal the unconscious biases in the human mind that often corrupt logical decision making, with profound ramifications for individual happiness and social stability.

If well-being were just a matter of having basic needs such as food, shelter, and clothing, the state could provide these things and be done with it. But Americans treasure the ideal of "making it on our own." It is a centerpiece of classical economics that people's choices reflect their desires, but this is more a matter of definition than of discovery. Economists tell us that people naturally choose the option that promotes their well-being, but that is pretty hard to prove by the decisions they actually make.

Like most ideals, this one crumbles when we see how real people handle genuine obstacles and opportunities in their lives. Despite its affluence and its large class of pending retirees, the United States has a net savings rate of about zero. And though fiscal responsibility is within the means of many, the majority of American households carry credit card debt, and the median amount exceeds two thousand dollars.[19] Americans must be very confident that they can pay off their debt, and incredibly relaxed about not saving for the future. And while half of U.S. households do not own any stocks,[20] the average U.S. citizen lost about $303 gambling in 2006—totaling about $91 billion.[21] Many employees don't pay the maximum into their retirement accounts, despite company offers to match employee contributions, thus walking away from free money. Some families don't participate in retirement plans at all, because they can't. For those who can, their money is often allocated recklessly into their own employer's stocks or unproductively into fixed-income vehicles with relatively poor long-term returns.

We discount our future physical health just as we do our financial health. Worldwide, obesity rates are high and rising rapidly, and along with them, levels of diabetes and other diseases. People with, or at risk for, life-threatening health conditions often fail to take the most rudimentary steps to protect themselves. In fact, over

40 percent of early deaths in the United States are related to people's behavior.[22]

Controlling these ruinous behaviors does tend to make us happier. But this is not a book of advice about how to lead a happier life. There is a self-help book and therapy industry for people eager to goose their individual happiness. Instead, this book is about how we can use tools forged by cognitive psychologists to design personal decision strategies and social policies aimed at making our lives better. What makes life better, of course, depends on where you start. If you don't have enough to eat, food will make your life immediately better than antidiscrimination laws. But if you are already near the top of the curve, your priorities may be different.

This book is guided by a vision of a society that treats everyone decently—with fairness and respect. It doesn't attempt a grand theory of justice or the good life. There is a place and time for abstract theories, but they would take us too far away from people as we find them. This book looks at people in their concrete and natural habitat. In our many environments, we humans are not the economist's perfectly rational actors, the philosopher's loners in the state of nature, or anonymous citizens behind a veil of ignorance. Instead, we are the cognitive psychologist's earthly decision makers, at once flawed, adaptable, bounded, and clever.

The science in this book is thoroughly modern, but the book's philosophical core is centuries old, inspired by the theory of natural sentiments found in Enlightenment thinkers such as David Hume and Adam Smith. Their vision looks soberly at the vulnerability of real humans, and views with awe our resilience and talents. Our best motivations don't result from an elaborate logical architecture of first principles or abstract theories of justice, but from a natural sense of our common humanity. Normal people care about their neighbors, about fair treatment and good options. This book details the psychological capabilities of ordinary people and their basic needs under normal stresses. As part of this quest, it seeks to uncover the standards for a decent life. But more than that, this book proposes a role for government that expands our effective capabilities, government in the service of human autonomy. We may disagree at the margins about what capabilities to value, but we can focus on those capabilities most everyone urges are good: literacy, health, financial security, education, art, and political engagement.

The big ideas of the book come from philosophy and the science of judgment and decision making. The weakness of our empathy and the strength of our cognitive biases is an accursed combination that makes us poor pursuers of our own happiness and even poorer custodians of the happiness of others. But by listening to this research, we can extend our judgment and empathy by using outside strategies. The result will be that we understand more about the nature of human well-being, and that this knowledge can be used to improve the lives of Americans. Though the needs of poor people are most urgent, the ideas in this book cut through demographics to an increasingly insecure middle class. The American middle class is suffering a new kind of volatility, and this leaves them open to financial shocks like never before. About half of the people without health insurance are above the poverty level, often well above it. Poor people are eligible for Medicaid, but many middle-class breadwinners work for companies that do not finance health care for their employees, and have incomes too low to cover private insurance.[23] Middle-class people cannot hope to make enviable choices under these conditions; all of the options are bad.

As a resource that is both an intrinsic good and an instrument for upward mobility, education is vital. But the cost of college has allowed only the most moneyed students to exercise their capabilities. A 1992 data set is still widely cited as a snapshot of unmet educational needs.[24] Of the students qualified to go to college, 84 percent from the highest quartile of socioeconomic status (SES) actually go, whereas only 45 percent of the lowest quartile do. The number of permanently disadvantaged kids is large; 140,606 low SES students who qualified for college didn't attend, and 193,038 low SES students did not attend a four-year college.[25] For most Americans, the costs of higher education impose severe constraints on their hopes

and capabilities. Eventually, some low SES students, though qualified for college, abandon the dream altogether. And when we don't
have any control over the grim quality of our options, we learn to
like what we have.

For middle-class people, their children's education will often
come at the expense of the parents' retirement, crippling student
loans for the child, or credit card debt. The strain of financial insecurity for the middle class continues. Since 2000, individual health
care premiums have increased by over 80.0 percent, and the cost of
family health care has skyrocketed 80.8 percent. Premiums are rising
twice as fast as wages and inflation. As a result, the typical family
health insurance premium in 2006 was $11,480 a year, compared
with $6,348 in 2000.[26]

Americans tolerate enormous economic disparities, but there are
limits. Fairness, justice, and equal opportunity are values sunk deep
in the belly of Americans, and this cluster of values is disturbed when
the disparities are too glaring. The United States is not a country of
modest economic and social imbalances, where impoverished people
languish beside a remainder of the population only slightly above
the poverty level. The inequalities in the United States are vast and
often meritless. A good and empathic society can tolerate common
and moderate inequalities, but such a society is incompatible with
enormous differences in well-being that are, from the perspective of
desert, arbitrary.

Compare the annual pay of the average CEO to that of the average factory worker. In the United States, this ratio rose from 42:1 in
1960 to as high as 531:1 in 2000, at the height of the stock market
bubble, when CEOs were cashing in big stock options. In 2005, the
ratio was at 411:1. Europe seems able to limit this ratio to about
25:1.[27] Alongside these inequalities in the United States the poor and
middle class struggle for their own security. This kind of struggle is
understandable in nations without resources, or those crippled by
tyrannical rule; they cannot minister to the satisfaction of their citizens. But the United States can. And with its enormous budget and
vast inequalities, an impartial observer could only conclude that

empathy is in peril here. In wealthy countries such as the United States, a double-digit poverty rate and a struggling middle class result not from natural laws but from government permission, a systematic empathic failure. These policies or government permissions change all the time, and not all nations play by them. That we control the treatment of people at the bottom can be seen by how we empower those at the top.

This empathic imbalance can be corrected, but it will take sentiment *and* science. To understand why psychological science is needed in policy-making, we have to understand why policy making goes wrong without it. With the high profile of economics in the discussion of inflation, banking, the stock market, and employment policies, citizens are used to accepting economics as the science of policy. But it is the scientific techniques in psychology that uncover the frailty of policy. We say we want to retire comfortably, but we fail to save when we can. We believe we want our society to work toward alleviating poverty and improving public education, but we wince at taxation. We say we want to be happy, but we make choices certain to leave us miserable. Why do we humans *routinely* make decisions that undermine what we say we most want, and what can we do about it, as individuals and as a society? These are the questions this book seeks to answer.

A reason to tolerate vast inequalities would be if such inequalities were necessary to produce a healthier economy from which everyone benefited. But there is much economic evidence that greater income equality is fully compatible with, and perhaps even causes, economic growth.[28] Whatever the precise empirical evidence, a good society doesn't require perfect equality of income, wealth, or opportunity. Modern political philosophy pressed the case that well-being involves more than income. It includes things such as education, health, and employment. All other things being equal, a person with a poor public education is worse off than one with a high-quality public education. Of course, that is true whenever one person has more than another—jelly beans, handsome sweaters, high-tech features on their stove. But some goods are more central to our well-being than, say, heated car seats; there are goods that contribute *significantly* to our well-being. Good health is probably more important to one's well-being than having a college education, and having a college education is probably more important than having a new car. In a decent society, access to the more essential goods can't be merely formal; it must be real and effective. This way of ordering goods—by their power to secure well-being in a society—captures the attractive idea that people must have both the capability and the opportunity to function. A disabled person might require more money or resources to have well-being equal to that of an able-bodied person, and a person from a neighborhood with poor schools or virulent racism might need more resources to have opportunities that are genuinely equivalent to those of others. But this inequality is more easily explained than remedied.

It would be naïve to suppose that there are substantial, universally agreed-upon goals for a decent society. There isn't even agreement within any single nation. Ours is a large nation of many cultures. Within U.S. borders, we have different religions, different traditions of music, different conceptions of the family, and different attitudes toward employment. We expect to disagree with other Americans over basic issues.

Yet everyone rallies around health, education, and equality, even if without the same fervor. People who value protecting children from HIV infection, for example, do not agree about the best way to do it. Often the issues inspiring the most intense disagreement don't have much to do with the general welfare. Citizens have deep and heated disagreements over gay marriage, drug use, abortion and contraception, capital punishment, and gun control, to name a few. But while these issues divide us, we don't have to reach a consensus about them to improve well-being overall. The most dramatic fights may happen at the extremes, or on highly moralized issues, but as the saying goes, policy is made in the middle. As a result, health care, quality public education, government reactions to poverty, the length of the work week, support for working parents, a dignified retirement—these concerns are relevant to everyone's well-being,

and none prompts all-out culture wars in the way that guns, gay marriage, or abortion does.

Policy has a friend in the science of judgment and decision making. Our best research can help us find a consensus about what citizens seem to like and appreciate in their society, and what it is
psychologically and socially *possible* for citizens to do or tolerate.
Some Americans are reluctant to support basic-needs programs for
the poor because they believe they will miss the earmarked money. If
we knew that painless giving was psychologically and socially possible, we might not be so averse to social welfare programs. Many
of the scientific findings that animate my well-being proposals may
contradict our most firmly held beliefs about ourselves and society. But that is what separates impartial science from seductive
intuition.

These questions of equality and well-being have a philosophical
ring, and much philosophical talent has been tested on topics such
as fairness and social welfare.[29] But too often, philosophers have
worked in glorious isolation from the science of human well-being.
And with rare exceptions, they could only venture the question that
economists and psychologists of decision making had already studied: How can people make decisions that enhance their own well-
being and craft durable policies that help others? These opportunities
form the basis of a decent society.

The kind of decency I have in mind, and that most people feel, is
not especially exotic, and it is surprisingly easy for us to agree on its
basics. Nearly every culture in the world has social norms, if not
philosophical theories, about distributing material excess. Most of
the homey advice resembles Old Testament wisdom: You "tithe of
thine increase," giving it to another who "hath no part nor inheritance with thee . . . the stranger, and the fatherless, and the widow."
(Deut. 14:28-29) This common empathic norm may be prompted by
a belief in a benevolent God, a sense of moral obligation to others, a
natural emotional reaction to human suffering, or an uncompromis-
ing taste for efficiency. Whatever the motive, it is worth knowing that

most material excess is largely irrelevant to the donor's well-being, and so giving it away is not a significant sacrifice.

This honorable image must be given practical legs. There are at least two goals of a decent society. First, it provides money or other resources to reduce human suffering, most often to cover the basic needs of the poor. This decency measure could take many possible forms. The most familiar is a social safety net that catches people whose income falls beneath a minimally decent floor. Behind these measures is a widely shared belief: If you can improve the well-being of those in peril or who are otherwise vulnerable or deprived, you should help them as long as you aren't thereby seriously risking your own happiness or well-being. This wholesome principle also expresses a simple source of agreement: Most of us would forego seconds at a dinner table when the starving child seated next to us hasn't eaten yet.

Second, a decent society pursues equal opportunity that is *effective*, not pie in the sky or merely formal. Formal equality is an important procedural guarantee, to be sure. Formal equality is what allows the rare child, sick or poor, to emerge from the shadows and achieve greatness. But opponents of well-being policies should not be coy about the weakness of this constraint. Equal opportunity is impotent without resources. And studies of both social networks and class trajectory back this up.[30] When the well-being of our children is at stake, then public debate should not pretend that everyone has equal *effective* opportunity just because no law can interfere with a person's legitimate pursuits. A decent affluent society should offer more than an arid procedural guarantee. It should honor the reality that people come into the world with different prospects—different talents, stamina, personalities, class status, and social networks. Achieving well-being should not demand heroism, as it does for so many of the poor. If we want to correct the blameless inequalities caused by accidents of genetics or birth, we will need serious policy proposals designed to promote effective opportunities for everyone.

Unless our country can craft laws and institutions that make good decisions easier for citizens to reach, then equality and basic well-being will remain shadowy ideals. Individuals want to reason accurately that their children can afford college or professional school, their friends' children can play in a safe and healthy environment, and their ailing aunt won't have to choose between food and prescriptions. The strategies for individuals are pretty clearly marked; they are about a particular person's finances, health, safety, and life prospects. But some of the facets of our well-being can be addressed adequately only by improving policies that govern us all.

When our flawed social policies are exposed—in a flood that devastates the poor and leaves the wealthy largely untouched, in laws that benefit banks that prey on the fantasies of indebted consumers, in crime policies that create easy targets and trap fearful people in their homes—it is time to ask how we can make decisions and forge policies that raise the overall level of individual well-being, while at the same time promoting the common good.

The first half of this book is about how we make these errors in reasoning, both at the individual and the social level, due to our inability to practice effective empathy, act autonomously, and reason without bias. These defects are not harmless embarrassments of reason. They cripple our most fundamental pursuits of well-being. The second half of the book fits us with prosthetics for our stunted judgment. It explains how we can bind ourselves personally to well-tested decision making strategies, support policies that are the cheapest and most effective, and not confuse plain old governance with meddling paternalism.

These policies, durable structures outside of the mind, furnish a practical plan for honoring the complex demands of citizenship in a modern, affluent democracy. In the United States, the existing committees of Congress—most important, the House Committee on Science and Technology—should consider and promote the use of scientific evidence from cognitive psychology, particularly the overwhelming and jarring evidence that biases in intuitive human judgment undermine effective decision making, both personally and in social policy. This should apply to all of the offices from which new policies and laws can originate: the executive, or cabinet; state legislature, constituency, or organization; or a House committee or subcommittee.

While its themes end with a practical plan, this book begins with an anatomy of empathy. Empathy is not an exotic reaction; every normal person responds to another's suffering in a way that expresses our common vulnerability. Everyone has had the experience of observing another person in a miserable job, in terrible pain, or in personal turmoil. And we answer with empathy, thinking, "That could have been me." By focusing on our reaction, we needn't be favoring moral impression over moral principle. Rather, empathy honors moral sense to advance moral principle. To see this, we need only recognize that empathy responds to the effects of violated moral principles. Empathy is alert to the humiliation and indignity of being treated differently for reasons that are morally irrelevant, such as race or class. Empathy responds to the strain of the overwrought, single, and erratically employed parent—not just to the child's well-being, but to the virtually permanent deferral of the parent's projects. Empathy registers our suffering when we are unable to care for loved ones adequately, for our parents far away or our friends and family nearby. Even when people have a home and a car—their basic needs met—our empathy joins them in their credible fear that they will fold under constant exposure to financial insecurity or health risk. Precisely because empathy propels us to envision lost hopes and prospects, it serves as a kind of political sentinel, announcing the unfair or harsh conditions that produce such sadness.

Of course, empathy is not omniscient; it misses worthy cases and agonizes over unsuitable ones. But empathy shouldn't be dismissed as juvenile sentimentality. When we watch a loved one or stranger die from a disease because their health care coverage was delayed or denied, what citizen hasn't wondered whether the deciding institution is an insurance company that grows stronger by denying coverage? When contemplating better alternatives, what citizen among us hasn't wondered whether our country really needs to choose between a strong economy and a higher tax rate? We don't really know, because we haven't really tried to place empathy at the center of policy.

Even so, empathy is one thing; follow-through is another. Empathy with a purpose requires that we think more practically, and ask, "What can we *do* about this suffering or injustice?" From recognizing our own vulnerability to misfortune, we decide how we would like to be treated were we in the same position. With an empathic reach so speculative, all it takes to dampen the helpful urges of well-intentioned people is a story, widely told in America, that we have free will. And the ultimate fate of people, because they have free will, results from their choices, not their circumstances.

This muscle-bound view of free will is unrealistic, if our best scientific psychology is any guide. If what we need are choices that are *effective*, and options that are *realistic*, we need plans that match our goals with the normal capacities of ordinary people. Humans are creatures of habit; human minds, automatic scripts triggered by familiar cues. Also, human minds seldom act alone. We are not only connected to our environments, but to other humans. We are also social animals, and we organize and school accordingly.

While it is individuals who display the poor judgment, it is policies that are responsible for setting the options. The status quo bias, for example, leads us to accept existing or "default" options over others that might be far more attractive. As a result, we end up making choices that are not in our best interest, in some cases because we have failed to decide, and have had the decisions of policy makers imposed on us—for example, when we die without a will. At the end of life, too, our fate may be guided by an advance directive, something we will have read and approved. But not so fast. Experiments on the framing of advance directives show that the very personal end-of-life medical treatments people approve for themselves are likely a result of their having to choose mindlessly among the default options on the form.[31]

We don't even have to imagine how default options influence our everyday choices. Many of our government and community institutions, as well as economic motives and consumer advertisers, shape our choices. These institutional, outside strategies are at least as old as the story of Ulysses. Ulysses didn't resist the tempting sirens by facing his weakness with a resolute will; he used an outside strategy, taking bold steps to control his behavior. Outside strategies are our ropes. Government agencies often provide these bonds. The Food and Drug Administration, the Federal Communications Commission, and the Securities and Exchange Commission all impose standards when we, as consumers, might otherwise weaken and make choices about matters beyond our depth. We all want to understand our habits of intuition that cause us to lose control. But we also want to reverse their effects, so that we can adhere to the speed limit, continue to exercise, and even limit our roles as germ vectors. Psychological research uncovers great advantages for those using outside strategies. Outside strategies are designed to make it easy to do the things that are good for us (such as exercise in public parks), and make it easy *not* to do things we shouldn't (such as run up credit card debt). Intensive deliberation, then, is not always a good thing. Yes, we want to arrive at accurate solutions to our individual and social problems. But there is no evidence that this is best achieved by individuals madly calculating. Sometimes it is better to use a simple but familiar rule, a forecasting custom, to predict how well a course of action will serve our well-being.

Outside strategies can promote the common good while respecting individual choice. In some cases, the balance isn't any trickier than seeing the wisdom of seat belt laws; after a few false starts, people realize that they are mistaking paternalism for plain old governance. On more controversial issues, however, we can engage in social experimentation to resolve the disputes of an uncertain electorate. If an implemented policy does not have the desired effect, it can be automatically retired. But in most cases, we can pursue policy changes without a new vision of the good—we can focus on the values we already agree about. We just need to notice what most acknowledge: poor health care, lack of access to education, crime, and poverty are important social problems.

Apparently, having the building blocks for solutions to many social problems does not automatically get the government's attention. This irony turned from curious to tragic as the U.S. government witnessed one of its most influential and productive researchers, Daniel Kahneman, receive a Nobel Prize for pathbreaking work on judgment and decision making in economics, yet largely failed to apply this research to policy, opting instead for the favored intuition-based policy. This disregard for scientific research is more character-istic of policy makers in a prescientific village, and all the more tragic now that we have the tools to live better in an age of empathy.

In order to present the vision of a government that aggressively pursues the means to improve human well-being, this book will take us through not just the triumphs of human psychology in policy, but also its embarrassments. Our government leaders seldom admit these failures, often because they don't recognize them. Our econ-omy may be twenty-first-century, but our political psychology is still state-of-nature.

If the themes of this book seem delivered with urgency, it is be-cause unreliable intuition currently dominates institutions of govern-ment, law, and medicine, and in the meantime, citizens, clients, and patients suffer the painful consequences of avoidable mistakes. We need new ways to elevate the quality of our choices, so that a strug-gling middle class won't have to choose between enjoying their chil-dren and enjoying their retirement, and those living on the edge between feeding their children and avoiding crippling debt from predatory lenders. All citizens endure policies of poor and biased judgment. But there are countless ways we can shape a society to make everyone's life more livable. By structuring opportunities that tilt toward our own common goals, a single policy can do the work of a million treacherous individual choices. Psychological science can light this path, but citizens must appreciate the larger purpose of applying the lessons of psychological science. The emerging science of reason can be applied not just to policy goals but to the creation of a more decent society. The empathic motive driving this grander purpose—to help others—reaches far back into our human cultural history, and even farther into our primate past.

CHAPTER 1

Bridging the Empathy Gap

The Tangle of Empathy

THE MEDIEVAL PHILOSOPHER THOMAS AQUINAS DEFINED empathy as mercy: "the heartfelt sympathy for another's distress, impelling us to succour him if we can."[1] And Adam Smith suggested that an empathic reaction such as pity or compassion is "the emotion we feel for the misery of others, when we either see it, or are made to conceive it in a very lively manner."[2]

Empathy is the capacity to accurately understand the position of others—to feel that "this could happen to me." When we are successful, our efforts at empathy reveal people's shared susceptibility to risk and harm. Empathy has as a goal to accurately understand another's inner states by placing ourselves in his situation or taking his perspective. Sympathy, on the other hand, is focused not on accurate understanding but on feeling. We might share the fear of a frightened person, but pity a beggar. Only the former takes the perspective of the other person. Psychologists have tried to refine the idea further. They often distinguish empathy from other responses, such as upset, alarm, distress, and anxiety, which are more focused on the self. Empathy, by contrast, is uniquely directed toward others.

People agree that empathy is a good thing. We usually like the people who display it, and take its absence as a sign of pathology. Well-adjusted people experience these feelings as a response to another person's suffering, but they don't go too far: psychologically healthy people have a calibrated system of empathy, with healthy limits and perspectives.

The psychologist Daniel Batson predicts that empathy will provoke altruistic or helping behavior, whereas those not feeling empathy won't act altruistically. The connection isn't perfect, of course. People don't always help when they feel empathy; they may otherwise dislike the person, or they may not have the time or the money. Nor do people always withhold help when they don't feel empathy. We sometimes spend money on projects that will assist people we don't know, or perhaps support people we don't like but who deserve the help. It is reasonable to expect help more frequently from people feeling empathy than from those who do not.

We empathize with those who lack the goods that a decent society should provide: effective opportunity for shelter, food, employment, education, and sound health, to name a few. In theory, the goal of empathy may be to mind-read. But in practice, empathy provides the motive to even things up, at least a little. We see a homeless person, and we give them money. We donate canned goods to the neighborhood food drive. And when we have the means and inclination, we send a check to a charity.

Empathy has a physiological component. The psychologist Ezra Stotland got subjects to imagine how a specific person felt when experiencing an apparently painful medical procedure. Subjects engaged in this exercise of imagination reported stronger feelings of empathy and displayed a higher level of physiological arousal than subjects instructed merely to observe the target person's movements.[3] When the person suffering is similar to us, empathy really ramps up: we experience stronger physiological arousal, report identifying more with the suffering person, and report feeling worse while waiting for the painful stimulus than subjects observing the same pain administered to someone not similar to them. We are even more willing to pay a personal cost to help when suffering individuals are similar to us.[4]

Empathy may be easy to feel when an individual suffers; we identify in some way with the sufferer. The danger in this egocentric pattern of empathy is clear. People who deserve our concern are often very different from us, and it would be more than a pity if our empathy reached only the parochial. A destitute Thai man is still jobless and hungry, even if his religion, his language, and his psychological reaction to his situation are hard for us to imagine. Though this man's condition may be explained by a variety of factors, the most important causes come from his circumstances, not his character. When facing another person's destitution, childhood poverty, and illness, we may not react with perfect kindness, but we can create a crash plan that responds with basic decency.

It may at first seem a slippery slope that carries us from empathy for an individual to an empathic social policy. But such a trajectory can be justified. Individuals suffer a collection of biases in judgment— systematically defective patterns of reasoning. Because we can see how such biases are shared by many, we can also appreciate how they lead to decisions that contribute to poor policies. For example, we are too optimistic about our future health, and as a result we too readily dismiss risks to our health from everything from HIV to heart disease to cancer. We treat our future self as too much of a stranger. And we also discount the risks to others. After all, that's not me—the poor guy living off frozen pot pies in retirement—that's a stranger. As a result, we undervalue future resources, and badly undersave for some of the most important and foreseeable events in our lives, ranging from the costs of health care to retirement. These biases of reason and emotion are not exotic; they afflict normal people in their daily routines. Their effects are both familiar and expensive: needless suffering from illness, poverty, and a nettle of less severe irritants, such as hunger and loneliness. Individuals want good strategies to block these nasty effects. This optimistic bias and irrational discounting costs our health care and social welfare systems billions of dollars annually in uninsured treatment and indigent services. When we plan for our future, it looks as if we often treat our future self not as a later instance of "me," but as a stranger.

Suppose some part of our brain drives us to favor our current self above all others, including the stranger in the present or the "me" in the future? This bias defines the normal limits on empathy. We should at least be forgiven the impulse for immediate satisfaction; after all, we can't control our impulses. This picture isn't far-fetched. In fact, our brain appears to have one neural system to evaluate immediate rewards, and another for delayed rewards. This is what a team of researchers at Princeton University found when they tested brain function during a decision-making exercise. They placed people in a magnetic resonance imaging machine and asked them to choose between two options—an item now, and a more valuable one in the future. Faced with such a decision, the prefrontal cortex busily calculates the various payoffs over time, lighting up with blood flow activity.[5] But when a person chooses the present pleasure, the limbic system—which governs emotions and spontaneous responses—also flashes brilliantly. We are biologically programmed to respond more strongly to present pleasures. Who wants eighty dollars in retirement when you can have ten dollars now? There may be social programs to address this grasshopper-versus-ant problem within us, but few of these fixes are trustworthy. Most are left too much to individual judgment, and so bend to the persistent temptation of immediate gratification.

Perhaps this bias has its evolutionary roots in the Pleistocene epoch, when goods were perishable and you had to take things when you could get them. But now we can smoke or freeze our meat and eat it later, or forego a savings account and instead purchase stocks for a long run that will offset the eroding effects of inflation. Even with this knowledge and our modern resources, we still fail to correct for our limbic impulses—the urges we feel as our emotions and motivation combine into immediate desires—and we continue to undervalue the future.

We can devise strategies to curb our Pleistocene appetites, but the stunted reach of empathy sneaks up on it when dealing with those we care about more abstractly, such as the child starving in another country, or a culturally distinct group. No one would turn away an injured person who appears on their doorstep, and we would swiftly challenge, if not dismiss, any moral theory that did not condemn such neglect. But then we quickly turn away and plunge into routine. There is a reason for this: People believe that if they can escape from the situation that produces the empathy, they won't feel the anxiety induced by another person's suffering. And, at least when it comes to a suffering person not in our immediate family, this is what we normally do.[6]

There must be a way to care for those who, through no fault of their own, present an imposing empathic barrier, a gap harder to vault with our imagination. As the individual pushes her empathic focus further into the future, it becomes more difficult for her to envision how she might feel as an older woman without much money or mobility. The empathy gap widens further as she attempts to understand, and in some sense participate in, the suffering of unfamiliar individuals far away, and groups spread out in a country. Empathy alone cannot tell you what to do with the more than thirty million people, or the eleven million children, in the United States who fall below the federally identified poverty line. For that, we need policies that cut channels of empathy, taking us from our compassionate feelings to the goal of ensuring well-being.

These channels must have capacity. The U.S. Department of Agriculture indicates that more than 36.0 million Americans are food-insecure, of whom more than 14.0 million are children. Farther from home, in sub-Saharan Africa, 194.0 million people lack adequate nutrition. In Latin America, there are 53.6 million (11 percent of the population). In the Middle East, 32.5 million.[7] Is there nothing to do but let them starve? Is there no way to organize assistance more effectively, collect money more successfully, treat those in need more immediately, or distribute resources more responsibly? An empathic outsider naturally feels overwhelmed.

Self-focus is not a biological inevitability. It may have a biological ingredient, but it either can be reined in, or go unchecked, by cultural norms. When Americans now turn away from the needy, they do so especially sharply from the distant needy—unlike, for example, most European nations, who give a far larger proportion of their

GNP to foreign aid.[8] But it is not American glands that are different. It is the opportunities and norms of empathy easily available to us. Later we will fill in the details of this puzzle at the center of human empathy, but for now let us look at the image of humane policies.

Thankfully, we won't need to suppress our empathy in order to achieve our own happiness and the common good. On the contrary, because our happiness depends so heavily on the ties of friendship and family, empathic people are likely to be a popular choice for positive social exchange. But our competence as citizens depends on *accurately* understanding and depicting the lives of others. So when our empathy gaps constantly mislead us into blaming innocents and fix our focus only on suffering in the present, or on a victim nearby, we cannot hope to find happiness and give others a fighting chance to secure it, the twin goals of any great society. Empathy can trigger the urge to help others, sure enough; but it cannot be the ultimate guide alleviating human suffering. It can be a place to start, but not to finish.

MAKING EMPATHY EFFECTIVE

It is rare to find an entire culture that lacks empathy. But it is common to find a culture whose most powerful members typify a disdain for empathy. Edwardian fiction captured this attitude among its aristocracy. In E. M. Forster's *Howards End*, Henry Wilcox dismisses empathy for those in poverty, even if it resulted from bad fortune: "It's all part of the battle of life . . . The poor are poor; one is sorry for them, but there it is." As the book unfolds, it is clear that Henry isn't simply a curmudgeon. He is a sick person; his life is badly out of balance.

Cultural habits of charity are often more effective, more foolproof, than personal plans or deliberate reasoning. In Indonesia, for example, the Javanese term *gotong-royang* captures the idea, common among different ethnicities in Indonesia, that everyone should pitch in on projects that contribute to the common good. If a poor person's house burns down, the community cooperates to rebuild it (or fund its rebuilding). Even government programs in Indonesia use this idea to improve life quality in rural areas. Local scouts, a government program for youths, for instance, will help clear trails as a preliminary step in road building. Or, consider the Muslim notion, which dominates in Indonesia, of regularly giving alms to the poor. You are not considered a good Muslim unless you routinely honor this practice as one of the five pillars of Islam.

Empathy may have given birth to these habitual cultural practices, but after a dozen generations, you don't have to feel someone else's pain to relieve it. Other cultures, such as the Japanese, idealize empathy (omoiyari). In Japan, people internalize the powerful social expectation that you will help those in need. As a result, they pursue the ideal not just because social norms impose feelings of shame, but also because failure to empathize carries a sense of individual guilt; you feel disappointed in yourself. In one interview designed to describe the nature of empathy, when asked about his own feelings of empathy, one little Japanese boy explained that he felt naturally obligated to help those worse off, in order to repay the kindness people had shown him. He explained that unlike so many, he always had more than he could eat and an education that his parents paid for. And, after all, he is kind and nice to others, and such a person would act empathically.[9]

Amish communities in the United States have no slick "Be like Ephraim" ad campaigns, yet they offer concrete help to other members:

> Perhaps the most dramatic form of mutual aid is the barn-raising. But there are many additional neighborly associations that result in exchange of services including sawing and cutting wood, erecting milk houses or remodeling buildings, painting, fencing, and butchering. . . . When the unexpected happens

such as a death, an accident, or illness, the community comes to
the rescue to take care of the farm chores, to harvest the crops,
or to care for the children.

The Amish community offers economic support for members
in need. Young farmers get interest-free loans, and fire insurance is
administered by the community. Older people are supported by the
community, living in two-household units (one for the young farm-
ing couple with children and one for the grandparents) in which
grandparents receive simple farm products for their modest needs.[10]
Amish people do not arrive at these norms by argument or conscious reaction to empathy. They don't pitch in because they feel empathy; it is just what they do, a habit sustained by cultural norm.
There is a compassionate thoughtlessness about this practice. After
all, sustained thoughtfulness regularly leads to inaction, a kind of
decision paralysis.

These practices are so well tuned, so immediate, that there is little
reason to pause to consider empathy. Empathy delays action and extends the suffering. It can also mutate into a kind of indifference that
has a familiar script. When people pause to consider the plight of the
poor, they can give themselves a million reasons to place the needy
beyond the reach of moral duty. They begin to measure the risk they
assume by helping. And that's no way to close a compassionate deal,
especially one that began with generous hopes. Closing the deal,
building a bridge from empathy to aid, first requires that we understand the psychological terrain empathy traverses.

BRAINS AND DRIVES

In the late 1970s, a homeless man, apparently ageless, haunted the
edge of the campus at the University of Pennsylvania. Stan the Vent-
man was what people called him. You would often pass him on the
corner, where he would be drinking his coffee or eating a donut.

Sometimes people would buy him more nutritious meals—a hamburger or sandwich—and he would occasionally bark out an order, or begin lecturing his coffee. Most people avoided him, no doubt because they found his appearance and manner repellent. He smelled bad, and his outbursts were pretty unpredictable. Drawing on the brain-imaging data, we might say that Stan was hard to empathize with. He was even something of an outlier for a homeless person. Yet, most people would agree that this was no way to live, and would have resorted to a policy that could have helped Stan, if only there were one. If an empathic outlier such as Stan can stimulate concern, how can more representative, psychologically normal homeless people—who simply fall into cyclical poverty—be so easily ignored?

Unlike the collectivist culture of the Amish or Japanese, where those less fortunate are cared for, our much larger, diverse, and individualistic society exposes us Americans to many risks. And this fact presents a persistent paradox at the core of humane social policies. How can people be both kind-hearted about those in need and compartmentalized in their decisions to help them? The answer lies deep in our drives, and is rooted even more deeply in our brains in the neuronal structures designed to lubricate the path to empathy.

In the human brain's anterior cingulated cortex, just behind the frontal lobes, are "pain neurons" that fire when, for example, we are poked with a needle. The curious thing about these cells is that they also fire when we watch *another* person being poked.[11] When MRI participants were shown pictures of feet in painful and nonpainful settings and told to imagine themselves, and imagine others, in the same settings, both self and other imaginings activated the same neural networks, including the anterior cingulate cortex, the parietal operculum, and the anterior insula.[12] While there is now powerful evidence that we use the same circuitry to process our own pain and that of others, these "empathy neurons," or "Dalai Lama neurons," as neuroscientist V. S. Ramachandran calls them,[13] don't *dissolve* the barrier between self and others. (After all, we don't feel the same *kind* of discomfort we observe.) Instead, they bridge it.

But we literally feel some people's pain less than others. Princeton psychologists Lasana Harris and Susan Fiske used magnetic resonance imaging, and observed a chilling phenomenon in the human brain. The medial prefrontal cortex is the area of the brain involved in the processing of social information, such as the categories class and race, and social attitudes such as pity, envy, pride, and compassion. For example, if you hear the sentence "The cup fell off the table," no physical changes take place in this region of your brain because no social information is conveyed. Hear instead "Mary *pushed* the cup off the table," and this region crackles with activity as you madly search for the psychological explanation for the action. In the research of Fiske and her colleagues, people were asked how different social groups are viewed by their society. When asked a series of questions about social warmth and the competence of different social and ethnic groups, the answers clustered around four emotional responses: pity, envy, pride, and disgust. For example, people routinely react to the homeless with disgust. This is puzzling enough. You might have thought people would *pity* the homeless, empathize with their position, and feel sorry for them. Not at all. And in a functional MRI study, when study participants were presented with pictures of members from each social and ethnic group, the medial prefrontal cortex—the site that registers the potential for an object's social action—popped for all but one group: the homeless. The homeless may be seen as human, but not fully so, not as social actors.[14]

While nearly everyone supposes that altruism evolved to support group behavior, as far as we know, humans are the only animals capable of empathy.[15] Fortunately, humans are also the only animals that can consciously construct social policies that overcome our most primitive and biased impulses. Beginning with our best intentions to help others, we can build specific practices to carry out those intentions without wrenching psychological involvement, so that we can live and enjoy our lives.

Because our most urgent desires don't reach far into the future, or far beyond our homes, our intentions to display long-range empathy are usually ineffective, as scientific research on judgment now reveals.[16] In order to close the empathy gap, we naturally employ a rule of thumb, a cognitive shortcut: we assume that others are like us. For example, in an experiment that has people read a scenario about a camper lost for several days in the wilderness, hungry people say the lost camper's dominant desire is for food. Thirsty people say it is for drink.[17] It seems that empathy is egocentric. When deciding whom to help, people tend to assume that they are the measure of everyone else's emotional or visceral states. This shortcut is at play in some of our most cherished institutions, such as the courts. For example, it leads to biased jury verdicts that grant higher damage awards to plaintiffs residing nearby.[18]

Despite the egocentrism of empathy, we usually agree that we should not tie our charity and funding decisions to our personal feelings of empathy for the afflicted group. Upon reflection, most people want to allocate money according to who is in need, not according to whether a *donor* happens to be hungry, angry, or depressed. Driven by visceral responses, an angry person may blame the poor, and decide not to donate. So we fail our funding goals when our decisions are dominated by our fleeting but powerful drives. Knowing this bit of psychology should influence individual and social funding plans.

Empathy's local reach may have served humans well when neighbors in need were right before us—when we foraged in small groups, or lived together in villages. But now we live in a vast land encompassing a diverse population—with people not like us, all in one nation. The gap widens as our nation is separated from others by laws, and by other cultures, in a world community of billions. It is far more difficult to get aroused by others' need, and far more complicated to execute a plan. In order to help needy people, and treat them fairly, we need to draw a bold line to empathy's target. After all, we may not personally know any hungry children, but this does not make them any less deserving, and it certainly doesn't make them any less hungry. Familiarity may breed empathy. This fact may explain our nearly exclusive concern for visible neighbors, but it does not justify the utter neglect of destitute people who just happen to be in a media-poor or forgotten country. A healthy empathic system, well calibrated to social needs, treats poor people as worthy of assistance even when their plight is difficult for us to imagine. After all, imagination is built to free us from experience, not to track it.

REAL AND IMAGINARY REACTIONS

When I was fresh out of graduate school and on the philosophy job market, I received a call from a dean at a small rural college where I had interviewed. After exchanging pleasantries, the dean explained that they wanted to make a hiring decision soon, that they had winnowed the list down to two candidates, and that I was their top choice. He then asked, "What would you say if I were to make you an offer?" implying that I would get the real offer if I said yes to the hypothetical one. I explained that I still didn't know; he hadn't made me an actual offer. I told him that I would think differently about the attractions of a job if I had an actual rather than an imaginary offer. At the time, I think I was mainly interested in letting the dean know that I recognized his question as a low-rent hustle; they didn't want to waste time on a candidate's offer that might not be accepted (potentially losing their other candidate in the process). The dean made an actual offer and told me I had four days to decide. I took another job.

Many of us wonder how our lives would have gone if we had had different starting points—had we been richer, better looking, more patient, or smarter. We also muse about how things would have turned out had we made other decisions, such as saying yes to an academic job at a rural college. Should I have considered the hypothetical offer, imagining the satisfaction of ending a stressful job search, fishing in the local river, and raising children where we could enjoy many hours hunting for fossils and catching crawdads? Or, had I answered yes, and gotten the actual offer, would I then have focused on different, more practical issues? There was, after all, little else to do there but fish, and search for those fossils and crawdads. It turns out

I was right to withhold my response to the dean's hypothetical offer. I correctly guessed what scientific psychology would soon reveal: people think (and act) differently about real and hypothetical circumstances. Fifteen years later a psychologist at the University of Colorado, Leaf van Boven, addressed a related question with two of his colleagues.[19] He asked students how much money it would take for them to dance to Rick James's "Super Freak" in front of the class. Students overestimated both their peers' and their own willingness to engage in that embarrassing display, and the overestimation was even greater when facing the hypothetical rather than real decision. For example, when asked hypothetically whether they would perform this dance for five dollars, 30 percent of the students said yes. The initial excitement is understandable; after all, "the girl's a super freak." But as the event drew nearer, more people balked. When given a real opportunity, only 8 percent signed up. In all likelihood, they began to think about the practical details of dancing in front of the class, and got cold feet.[20] And like the dare to dance, our feet get colder as the time grows nearer to pony up on our commitment to others.

When considering situations we believe are unrealistic, it is easy for us to say what we would do. It is harder to follow through. What would you do if you had a million dollars? If you were on your deathbed? If you were suddenly rendered a paraplegic? If you fell into abject poverty? For each of these challenges, it is easy to say, in turn, "I would give ten thousand dollars to each of my close friends," "forgive all my enemies," "look at the bright side of physical confinement," and "use my wits to emerge from destitution." When there is little chance of ever knowing the real answers to these questions, we may as well make dramatic, overconfident, and usually self-serving pronouncements.

Do imaginings like this ever help us to identify, and act on behalf of, those in need? How reliable is our ability to appreciate the situations of others, and so to use empathic procedures to make accurate attributions? Obtuseness of attribution descends from the basest of human desires. In particular, we are subject to what psychologist and economist George Loewenstein calls the hot-to-cold empathy gap. We think about the same events differently depending upon whether we are in a "hot" state (angry, hungry, fearful, sexually aroused) or a "cold" state (composed, quiet, and reflective). This is due not to *moral* differences between the events, but to morally irrelevant differences between the evaluators. People in a cold state have difficulty imagining what they would be like in a hot state, and so tend to underestimate the influence hot states would have on them, and on people generally. As a result, they fail to see how circumstances might have provoked regrettable behavior via anger, misplaced pity, jealousy, or outrage—all hot states.

STUDYING HARD IN BERKELEY

Ordinarily, we assume that if we coolly think about our situation or that of others, we will face few surprises; we can predict our behavior and that of others. But this isn't true when the behavior is produced by hot, visceral states—as when we are emotionally or sexually aroused. We don't plan for these surprises. But we should. Citizens and legislators are prone to these visceral influences, and their actions may tell us more about their state of arousal than their considered political beliefs. As a result, our policy choices may reflect the unreliability or caprice of the situations that prompt them. How vulnerable is our behavior to the mismatch between the hot states we may be in and the cold states we are thinking about, and vice-versa?

We didn't ask for this empathy gap. It came prepackaged. But we don't need to accept what's inside. We don't have to neglect the destitute any more than we must ignore our retirement savings program. But we are not quick to admit our psychological limitations, or our embarrassingly bad judgments. Instead, once we satisfy our drives, cognition starts a hasty cleanup operation with a clever cover story. If our behavior seems out of character, we cobble together a story about how we intended the outcome all along, that it was the result of a deliberate and freely chosen course of action, or perhaps even that circumstances forced us to the unusual act.

But how powerful are the different influences on our behavior? How impressive is our self-control? This was the topic of an intriguing study by economists Dan Ariely and George Loewenstein.[21] They collected Berkeley undergraduate males willing to masturbate for pay under controlled conditions. Some of the volunteers had instructions to answer questions "while in their natural, presumably not highly aroused, state." Others "were first asked to self-stimulate," and were then "presented with the same questions only after they had achieved a high but sub-orgasmic level of arousal."

The screen before the subjects displayed a long series of survey questions. Some asked about the attractiveness of different sexual activities, items, and opportunities. Among them were women's shoes, a twelve-year-old girl, an animal, a fifty-year-old woman, a man, and an extremely overweight person. Other questions probed the risks the subject would take in order to obtain sexual gratification. Outfitted with a keyboard designed for one-handed operation, the subjects were instructed to press the computer's Tab key if they ejaculated.

Ariely and Loewenstein's findings are dramatic, though after the fact we may believe they simply cinch what most people already believe about all young men. When aroused, young men (1) become sexually attracted to objects that are otherwise off-putting, (2) grow more willing to engage in morally questionable behavior that might lead to sex, and (3) are more likely to have unprotected sex. One unsurprising conclusion is that "sexual arousal influences people in profound ways."[22] More important is the lesson that "Efforts at self-control that involve raw willpower are likely to be ineffective."[23] This moral is true in virtually all cases of weakness of will—in gambling, investing, risk assessment, even eating donuts. The objects of our desire are in the here and now. So if we want to grasp at goods in the future, we better have a plan that keeps both hands on the keyboard.

VOTING ON AN EMPTY STOMACH

In a widely read obituary for the thirty-eighth U.S. President Gerald Ford,[24] biographers wondered at a contradiction in his character: his generosity when facing a poor person, and his apparent indifference to the poor as a matter of policy. Speaking of Ford, one biographer commented: "[T]his guy would, if he saw a school kid in front of the White House who needed clothing, if he was the right size, he'd give him the shirt off his back, literally. Then he'd go right in the White House and veto the school lunch bill." Another biographer had spent a week with Gerald Ford, and asked in *The New York Times Magazine* of April 20, 1975, "What is it in him?" "Is it an inability to extend compassion far beyond the faces directly in view?" "Is it a failure of imagination?" While it would be nice to believe that empathy is just a matter of *imagining* we are walking in another person's shoes, that is voyeurism, not empathy. The fact is Gerald Ford isn't so unusual. It might be comforting to mock this contradiction, citing it as a result of a disordered personality. But that would be too easy, not to mention hypocritical. We would all feed the proverbial hungry child at the dinner table, and then accept policies that neglected the unseen poor.

The difference between imagination and voyeurism has practical and far-reaching effects. When presented with a hypothetical scenario involving the sexual infidelity of their partners, men without sexual experience predicted that they would not be angry at their partner's sexual infidelity, and men with much experience predicted they would.[25] The lesson may be that experience matters (along with the sense you make of this experience). Two professors at the Wharton School of Business showed that when people know a victim, they are more likely to donate money or time to *other* victims of the same misfortune—be it AIDS, Alzheimer's, or cognitive disability.[26] We help those we know, and those like them, more readily because our experience with them decreases the social distance between us.[27] So we feel more responsibility for their well-being. This sense of responsibility for people we know is a marker of what Harvard public policy professor Robert Putnam called "social capital," a commodity in greater abundance in some areas of the United States than in others.[28] At the same time, it is hard to achieve genuine understanding of others' hardships while studying from a distance. Reading fiction, or narratives about people unlike us, goes only so far. We don't learn the joys of love, the pain of cancer, the frustration of unfair treatment, or the ravages of chronic hunger merely by imagining it. To make matters even more difficult for the earnest empath, psychological research, including the "Studying Hard in Berkeley" experiment, shows that our ability to act properly on our priorities, and to correctly predict that we will, depends on whether we are emotionally aroused when we make the judgment.

If experience and arousal matter so deeply to accurate decision-making, then the American electorate is in a serious bind. Victims of poverty are in a special predicament. Members of Congress, for example, earn $165,200 annually. In addition to this personal salary and social perks, they typically enjoy a financial background and trajectory bound to isolate them from the poor. Their social distance from the poor will make it difficult for them to appreciate the personal impact of poverty. As challenging as their jobs must be, it is a good bet that none of them misses a meal, let alone experiences chronic hunger. Scientific research on the empathy gap, then, supports an intriguing prediction: Comfortable and full, members of Congress will unwittingly discount hunger and its effects when they make that judgment, just as their experimental counterparts do. How should Congress respond to this empathic challenge, when critical reflection just won't do the job? Should they be hungry when they vote on poverty measures? Should they be sick when they vote on what to do about the forty-five million Americans without medical insurance? These particular proposals may seem outlandish on a practical level, but not from a scientific perspective. The real problem is how to make such proposals workable, without having to actually starve or infect Congress. Outlandish or not, there is now a growing sense that governmental bodies should receive empathic assistance.

Popular legal literature now argues that jurors must be in the "right emotional state" when considering certain kinds of issues.[29]

Once again, experience matters. Nothing gets you into the right emotional state like concrete personal contact with those suffering pain or injustice, as long as you feel you can do something about it. Members of Congress can do something about it. Yale economist Ebonya Washington recently showed that congressmen's voting records on women's issues were predicted by whether or not they had daughters, and how many. The more daughters they had, the more likely they were to have a liberal stance on issues such as reproductive rights.[30] The obvious explanation for this pattern is empathy. And this empathic influence overpowers ideology. Wherever there is a voting record, "the daughter effect" can explain even the most vexing inconsistencies. The late chief justice of the Supreme Court, William Rehnquist, was widely viewed as a champion of states' rights. So Supreme Court watchers were deeply puzzled by his inexplicable decision in 2003 regarding medical leave, in which he argued that discrimination in the workplace regarding childcare issues was so serious that fair enforcement could only be trusted to the federal government. Why the sudden and uncharacteristic solidarity with his working sisters? It seems that, at the time, the chief justice was facing those issues up close and personal. His daughter also had a demanding government job, and he often left work early to pick his granddaughter up from daycare.[31] Not surprisingly, men who actually have daughters can more easily and accurately think about the challenges facing women. Empathic imagination isn't as necessary when you are looking at the real thing.

So, high-minded theoretical debate can be window dressing. The real question is why poverty and sickness have to *touch* us personally before we *take* it personally. If childhood poverty were reduced by 50 percent overnight—from 22 percent to 11 percent, elevating about six million children—how would we know? Everyone knows it would be a good thing, but the difference would be hard to detect for those of us not threatened with poverty. Certainly we can read the numbers. There are more than eleven million children living in poverty in the United States, and we seem to notice and regret this condition. After all, even people who don't have children often like them. The same could be said for impoverished adults, of whom there are at least twenty million in the United States. People shouldn't need close personal contact with poverty to appreciate the undeserved suffering it causes. By comparison, it is much easier to find members of Congress whose personal experiences with health issues have made them advocates, because illnesses strike families regardless of their congressional status. For example, Alan Simpson was an advocate for the cause of schizophrenia, and Ted Kennedy and his son for depression. But poverty isn't like a lurking health problem in your lineage. It effectively excludes you from congressional membership. Poverty is not uncommon in the general population, but no member of Congress lives at or below the poverty level, and few members were impoverished as children. If the most potent form of empathy issues from personal contact, poor and middle-class people will once again be at the back of the line. In the halls of power, many issues will take precedence over entitlements for those who find it difficult to satisfy their basic needs.

This isn't news to poor people. The news is that empathy is, at best, only a start. Our competence as citizens depends on *accurately* understanding and depicting the lives of others. So, for example, when our empathy gaps constantly mislead us into blaming or ignoring the poor, we cannot hope to find happiness and give others a fighting chance to secure it—the twin goals of any great society. Empathy can trigger the urge to help others, sure enough; but it cannot be the ultimate guide. Instead, it is a place to start. Unfortunately, many are paralyzed before the finish.

PARALYZED BY EMPATHY

The tendency for someone to turn inward when helpless finds expression in Bertrand Russell's *Autobiography*, in which he says love, knowledge, and pity are the three forces that have driven his life:

Love and knowledge, so far as they were possible, led upward
toward the heavens. But always pity brought me back to earth.
Echoes of cries of pain reverberate in my heart. Children in famine, victims tortured by oppressors, helpless old people a bur-
den to their sons, and the whole world of loneliness, poverty,
and pain make a mockery of what human life should be. I long
to alleviate this evil, but I cannot, and I too suffer.

Like Russell, we too can be crippled by excessive empathy. And
when you, as an observer, feel as much pain as the victim, your
thoughts return to yourself.[32] Rumination punctuates helplessness,
which can be reversed only by evidence of effectiveness. Like the subjects in Stotland's experiment (who were asked to imagine someone
else undergoing a painful procedure), people who are shown that their
action improves the lives of an afflicted group can end their rumination and paralysis, once again directing their action to assistance.[33]

Charity isn't an effective long-term answer to the challenges of
poverty, inaccessible or poor health care, inadequate education, and
rampant crime. Fighting poverty with charity is like fighting a battle
with weekend warriors. By and large, impoverished and working people have inferior educational preparation, worse health, and a less influential political network. When facing systemic disadvantages such
as these, erratic charity can't even things up. At best, it may provide
some small and immediate relief. But in the end, the problem is too
large, the coordination of individuals too clumsy, and the outcome
too important to leave to the fragile motives of individuals.

Cynicism is another source of paralysis. Like many others, donors tend to blame the poor for their situation.[34] This bias—known
as the fundamental attribution error—frequently is reflected in their
behavior. We can see the fundamental attribution error at work not
just when people blame the victim,[35] but also when they decide
not to assist those in need. One reaction is based on lack of personal responsibility for the needy's situation ("I didn't cause their
lot"). Another is based on desert ("They aren't doing anything to help
themselves, so they deserve what they get"). If people are poor, suf-

fering, unemployed, ineffective, unhappy, etcetera, they have failed to exercise adequate skill, stamina, reason, and so on. We may have a social responsibility to assist those people, as long as we are clear that this is charity—the tender call of beneficence—not moral obligation. Whatever the remedy, then, in the individualistic West the fundamental attribution error leads us to blame poor people for their poverty, rather than explain their situation in terms of social, economic, or cultural factors.[36]

In fact, the fundamental attribution error is a largely a Western individualist phenomenon. It is not as prominent in Eastern, more collectivist cultures, a distinction intimated earlier.[37] People in poor nations are actors, and the donors in developed countries are observers. As we might predict, then, Westernized Australians are more likely than Malawians to explain poverty in terms of characteristics of the poor rather than their circumstances.[38] Perhaps donation marketing can twist arms, or at least wring out some guilt. But while guilt-arousing foreign aid campaigns may force a few to donate, "guilting" people into giving usually raises donor hackles. In one study,[39] guilt tactics prompted far more donor suspicion than tamer marketing strategies, leading potential donors to insist that foreign aid didn't reach its target, and reinforcing the view that poor people deserved their lot.

It is little wonder that nations and nongovernmental organizations donate at much higher levels to nearby rather than distant nations.[40] We needn't be perfectly impartial when we open our wallets; a nearby country may be bound up with our nation's projects, or may be cheaper to deliver aid to. But the descent by distance is steeper than you'd expect. We make these geographically biased judgments at every stage of donor decision making, from identifying eligible countries to writing the donation check. We may trust, correctly or not, that more local needy will actually receive the donation. Or maybe this geographic bias may dominate a more impartial empathy. Whatever the case, our decisions reflect the way we think about the needy. But most of us aren't needy—at least not in that sense. We can only imagine what it is like to live in poverty. So if we want to improve the poor's condition, we had better imagine correctly.

THINKING ABOUT (AND EMPATHIZING WITH)
STATISTICAL PERSONS

When we try to empathize, a debilitating sympathy often comes along for the ride. In fact, in any given individual, the difference between pursuing and abandoning our empathic efforts is measured in just a few centimeters in the brain. Nestled behind the forehead is the prefrontal cortex. On the left side is the area that activates our eagerness ("pre-goal attainment positive affect"), the positive emotion we get when we approach a goal. But when our almond-shaped amygdala gets activated, so do our negative emotions. We then lose interest in topics, we lack motivation, and we enjoy ourselves less. Not surprisingly, then, negative emotions interfere with our pursuit of positive goals. The empathic processes in the brain impel us to feel good or bad for others, but they don't tell us what to do in response to that feeling. For that, we need our problem-solving skills.

This "sympathetic paralysis" is most obvious when we are faced with children in desperate need. When University of Wisconsin neuroscientist Richard Davidson placed people in a functional magnetic resonance imager and showed them pictures of starving children, the amygdala tagged the stimulus as negative. Once encoded as aversive, such an image, when retrieved from memory, can bring psychological pain, prompting the self-protective reaction of neglect. In other experiments, a highly active amygdala coincides with feelings of helplessness, as when confronting an insoluble problem.[41] In short, negative imagery of the poor prevents us from eagerly tackling the challenge of assisting them. This anxiety can't be compared to the stress of actually being poor. But it does explain why people are not quick to handle the problem.

Nature's wisdom has enabled us to turn off our empathy before we become overwrought and crippled with unhappiness at the suffering of others. At the same time, that wisdom also made us smart enough to lay plans—e.g., plans to care for people far away or out of sight. But there is more than one way for the needy to seem far away or difficult to perceive. Abstract concepts, such as a statistical victim, are difficult for people to warm up to. We seem to care that our efforts help *particular* victims. But when it comes to reasoning about *how many* people are victims, our concern is little different from reasoning about *whether* people are victims. The weight we place on *identifying* a victim seems little more than sentimental attachment to things close or familiar. Thomas Schelling first named the now familiar "identifiable victim effect," in which the death of a specific person produces "anxiety and sentiment, guilt and awe, responsibility and religion, [but] . . . most of this awesomeness disappears when we deal with statistical death."[42]

In a way, we were already aware of this familiarity bias every time a relief campaign on late-night television challenged us to help a particular child or allow her to starve by changing the channel. Seeing the individual in distress removes many of the self-protective barriers to empathy, and we immediately feel desperate and often paralyzed by that image. Putting a face on desperation makes the victims seem more familiar. But we had no idea just how powerful identification could be, and how passionless the reaction to statistical victims. So psychologists ran experiments. Even when very little specific information was provided, people contributed more to a charity when they were told that the family to benefit had already been selected from a list, rather than that they *would be* selected from a list.[43] This is an extremely weak form of identifiability—we don't know what the family looks like, the parents' occupations, the family members' personalities, and so on. And yet our empathy places a firm grip on the slim reed of familiarity. This has of course been noted anecdotally. Nobel laureate Albert Szent-Gyorgi, a biochemist, said,

I am deeply moved if I see one man suffering and would risk my life for him. Then I talk impersonally about the possible pulverization of our big cities, with a hundred million dead. I am unable to multiply one man's suffering by a hundred million.[44]

Stalin appreciated the irony as well: "The death of a single Russian soldier is a tragedy. A million deaths is a statistic."[45]

These examples display biases of identification. Knowing about this familiarity bias doesn't make it go away; it simply creates another one in its place. Once we are made aware of this familiarity effect, we correct for it by giving *less* money to the familiar victims without, at the same time, increasing our giving to undescribed individuals. So informing people about the bias has an ironic effect. We give less money overall, producing less total well-being.[46] The same bias toward the familiar occurs when we want to punish; we are more likely to punish identifiable rather than undetermined individuals, even when the identifying information is very general, and practically useless.[47]

When faced with equally deserving victims, why are we so prone to favor those described uselessly over those not described at all? The legal scholar Cass Sunstein suggests that we use heuristics—simple rules of thumb—not just in the cognitive domain but also in the moral realm. But like cognitive heuristics, moral heuristics, often handy, can be very unreliable. People may use the cognitive heuristic that we infer that a crime is worse if we have heard about it. A moral heuristic may lead us to infer that a crime is bad if it induces outrage. According to Sunstein, when a company responds to an emissions law by paying the fine and continuing to pollute, our reactions are uniform: "People should not be permitted to engage in moral wrongdoing for a fee." When safety products such as airbags malfunction from negligence, we lash out at the manufacturer in court, enforcing a betrayal heuristic: "Punish, and do not reward, betrayals of trust." Both are linked to a generic *outrage heuristic*: "People's punishment judgments are a product of their outrage."[48] In each case, it is easy to show that people are willing to embrace these terms no matter what the consequences, even when it is very costly to the enforcer and will not improve the offending behavior.

This outrage is genuine, but there is no reason to think it lines up with the seriousness of the offense, or with the cost of the reform. We don't really have a good sense of how to balance the kind of harm (reckless, intentional, accidental) against its magnitude. We may be equally outraged by a poor scammer exploiting a welfare allowance of a few thousand, and a CEO scammer who bilks a company and its employees and shareholders of millions. In the former case, few are harmed; in the latter, perhaps thousands. We simply can't expect our empathic reactions (the clean-cut executive may be more familiar to us) to do the work we expect of them. In states with a "three strikes, you're out" law, conviction for a defendant's third felony can mean jail for life. But juries are not made aware of prior felonies; they decide only on the alleged crime in the case before them. It is no wonder, then, that when jurors (or for that matter, the public) discover that their verdict of guilt was the defendant's third felony, they can feel genuine regret and principled misgivings about their role in the outcome. After all, the punishment of life in prison is hardly proportional to the harm. Does our outrage at chronic law-breaking, we might wonder, really justify a life sentence when the criminal's third felony is theft of a shopping cart used to store his belongings?[49]

The route to laws such as the "three strikes" law is an ironic one. Public and personal outrage at crime—moral outrage—drives such laws. But when people see the consequences of these laws, they are horrified, presumably because the punishment so far exceeds the harm. Perhaps the principle of the proportionality of punishment to harm, too, is a heuristic, just like outrage.[50] That may be so, but at least assertions of proportionality can be rationally assessed. A drunk driver pulled over for merely driving erratically is punished far less than one driving equally erratically but who kills a pedestrian. That difference descends from a judgment of proportionality, not impulsive outrage.

We don't really transform our intuition into moral principles. Instead, we ignore the evidence and then employ rationalization. But we may be as inept at assigning credit as we are at issuing blame. Many of the examples of assistance that leap to mind involve dramatic risk or high costs—rescuing a child from a burning building, diving into icy waters to save a drowning victim, or tithing to the poor until you are at subsistence level. These are acts of heroism, but there is no reason to think that assisting the needy requires heroism. Assistance may require little more than the sober administration of transfer policies, such as we find in Denmark, Sweden, and other welfare capitalist countries. Actually, great personal sacrifice for the needy is a sign of a bad plan. Even if distance does determine our judgments of neediness, giving the nearby needy the edge, this fact needn't determine our decision to assist. When we don't assist, *why* don't we? Is there a better reaction to distant need than rumination and helplessness? There is, but the answer does not lie in mobilizing charity, but rather in civilizing policy. In a country where citizens pursue money as a means to happiness, they may treat having money as a kind of insurance policy that moderates the risk of unhappiness. Put this way, we can understand how people might think that giving their money regularly to others might threaten their own happiness, or at least expose them to a greater risk of unhappiness. And this reaction is too bad because, as the introduction shows, once we are substantially above the poverty level, our happiness absorbs substantial shocks to our financial condition. We could give large sums to treasured causes—either through charity or tax policy—and never feel a downside.

THE KINDNESS OF STRANGERS

In order for any significant policy to be successful, we first have to make it a priority, and then it must be taken out of our hands, beyond the reach of our psychology. When we do, the results are striking. In an attempt to compensate for the damage that the United States wrought in Iraq during the 2003 invasion and the sustained occupation thereafter, the U.S. Agency for International Development supported health initiatives. Aid programs were put in place to help the sick and the poor in Iraq, a project run in tandem with the creation of a U.S.-friendly government. At more than 2000 community-based centers in almost every province, USAID partners trained 11,400 staff in managing malnutrition in children. More than 600 primary health care centers were provided with "clinic in a box" kits containing key equipment and furniture; more than 2,500 primary health care workers were trained for this purpose. Helping to strengthen health care services in Iraq was seen by the United States as vital to gaining the trust of the new democracy. So the cause was made a priority, and was supplied with labor, money, and protection.

As part of this effort, in July 2003 an immunization campaign was begun. Under far more difficult circumstances than are found in the United States, by the end of 2005 Iraqi children aged one through five soon after implementation had a 5 percent higher immunization rate than U.S. children. (The rates were 98.0 percent for measles, mumps, and rubella [MMR] in Iraq versus 93.0 percent in the United States. For polio, the difference in immunization rate is 97.0 percent in Iraq and 91.7 in the United States.)[51]

These figures stand as one clear example of how, when given priority, a policy can bridge the empathy gap. And as far as Iraq is concerned, the gap could hardly be wider. Culturally, economically, and geographically, the United States and Iraq are vastly different. In addition, the Bush administration had effectively blacked out any news that would humanize the Iraqi people—there are no images of sick or maimed children, and no televised Iraqi mothers crying over their soldier-sons.

Back on the homefront, not only do U.S. children have lower immunization rates than Iraqi children, but poor children in the United States suffer a greater measure of neglect. From the summer of 2003 through the summer of 2006,[52] the immunization rate for U.S. children beneath poverty level fluctuated around 91.3 percent. For polio, the figure is 89.8 percent. If immunizing poor children in the United States has the same priority as immunizing children in Iraq, these figures are hard to explain. It can't be a *more* noxious task to immunize children in the United States; among other things, an aid worker in the United States is far less likely to get shot or blown up. And it can't be that we care more for Iraqi children than for our own— this would contradict everything we know about the psychology of discounting, the steep rate at which individuals devalue culturally unfamiliar people in distant lands. The responsible error here must be the status quo bias, the tendency to overvalue existing options by sticking with them, even when there are overwhelmingly superior alternatives. In this instance, the status quo bias leads us to persist at current levels of inoculation in the United States. We will soon examine the anatomy of these biases in dramatic detail.

Many countries have made poverty a real priority.[53] Austria, Denmark, Finland, France, Germany, Italy, the Netherlands, Norway, Sweden, and Switzerland all give more per capita GNP to domestic aid (the Organisation for Economic Co-operation and Development [OECD] calls it "social protection") than the United States—in most cases by a very large margin. In the United States in 2003, 13.98 percent of per capita GNP went to social protection, whereas the European average was nearly twice that, at 26.58 percent.[54] These are not countries of drab wardrobe driven to social obligations by a grudging discipline or a religious search for redemption. These are successful, vibrant societies with market economies and the usual ups and downs that go with them. They recognize that policies responsible to the poor don't require religion and don't cost them happiness. Denmark, Norway, Sweden, and Switzerland, to pick just a few, are all secular nations that register at least U.S. levels of citizen happiness. And the high rate of domestic aid in Europe is not because its countries have fortified their domestic barriers, caring only for their own. Their generosity extends to their remote neighbors as well. Taken together, Denmark, the Netherlands, Norway, and Sweden average 0.81 percent of gross national income in foreign aid, well over five times the 0.14 percent of the United States.[55]

Yet even these more generous Westerners treat the suffering of their closer kin (siblings, mother, father, etc.) as more urgent than the suffering of non-kin, just as we treat our remote futures as vanishingly less important than our present states. More Eastern-influenced, collectivist cultures may find concern for non-kin more natural than in the United States. In one study of this topic, people in the United States and India were given scenarios about individuals who needed help. Researchers manipulated closeness of relationship and severity of need.[56] In the "extreme need" scenario, there were no cultural differences; everyone reported that they would help. But the "less severe need" scenario revealed large differences in Indian versus U.S. reactions. This situation involved a person who would not stop reading a gripping book when a friend asked him for local directions. Ninety-three percent of the Indians maintained that the reader had an obligation to assist, but only 33 percent of the Americans thought so. In the case of the strangers in need, the difference was 73 versus 23 percent for Indians and Americans, respectively.[57]

These findings suggest that, like spans of time and geography, cultural distance, too, is an imposing barrier to empathy. In fact, this psychological distance seems to explain why misunderstandings arise from cultural differences, and why it can prevent us from feeling empathy for others. There are norms characteristic of many Asian cultures, such as the modest sharing of individual accomplishment, public officials' receipt of monetary gifts, and concern that friends remain dependent on one another. When these norms are violated, it is common for Asians to feel distress. When Americans witnessed the distress induced by an employee's individual recognition, a friend's closeness to other peers, a schoolteacher at not being given cash gifts by parents, they failed to empathize. Not having internalized collectivist norms, Americans couldn't empathize with the distress because they could not adopt the culturally different perspective.[58] And perspective taking may be too voluntary or discretionary an activity to be a stable empathic response to another's distress.

BRIDGES TO WELL-BEING

Empathy is a sweet emotion, sure enough. But it is too blunt and volatile for the surgical task of identifying and distributing help to those most in need. Many countries lack the GNP to raise their poor above the poverty level. The United States is not one of those countries. There is no shortage of policy ideas to assist the poor. But to put it simply, the United States has not made the eradication of poverty a priority. It has at once the highest per capita income in the OECD and the second highest child poverty rate.[59]

There is only one effective psychological strategy to elevate poor people, and it isn't empathizing with them. It is taking out of our hands the decision to help and placing it in the caring hands of fair policy. Empathic imagination is a lousy guide to acts that would promote the priorities we value. It would be difficult to shed this habit of thought, not because it is essential to our nature, but because without outside intervention, heuristics, like habits—nail biting, stewing over personal insults, and berating outcasts—are generally hard to abandon. Any personal commitment is likely to be unprecedented and unsustainable.

Compare the condition of children in Sweden and the United States. As industrialized countries go, Sweden is comparatively small and culturally homogenous. The United States has about thirty times the population of Sweden, with a rich collection of different cultures—African American, Mexican, Chinese, Russian, Irish, Japanese, Italian, Korean, and Indian, to name a few. With this heightened awareness of cultural differences comes an exaggerated perception of free riding—the fear that members of "other" groups will steal some leisure on the backs of our hard work, or sneak comfort from our sacrifice. So it is no wonder that U.S. citizens support policies designed to catch free riders. There is nothing wrong with the idea that every able-bodied adult who benefits from society should contribute to it. And while it would be unjust to prevent individuals from benefiting fully from, say, insurance for reasons that are not under their voluntary control—such as race or gender—it may be reasonable to customize health insurance rates to a chosen lifestyle.[60] But the calculation isn't straightforward. Perhaps smokers may legitimately pay a surcharge, but what about someone whose cholesterol is high owing to a combination of diet, poor exercise, and genetic factors? Whatever the correct response in this particular case, we should not formulate policies that force us to choose between discouraging free riders and supporting impoverished children.

Some people are energized by empathy to act. They first address the question of whom to help and how: Creating a center that distributes diapers and formula to impoverished mothers with infants? Building low-income housing on discounted land from donated materials and labor? Providing on-site medical care for the isolated rural poor? Setting up shelters and food for the homeless? Once they determine the need, effective people roll up their sleeves and dig into the community, and into the pockets of the well-meaning but distracted. They locate and open centers, and organize work schedules for volunteers. Empathy may light this flame, but only discipline keeps it going.

While not a substitute for decent policies, charity should be an option available to those who have special causes they would like to advance. As a microcosm of an empathic policy, let's begin with a personal plan for charity. If we tend to value the money we have today more than a slightly greater amount we'll have later, we may find it easier to make charities wait until next year, when we expect to have more money. But given the impulse for immediate gratification, this will always be the case—we will always feel that we don't have enough to give. What is important to the needy recipient, however, is whether you have enough to give, not whether you *feel* you have enough to give. So people are better off saving for charity as though they belong to a Christmas club, using disciplined strategies of automatic deduction to fund the holiday till.[61] The poor don't need a potential donor's empathy after all; they need the donor's discipline.

A great example of this discipline comes from our own private finance. One reason Christmas clubs work is that, like any automatic savings plan that starts small, we put the money aside without ever putting it in our pockets. We then adapt to our slightly reduced income, and it doesn't make us any less happy. So maybe we can edge toward the limit of our adaptation.

Unfortunately, we have no real way of knowing just how far

charity will go in the eradication of poverty. Even if all of the private
charitable sources have been tapped, we may well fall short of satisfying the basic needs of the poor in the United States. The countries
that are most successful in dealing with poverty in the present—
countries with the lowest poverty rates—do not leave the fate of millions to the discretion of charitable individuals who can, for any
reason, set the terms of the gift, or decide not to give at all.[62] The only
reliable alternative, then, is a social contract that guarantees basic
needs to those who would otherwise not have them. This measure is
an example of empathy memorialized in policy.

A social contract can require taxation. And people adapt to taxation. There is nothing to be gained by rhetoric that talks of taxation
for basic needs as theft. It is no more theft than the taxes that go
toward a prepared military, a watchful Securities and Exchange Commission, or proper water and highway services. Basic-needs revenues
can be distributed to assist the poor. If it helps blunt the punditry,
domestic government aid is more like compulsory insurance, a benefit that would be available if any citizen fell beneath the poverty
line.

With proper awareness of the uses and limits of empathy, we can
appreciate the need for a compulsory basic-needs policy. It is oddly
punitive to give people the option of ignoring impoverished children
and then blame them when they, predictably, do. A civilized response
to poverty focuses on filling empty stomachs and reversing hopeless
prospects, not fanning sentimental mercies. We should be more like
the Amish: identify the most potent causes of human suffering, create institutions and norms to counteract them, and dispense with the
tradition of empathic assessment.

THE ROAD AHEAD

Judging by many of the important individual and social choices we
make, our concept of a good life is grotesquely imbalanced, even by

our own standards. Our empathic organ acts like a switch that turns the emotional heat on or off. It doesn't regulate the temperature of the system. As a result, people display undue concern about events in the present, about people nearby, about easily imaginable individuals rather than statistical populations, and about the suffering of those most like us. And this imbalance creates perverse "coincidences." We favor ourselves over others even when we risk nothing by putting others first. We give a lot of resources to people with a name we know, while unfamiliar people much worse off get ignored.

The normal products of empathy are healthy and effective. Any biases that quiet the impulse to help, any ways of framing poverty that make the problem appear hopeless, any excuses designed to politely silence or deflect charity activists, should be traded for strategies that simply ensure that help will reach the target. Humans are not *short* on empathy. We simply overindulge our sloppy responses to human suffering. Like our reaction to other automatic psychological processes, such as intuitive judgment, we just can't believe that our empathic intuitions place our priorities on a crash course.

Our preferences are routinely inconsistent and, when we frame issues in a slightly different way, easily reversible. These phenomena are now well known but have not yet fully influenced political action. As Paul Slovic recently pointed out,[63] the president and members of the two other branches of government correctly honored Rosa Parks upon her death. But at about the same time, the U.S. Congress stripped $50 million from a Foreign Operations bill that would have funded African Union peacekeeping efforts in Darfur. The United States has been perfectly willing to involve itself in the internal affairs of other nations, and yet lawmakers voted to do less than they might to stem what Colin Powell referred to in 2004 as the "genocide" of four hundred thousand Africans. This grudging congressional funding decision occurred while U.S. officials were publicly celebrating the life of Rosa Parks in a manner designed to reflect the value the United States places on its citizens of African heritage. These two acts are not strictly inconsistent, but they coincided without any explanation. The scientific research certainly suggests an explanation for this tension: the empathy gap. Like daughterless congressmen voting on women's issues, or wealthy congresspeople voting on poverty measures, lawmakers vote for what they value, and they value what they know. And to make matters worse, it is just too hard to imagine the significance of Darfur-size numbers. Human empathy evolved to respond to a victim we knew, not to a mass slaughter whose dead equaled in number the entire population of Oslo, or Lisbon, or Oklahoma City.

Genocide notwithstanding, hunger and illness are the most certain routes to misery, and reducing both is the surest path to life satisfaction. If securing a chance at life satisfaction is a social priority, then our resources should be more squarely devoted to eradicating poverty. Economically less productive nations have been able largely to eliminate these problems. Wealthier nations, such as the United States, have not been able to generate public support for entitlement programs that would do better than leaving eleven million children impoverished and forty-three million people without health insurance. A number of European nations could act as models. If the United States is unwilling to study their lessons, it is only because eliminating the chief sources of human misery is simply not a priority, or because we have turned away from the problem. It is worth at least acknowledging this fact before attempting to tackle the obstacles.

Empathy may originate as a warm feeling, but it has the best chance to retain its glow, and to reach its needy target, if its delivery is arranged by those in a less passionate state. So, we need empathic leadership and guidance. But there are occasions when Americans notice failures in such leadership. While many of the disasters caused by Hurricane Katrina could have been averted by effective policies, it is the neglect, and apparent indifference to the human suffering, displayed by President George W. Bush in the days and weeks following the devastation that will be long remembered and reviled.

We can either vault the barriers to empathy or punch through them. The empathy gap can be bridged; we can connect our primitive and capricious emotional reactions to our clearly viewed priorities.

We can also cut through the tangle of empathic emotions with the blunt instrument of habit.

Empathy serves its purpose when we allow our tendencies toward fellow feeling to move smoothly, automatically, and habitually. The sure hand of habit, initially moved by empathy, will guide us to our best choices. Our individual habits may not connect directly with public policy, but they can be important tools of personal judgment and planning. But we can't appreciate the virtues of habit when the anthem of free will is always playing so loudly. The next chapter turns down the volume.

| CHAPTER 2 |

The Trappings of Freedom

Intuitive Feelings of Freedom

YOU CAN'T GET CREDIT, AND YOU CAN'T RECEIVE BLAME, unless you can act freely. The idea of free will underlies our every conscious choice and every deliberate movement. It grounds the U.S. corrections system, and the economic system constructed to reward contribution and effort. It powers the myth of the self-made man and the self-made nation. In fact, Americans are thought to put more weight on this concept than are people of any other culture. This view may be accurate. Americans value the ability to choose and pursue their own conception of the good life, and to design a life of moral integrity.

Free will is also a necessary condition for free choice, and choice is central to psychological well-being. We love the feeling that we are the authors of our own behavior. It is no accident that the happiest countries are also the most free; they rank highest in the Freedom House ratings, the standard evaluative tool for civil liberties, political rights, and economic freedom in nations throughout the world.[1] That is not to say that free countries always breed individuals with a robust personal feeling of freedom, or that individuals who have such feelings are always found in politically free nations. But the traditional story of political freedom in the United States has always been based on the drive for individual freedom and the idea that you can control the events in your life. Of course, we can all control some of those events, but Americans have a truly exceptional view of our ability to do so. The grand political historian Tocqueville claimed the centrality of this view to American life as a defining feature of America's superiority among all nations. As Tocqueville put it, Americans "acquire the habit of always considering themselves as standing alone, and they are apt to imagine that their whole destiny is in their own hands."[2] This idea is abetted by the Protestant ethic, which says that "one's fate will eventually mirror one's character, and one's personal traits and abilities will ultimately prevail over circumstances."[3]

The attractive feature of this individualism is the feeling of efficacy or competence it conveys. When people could have the same object either imposed on them or self-selected, they prefer being the chooser. Decades of scientific research documents that when given choices, people have a greater sense of control and internal motivation, better mood, and better physical and psychological well-being. At the same time, this priority on individual autonomy can develop people's natural social ties, a deep source of meaning in our lives.[4] Not surprisingly, then, other cultures are quicker to emphasize the downside of individualism. Anthropologists report that their Hindu acquaintances express "the idea that most people need to be protected from their own vulnerabilities," and reject "the idea of autonomous functioning and self-sufficient voluntarism."[5]

With all of these benefits, it is no wonder that Americans idealize free will. Like any idea we respect, free will deserves a hard look. If it is more than myth, it will hold up. If we replace worship with simple recognition, free will takes a more human form. We have habits that are practically impossible to break, prejudices we can't undo, unconscious motives we can't guide, and normal mental boundaries we can't surmount. Many of these behaviors are culturally influenced. And if free will is less than we thought, its mythology has great political consequences. It gives us the power to blame victims who have no real choice, and to dismiss the helpless who have no real chance.

It would be easy to dismiss Tocqueville's praise as prescientific romanticism about human freedom. After all, the idealization of free will predates a mature scientific examination of our individual and collective actions and motivations.[6] It arose before cognitive science revealed how easily we are carried away by biases, and before science detailed the mechanisms and processes that so swiftly and unconsciously shape our decisions. It emerged before we really knew the causes of our empathy gaps, or the magnitude of suffering they could bring about. The conclusion of cognitive scientists is complex: We are neither purely free agents nor sheer automatons. We are capable of planning and directing our behavior, provided that we have enough time, information, and preparation—in short, enough resources. We may have free will in some sense, but its proper exercise requires the right resources if we are to satisfy our goals and assist others in securing theirs.

In the practical politics of America, however, the idea of free will alone does most of the heavy lifting. It is used to justify the goal of ever-expanding choice in the pursuit of well-being, and to locate ever more sources of blame when sharing the burdens of social welfare. For example, slightly more than half of the people in the United States think that poor people lack motivation; like drug addicts, compulsive gamblers, nailbiters, and alcoholics, they could help themselves, if they wanted to.[7] Could they, routinely, counteract their self-destructive or unwanted behavior without the help of others?

There is a paradox at the center of these claims of choice and free will. In truth, the idealized story of free will that we believe and recite is a crass invention. Yet a large portion of the U.S. population turns this baffling notion loose on the poor—who command no resources and few options—and belittle a proposed safety net for millions of people. Many of us empathize with the poor. And so charities give millions of dollars to the poor in the hope that a little more food, a little better shelter, and a reliable system of health care could lead them toward a happier existence. But if humans have free will, aren't we all responsible for the choices we make, and for the decisions we don't? Why should we feel bad for the poor if their condition results from acts freely chosen?

After thousands of years of analysis and discussion of free will, it doesn't look like we are about to turn an important corner.[8] True, philosophers have filled tomes on this slippery concept, but there isn't much of a consensus about the nature of free will, about its mechanisms or causes. On the other hand, psychology has done a lot to dress down the notion of free will, to show that its cues are unreliable. And many of our thoughts and actions, which feel free to us, are eerily habitual and automatic, driven by our environment. In the end, one conclusion seems warranted. Free will is a bit like a sheep. There really is an animal there, but it's amazingly skinny when you've shaved all the wool off.[9] Most of us concede the truism that the broader environment shapes our choices, but we still wince when science puts meat on those bones—when scientists show, in detail, how a particular choice was triggered by an unconscious goal, an automatic association, or a mindless mental script.

FREE WILL IN THE SHADOWS

A big part of clarifying a problem is knowing where to look. Philosophers have tended to look inward, in the theater of their mind, for the source of their freedom. It is the feeling of freedom that philosophers have tried to deny, that special sense that I could do (or not do) anything, at any time. Not even the most hardened determinist can explain the striking feeling that if he wants a beer, he can get up out of his chair and get one or stay put. Aristotle, too, emphasized this internal control in free will: "when the origin of the actions is in him, it is also up to him to do them or not to do them."[10] René Descartes claimed that the will and freedom of choice both consist in "the ability to do or not do something,"[11] and that the nature of the will is to be "so free that it can never be constrained."[12] The Scottish Enlightenment philosopher David Hume describes liberty or freedom of choice as "a power of acting or of not acting, according to the determination of the will."[13]

Over the centuries, philosophers have lined up to take their stabs at free will, because it is a concept that has been invoked to explain every kind of human state and conduct, from murder and entrepreneurship to suicide and poverty. In fact, we appeal to it so frequently that we forget that we are just pretending we understand what it is. Of course, we haven't the first idea, not an inkling, of what it is. After nearly 2,500 years of sustained study, we still don't know how free will arises, whether it is a biological or psychological phenomenon, whether it can be explained in terms of physical laws, or whether it is irreducibly mysterious—so mysterious, in fact, that you can open philosophy journals and still find philosophers asking a favorite question from the Dark Ages: When we experience free will, is it God working his will or is it Him giving us permission to work our own?

Since the time of Aristotle, philosophers have made more distinctions, but no real advances, on the topic of free will. We don't so much understand free will as put it to work. And, ironically, we seem to have no choice but to use it. We have to have some way of praising or blaming people for their behavior. While the responsible use of antibiotics awaited our understanding of bacteria, we show no similar patience when it comes to wielding the idea of free will. As Nietzsche put it, "Men were considered 'free' so that they might be judged and punished."[14]

You don't have to be a cynic to believe that free will is less free than introspection might suggest. If you kept a diary of your daily activities, you would find that nearly half of your behavior was repetitive or habitual, performed without deliberation or explicit choice.[15] True, the internal force of habit is not the same as the external constraint of coercion. We may have chosen to pursue our profession and our family life, but we seldom choose the litany of actions we must repeat in order to participate in those things: reading into the evening, having a late-night snack, showering (using the same sequence of steps), and catching the train every morning. These actions require schooled motor controls. And these habits can be our curse or our salvation. A schedule of exercise, or the regular impulse to listen to our favorite music, can make our lives better. But a bucketful of cocktails every night can make it worse, just as heroin will, or chronic overeating. All of these behaviors are repetitive. But the reason for this repetition is humbling. It is not because we *decide* or *intend* to perform these behaviors over and over. Instead, the reward of relaxation and reduced inhibition *drives* us to reach repeatedly for the gin, as we pick up the environmental cues that trigger our actions.

Relying on habits, and not getting distracted by endless choices, is an important part of our well-being. If we can hand over the cognitive housekeeping to the choiceless unconscious, we can get some real thinking done. More than that, rumination and self-absorption are excellent examples of automatic behaviors, behaviors that are triggered by a cue (such as an awkward social exchange) and that then proceed unconsciously and repetitively. These particular automatic behaviors of self-absorption and rumination are socially isolating, and typically make for less happiness. No one wants to socialize with a person who can talk only about himself, in a relentlessly worried and desperate tone. By contrast, happy people don't engage in much rumination or social comparison (as in "Does that person have more money, talent, friends, and so on, than I have?"), and they are more concerned about the well-being of others, less self-focused. Perhaps not surprisingly, the most refined ruminators of all—poets who use the pronoun *I* a lot—are far more likely to commit suicide than those who do not.[16] So it is not automatizing alone that makes for a happy person; it is automatizing the right kinds of behavior— spending time with friends and loved ones, and devoting time to your hobbies, for example.

With the notion of free will in such a persistent mess, perhaps our salvation is found in behaviors that are not free but, rather, rigid and habitual. Can we harness automatic behaviors to achieve our higher purposes? To be happy, we must be free from persistent worry, excessive rumination, endless deliberation, and constant doubt. An occasional bout with these assorted ills is fine, but if they consume us, we will tilt toward anxiety, pessimism, and social isolation. We need to be able to empathize, to recognize genuine danger or unwarranted confidence. So some introspection is healthy. The key is to understand the costs and benefits of mental autopilot. A good part of the pursuit of happiness depends on balancing mental autopilot, with its satisfying feelings of fluent behavior, and the rewarding sense of deliberate and conscious action. Self-determined conduct may require some form of free will, but none that would justify the neglect of those buried under obstacles not of their making.

UNMASKING THE VILLAIN: FREE WILL TAKES A HIT

Because we really have no idea what free will is, but put our faith in it nonetheless, many of our beliefs about the causes of our behavior are likely to be wrong. And our decisions reflect these errant beliefs. Free-will enthusiasts identify a satisfying sense of control as evidence that they are the authors of their own behavior. One of the funniest and most widely studied of these false beliefs is the illusion of control, which causes people systematically to overestimate their control over the outcomes of their choices.[17] The earliest studies on the illusion of control began with a pool of lottery tickets. People were given the option of either selecting their own lottery ticket or being assigned one. Members of both groups were then given the option of exchanging their tickets for ones with better odds. Members from the group who had selected their own were less willing to exchange, despite the more favorable odds. People obviously don't want tickets with lower odds, but their illusion of control is so powerful that they think that their having selected their own ticket makes it more likely that it will win. Because people overestimate their control over events, they overestimate the extent to which they are to be credited for random events that happen to favor them.

Now suppose that the situation is even worse. Suppose people not only have the illusion of control, but also don't even know who is driving the car—don't know what agent, if any, is the author of their behavior. In his research on conscious control, Benjamin Libet asked people hooked up to electrodes to move their finger. Before people experience the conscious thought to move their finger, there is already action in the motor cortex designed to produce this movement.[18] So the measurement devices of science demonstrate that the finger moving action is initiated before people even have the thought. But our folkish impression of this sequence is exactly the reverse. People's subjective impression of their decision misplaces it as occurring *before* the motor movement. The general lesson is inescapable: Some of our actions start before we consciously intend to perform them, and these intentions carry with them the illusion that the intention is causing the movement.

A number of experiments show just how susceptible adults are to the subtle twisting of their decisions. We all have a "mental autopilot" that allows us to do more than one thing at a time: walk and talk, drive and think, listen to our child while remembering to pick up her prescription. But these automaticities can work against us, generating behaviors that are not always in keeping with our chosen goals. For example, in a lab at New York University, psychologist John Bargh and his colleagues asked student subjects to play a word jumble game using words we normally associate with an elderly person (e.g., *Florida, bingo*).[19] Subjects in the control group weren't exposed to elderly-person words at all, and even in the treatment group, only some of the words in the jumble game were elderly-related. So all of the participants thought they were simply playing a word jumble game. At the close of the experiment, participants were instructed to take the elevator to the first floor and leave the building. Unbeknownst to them, a student in cahoots with the experimenter was timing the subjects' walk from the lab to the elevator. The subjects who had been exposed to the "old person words" *took longer to get to the elevator* than those who had not. In short, the old-person words unconsciously activated or "primed" a mental stereotype of the aged, and this image in the brain influenced the subjects' motor controls, causing them to walk with a pace nearer that of an older person.

Following Bargh, Chen, and Burrows,[20] two Dutch psychologists, Aarts and Dijksterhuis,[21] primed participants with the names of either fast or slow animals (e.g., *cheetah* or *snail*). Those primed by the fast animal name walked to another room more quickly than those primed by the slow animal name. The word perception activated knowledge of the animal's movement, and this representation of fast locomotion activated the matching motor schedule. And while these shocking effects of temporary priming vanish in moments, chronic exposure gives the effects real staying power: people with a lot of prior contact with the elderly performed worse on a memory test when primed with the elderly stereotype, and merely thinking of old age can produce memory loss.[22]

At no point did the treated subjects *decide* to walk slowly; this is a pure case of situational priming. Like the new teaching assistant of mine who once finished our phone conversation with "Love you," the situation drew the action out of them.[23] Their surroundings contained cues that unconsciously triggered their behavior. My own reaction to my teaching assistant's comment was less automatic, and therefore less affectionate.

Cognitive and social psychologists have names for the processes that generate automatic versus deliberate behaviors: System 1 and System 2. System 1 processes are fast, automatic, effortless, associative, and emotional. Some automatic decision making seems to occur in this perception-like system. System 1 processes include impression formation, one-on-one communication, and much group behavior. System 2 processes, on the other hand, are slow (in the deliberative sense), controlled, effortful, rule-governed, flexible, and emotionally neutral. Reasoning is a characteristic System 2 process. While the paradigm case of decision making, such as selecting a new car or a retirement plan, is voluntary and deliberative, many cognitive processes are involuntary and automatic.

In the Bargh study, the old-age words activated a certain script, conveniently stored for retrieval. Subjects then acted out delay, intention, or awareness. If this material made youngsters act like oldsters, maybe a similar trick could make us smarter. Dijksterhuis and

Van Kippenberg[24] used a game of Trivial Pursuit to uncover a similarly jarring effect. Subjects instructed to think about the concept of professors (as a group) scored better on questions from Trivial Pursuit than subjects told to think about soccer hooligans. Furthermore, a cooperation script made people more helpful. Macrae and Johnston[25] found that unscrambling sentences about helpfulness made people more prone to pick up dropped objects for an experimenter. If the subjects in these experiments weren't told afterward about the point of the study, they would never know how helpful unscrambling had made them, and how much smarter they became from thinking about little-known facts rather than vandalism. The experimenter did not impose specific demands on the subject, and the subject did not resist. Instead, the situation passively and unconsciously channeled the subject's behavior into more desirable, pro-social forms of action.

Anyone who supposes that choice always promotes human well-being should care about these findings because they show how the environment often controls us, and how our psychological economy supports our well-being. In our daily activities, once these automatic processes get activated, we continue acting in that way unless acted on by another force—a kind of psychological inertia. And the simple fact is, we are not effectively free to monitor this constant motion. This research shows that as long as we aren't aware of these automatic processes, and sometimes even when we are, the conduct they produce lacks many of the distinctive features of free action, such as spontaneity, intention, and conscious control.

If the participants in these experiments couldn't even identify their own "free" will as the author of their behavior, you have to wonder what confusions are behind our ordinary concept of free will. Our experience of free will is not a haphazard confusion; it has the systematic structure of an illusion. We may be able to act freely, but the feeling of free will is like the glimmer of fool's gold. The real story behind the illusion of free will is that it blinds us to the influences of the environment on our behavior.

These experiments, then, demonstrate that people have false

experiences of willful control. Do we have any idea how often our feelings of control are counterfeit? We often have the feeling that we've solved a problem or made a decision on our own when, in fact, our solution or decision resulted from external situations or suggestions. These mistakes at first seem innocent, but they drive us to compare ourselves favorably to others in the struggle for success, and to blame the less fortunate.

Even our most high minded states, our awareness of moral guilt and regret, are tied by unconscious causes to automatic behaviors such as hand-washing. Like Lady Macbeth or Pilate, when a person's moral purity is challenged, he attempts to achieve redemption, quite literally, by washing his sins away. To make matters worse, the cleansing appears to relieve him of any residual sense of obligation to help others. People who clean themselves are less likely to help another.[26]

We also believe falsely that we have introspective control over which processes to select and focus attention on in our self-reflection. These processes have a characteristic irony. We get anxious when trying to relax, lie awake when most trying to sleep, get depressed when trying to be happy, and so on. Suppressed thoughts are hyperaccessible, just as thoughts on which people are asked to concentrate become evasive; when trying not to think about someone you dislike, unwelcome thoughts of that person invariably force themselves upon you.[27]

So we feel willful control over our behavior when we don't have it, and we fail to feel it when we do. The result? Our introspective experience of having willed an act, though woefully inaccurate, is so compelling that people exaggerate their influence on outcomes, and underestimate the impact of situations or circumstances on behavior.

Why do we find these weird and uncontrollable, these unconscious and motivating, effects? They may not be the result of the best design. Our evolution may have left us with an array of unwieldy body parts and mental strategies, making us poorly designed when we overreach. Walking upright may be good because less energy is demanded, but it leaves our armorless gut exposed to injury. Automaticity may allow us to multitask, but it causes healthy rituals, such as washing and the avoidance of toxins and decay, to leak into domains where they don't belong, such as in moral evaluation. Our naïve ideas about free will may capture some basic requirements of self-determined behavior, but they then seep uncontrollably into our judgments about what we (and others) deserve.

Many people take great pride in the futures they forge with their choices. Or so it seems to them. But they, too, are unaware of the spreading effects of automaticity. And this, ironically, is a threat to their personal freedom. If you don't know how or when the environment influences your action, you are likely to be clueless about how others can shape your choices.

BIG BROTHER, BIG BUSINESS, OR JUST CHOICE SHAPING?

If situations more than character cause our behavior, then our unqualified bonds to free will begin to unravel. Consider how we fail to recognize when, and how often, the environment rather than the force of our will shapes our choices. Our lives are a seamless drama, and multitasking is a way of life—talking on the phone while feeding the child, driving to work while considering a deadline, backhanding a ground ball while preparing to throw to second base. So we normally pursue a course of action without making an explicit choice to do so. This automatic activation of thought and behavior has an important function. It lubricates the otherwise dry connection between thought and action, a connection with an evolutionary origin: "In primates, the aim of the motor system is to create internal copies of actions and to use these internal copies for generating actions as well as for understanding motor events."[28] Internal copies of behavior are, in effect, blueprints for action. It is not surprising, then, that many imitative and other social activities are automatic: Once exposed to these environmental cues, we don't evaluate our options or calculate the utility of each contingency. Instead, we simply race down the "perception-behavior expressway."[29]

And somebody is directing traffic. The people at Campbell's know that if they arrange soup cans out of alphabetical order on the store shelves, they will increase sales by 6 percent. The rationale is *Mmm-mmm* good: if you have to search for the Chicken Noodle, you are more likely to also happen upon, and be seduced by, the tempting Beef Vegetable.[30] Buying the Beef Vegetable soup is not a choice we would otherwise have made. In fact, there are many unconscious means to unwanted choices. For example, music in a store can reduce the shopper's blink rate from the normal average of thirty-two times a minute to a hypnotic fourteen blinks a minute.[31] With reflection craftily dodged, the store's carefully placed displays mollify us, and our narcotic state makes us more suggestible to impulsive purchases.

There is, of course, a great deal more at stake than our grocery-purchasing habits; our happiness is on the block. If we could identify the situations that provoked positive and constructive behavior, then we could build environments that bent our lives toward happiness, and helped us become the kinds of people we wanted to be. If we don't craft that humane terrain, others—merchants and marketers, for instance—will be happy to make us into the people *they* would like us to be.

This choice shaping happens as often as we watch a commercial, hunt for a new car, or ask which mortgage we can afford. While it may be illegal for a company to misrepresent a product to the public, there is nothing illegal about disabling a consumer's resistance. If you wanted to wipe out a group of people, the best way would be to disable their immune systems, making them ready victims of illness. You wouldn't build their resistance by exposing them to the disease and strengthening their immune system. By the same token, if you want consumers to purchase alcohol and cigarettes, to gamble and eat foods that cause obesity, there is no reason to present information about its dangers and therefore give consumers a fighting chance. Any marketer would be fired for creating ad campaigns that gave people a chance to deliberate on the purchase and perhaps walk away. Instead, an effective marketer offers teaser rates that are attractive to naïve, first-time credit card users, for example, and irresistible to a person already drowning in credit card debt. Marketers tempt Internet users with the promise of gambling winnings. They subliminally plant desire in people's minds by placing product names in popular books and movies, when the reader or viewer's critical scrutiny has been disabled by the escapist drama. One entertainment company even has a Branded Entertainment Division, which shapes our children's choices by "delivering the brand" to them. The same company contracts attractive talent and "helps" create film, TV, Internet, and online gaming—human inventions designed as vehicles for a sponsor's ads. They even arrange product placement in books for teens, and create the very media that can make tweens furious or despondent if they don't have a particular brand of cellphone, blouse, car, or soft drink. This company looks after the consumer needs of our youth, working to "facilitate brand integration or product placement within popular youth media."[32] Parents may see the materialistic effects of this furtive intrusion in our children's lives as the result of callow and suggestible youth. But adults aren't free from the influence, either.

Whether through powerful but invisible force of social norms or through downright deception, these forms of choice shaping *feel* inconsistent with the treasured slogan in democratic theory, that "justice must be seen in order to be done": Any measure that restricts or otherwise shapes our choices must stand up to public scrutiny. It is a conviction, sometimes reified as the publicity principle, that can be traced at least as far back as Cicero, through Montesquieu, Kant, Tocqueville, and Mill, and to modern figures such as Rawls.[33] The same people who treat the publicity principle as a requirement of responsible governance must also appreciate the power of all institutions—public and private—to shape our choices.

Choice shaping is the product of learning and not a rare one. If it seems like choice shaping requires unusual efforts of devious manipulation, it is only because the actual process of choice shaping, like so much learning, is unconscious. And our unconscious processes don't discriminate between shaping that issues from government institutions and shaping that results from influences of private industry.[34] A plan to improve our well-being should be wary of both sources of control. But no matter what the source, people believe they are the masters of their choices, invulnerable to automatic and unconscious influences. Why do we feel so sure?

STORIES WE TELL OURSELVES

The evidence of free will we find most compelling is introspective. We "feel" how the thought of a cold beer, together with our desire for it, causes us to get one from the fridge. If this kind of introspective evidence is unreliable, then we may truly be "strangers to ourselves."[35] We believe that we exert conscious control over our actions far more frequently than we in fact do.

Given the counsel of introspection, it is difficult for people to persuade themselves that the distinction between thought and deed does not have the implications they imagine. We all have the experience of controlling our dispositions. We may dislike our boss, but suppress the urge to kill her off. Even some addictions and compulsions, such as smoking, can sometimes be broken by a strict regimen of behavior modification, or by removing the addict from his or her environment. With this distinction so familiar, is it any wonder that people assume that intelligent social and individual behavior is usually free from the grip of automaticity? Unfortunately, it proves nothing that we can imagine situations in which we see the cigarette and feel no compulsion. We can also imagine that we jump and never come down. Mere imaginings don't imply realistic possibilities. The same goes for the link beween decision and action. The mere possibility that we can exercise more, eat more healthfully, save enough to live in a safer neighborhood with better schools, does not imply that, in the real world, we actually could have done otherwise.

Acts are neither simply free nor simply unfree. Human action is complex, and the medley of neural activity realizing it may be inevitable, or yield to detours. How can we know that some of the behaviors we supposed we had willed, we in fact had not? The answer is to find examples of "counterfeit willings," in which we have the intuitive feeling that we willed an action but could not have done so due to the sequence of events.

People concoct heroic stories of our steely will—will that propels us from rags to riches, from a drifting youth to focused adult, etc.— and we do it with impunity because we seldom get quick and unambiguous feedback that would reveal our inaccuracy. We can't lead a separate life and see how things would have turned out had we made different decisions. Because the causes of our behavior are not easily observable, when we need a causal story, we simply make one up. Nisbett and Wilson[36] show that in the case of self-explanation, individuals supply erroneous reports about the influences on their behavior. First, the researchers presented one half of the subjects in their experiment with an array of word pairs. Some were closely associated, such as *ocean-moon*; others were not. Subjects were then told that they would be performing a recall task. The real agenda, however, was to ask the subjects to name a laundry detergent, with the expected result that more participants exposed to the *ocean-moon* word pair would reply, "Tide," than participants not exposed to that particular word pair. Of course, because that word pair appeared on a long list of others whose members were unrelated, subjects were unaware of the real purpose of the task or the association in the pair. The anticipated effect emerged, and participants were asked why they thought that they had given each of their responses to the word-association task. Unaware of the association, they simply concocted a connection that rationalized their performance, saying, "Tide is the best-known detergent," "My mother uses Tide," or "I like the Tide box." These statements may be true—but significantly more participants came up with the detergent brand Tide in the group exposed to *ocean-moon* than did those in the group not exposed to that word pair. However counterfeit, the subjects' stories carry a bonus for their self-esteem: they allow them to believe that they are always at the helm of their consciousness, always willfully and freely determining their behavior. But that is all after the fact. The experiment ensured that the subjects were unwitting stooges. And so they struggled heroically to reject the obvious but undignified conclusion: that the answers they had "chosen" were in fact arrived at unconsciously, set off by persistent cues and carried out by spiritless mechanisms.

The desire to save the appearance of free will is a human preoccupation. And while it is easy to draw a line of intellectual influence from Plato through Spinoza and Kant, the systematic empirical study of free will has a more recent pedigree traceable to the early days of scientific psychology. In 1931, psychologist Norman Maier published a now-classic study in which subjects were shown two cords hanging from the ceiling of a lab. Also at hand were items such as poles, chairs, pliers, and extension cords. The participants' task was to tie the two ends of the cords together. But the cords were set far enough apart that a participant could not, while holding onto one cord, grasp the other. Maier's subjects immediately arrived at three of the possible solutions, such as tying an extension cord to one of the ceiling cords. Each time a participant arrived at a solution, Maier said, "Now do it a different way." The most difficult solution was one that the subjects could not figure out on their own. After a few minutes of unproductive reflection, Maier, who had been wandering around the room, began casually tapping one of the cords, setting it in motion. Normally, in less than a minute of witnessing this cue, each subject took a weight, tied it to the end of one of the cords, set it swinging like a pendulum, ran to the other ceiling cord, grabbed it, and waited for the first cord to swing near enough to be grabbed. Following this solution, Maier immediately asked each participant to recount the experience of grasping the idea of the pendulum. Some answered, "It just dawned on me," "It was the only thing left," or "I just realized the cord would swing if I attached a weight to it." One cue Maier gave— twirling a weight on the end of one cord—turned out to be useless; observing it did not improve the subjects' problem-solving performance. Some subjects received this useless cue before the truly helpful cue (the swinging). Ironically, every one of *those* subjects said of the useless cue that it had been helpful, and rejected any suggestion that the genuinely decisive cue had helped them at all to arrive at the solution.[37]

Indeed, in the case of one subject, a professor, his story behind arriving at the solution came complete with a description of his thorough reflection and brilliant imagery: "Having exhausted everything else, the next thing was to swing it. I thought of the situation of swinging across a river. I had imagery of monkeys swinging from trees. This imagery appeared simultaneously with the solution."[38] If this first-person report were all we had to go on, we might be led to believe that this professor had heroically wrestled with this dark problem and illuminated it with his radiant intelligence. Thankfully, we know better, since the subjects not exposed to Maier's swinging the rope could not arrive at the more "difficult" solution. So the professor had most likely watched the experimenter absentmindedly swing the rope. Yeasty imagination had nothing to do with it. Neither did monkeys.

The point, then, is not just that people are bad at evaluating influences on their own behavior, but also that they are enormously resourceful at dreaming up credible-sounding causes for their performance. So we cannot count on the accuracy of an introspective report. In fact, we can assume that the inaccuracy will be systematic. Our fabrications portray our behavior as the consequence of our internal will rather than of another's contribution. Free will narratives make a better story.

SPLIT-SECOND DEMOCRACY

One good story is that our political choices result from free deliberation of our options. But the experimental evidence is less optimistic.

Surprisingly automatic behaviors turn up in other unexpected places, such as elections. In a democracy, the process of selecting a political leader is viewed as a hallmark of reflection, soul-searching, and deliberation—a classic System 2 process. But Princeton psychologist Alexander Todorov and his colleagues found that, when asked to make inferences about the competence of senatorial candidates solely on the basis of a one-second exposure to the candidates' faces, people's judgments of competence predicted who would be elected (68.8 percent of the Senate races in 2004). People's actual voting behavior is heavily influenced by their judgments of competence. In a later study, Todorov and Charles Ballew showed that inferences about competence were fast, intuitive, and unreflective. Could it be that we elect a senator or governor because, at a glance, "they look like a nice, trustworthy boy or girl"? Ordinarily, we suppose that our voting behavior is a deliberate and rational process, if anything is. So it is humbling to discover that people's fast, unreflective trait inferences—in this case about competence and gleaned instantaneously from faces—contribute substantially to their voting choices.[39] In fact, people's predictive accuracy in selecting the winning candidate erodes as they take more time to deliberate over the options.[40]

Our political decisions are also determined by how the options are framed, and this mechanism, too, can make a mockery of the feeling that our democratic choices proceed by ordering our desires or preferences. Political conversation evokes a range of loosely connected attitudes. In three successive years, researchers from the General Social Survey asked whether we were spending "too much, too little, or about the right amount" on a variety of government programs.[41] In each year, 20 to 25 percent of the respondents said that too little was being spent on "welfare," but 63 to 65 percent said that too little was being spent on "assistance to the poor."[42] Once again, if our democratic choices were based on the ranking of preferences, our decisions wouldn't be affected differently by the terms "welfare" and "assistance to the poor." But these two concepts could certainly tap into different aspects of our attitudes toward this assistance. And we may resist these findings because they conflict with a story we hold dear about free will and choice—in this case, democratic choice.

So it would appear that what we know from science is at odds with our rhetoric of liberty. Are the acts of voting, performed by a citizen observing a candidate's face for under one second, really "up to him to do them or not do them," as Aristotle put it? Deep in this web of causes, free will has little room to explain much of anything; it is just a name for a process we don't understand, just a term we use when we are ignorant of behavior's causes. It isn't a sensible enough concept to explain most of our behavior most of the time. But our desire to explain, and often to blame, overwhelms us. We have learned that we can at least keep what we have, and perhaps even advance our position, if we oppose sacrifice or social adjustments. In America, the pretext for doing so is ready-made. Harvard economist Alberto Alesina reminds us that "the United States was created from an anti-government revolution, and its history includes a civil war in which roughly half the country fought against the federal government."[43] And the rugged individualism lionized by Tocqueville and spotlighted in American exceptionalism justifies leaving others on their own to sink or swim. In this setting, "keeping what's mine" is a hardened value, not well placed for discussion or negotiation.

So some citizens, many of them in Congress, ignore all of this machinery of decision making and insist instead that it is not the government's role to help the poor. After all, they are poor because they made the wrong decisions, and they could have acted otherwise. Everyone has free will. Can we count on political representatives to moderate this exaggerated image of free action? We may not see the need to moderate this image, because we may not be aware that the influences on it are immoderate. But one reason we don't follow through on our empathic responses is that distraction makes us less determined in that effort. The kind of deliberate judgment entrusted to our politicians is undermined by simple distraction. People concerned about the plight of others, and made sad by it, may intend to help. But if we allow them, other forces can intervene to quash that empathic response. It is not that inattention is the force holding back compassionate solutions to poverty. But we are unaware of eroding effects that time pressure and attentional demands have on our empathic behavior. In a simple experiment, Small and Lerner checked to see if sad people would still support social welfare to the same extent if distractions intervened, and they were prevented from feeling empathy about a welfare recipient.[44] It turned out that once distractions prevented the sad person from thinking deliberately, the difference between sad and angry observers vanished; the sad persons, once distracted, judged the welfare recipient in the same way the angry subjects did. And this is what happens when people *already* care. It is hard to imagine that a busy, preoccupied, or agitated politician, or ordinary citizen, would be any different.

Yet our intuitions disavow these findings. Our empathy, our friendships, our self-concept, are all dominated by an arrogant pronouncement: "If I don't like the contents of my belief, I will simply change what I believe." We hear at our parents' knee: "Don't judge people," "Treat people like individuals," and "Keep an open mind." The adages are so common and potent, we begin to think we can follow them. But while we may aspire to these ideals, our performance falls short. We are as free as we can be, but not as free as we think.

FREE TO HAVE OUR CHOICES SHAPED

Technical discussions of free will are for philosophers, not nation builders. The Founding Fathers were carried away by the heady dream of a democratic America that was free at least from the king, if not from a rising aristocracy. Their first priority, then, was to secure freedom, not to define it. So the Preamble to the U.S. Constitution calls for a government to "promote the general welfare, and secure the blessings of liberty to ourselves and our posterity. . . ."

It turns out that *freedom* is difficult to define. But most people have strong feelings about what it requires, and what it prohibits. As part of the caution about tyranny, the Constitution decries the legislation of thought and behavior. But its rhetoric portrays our actions in this new country as originally without constraint—free from unchosen causes. Behind the Constitution's unrealistic optimism about the sources of behavior is its folksy eighteenth-century view that humans are not just free, but hyper-free. The language suggests that we are free not only to think anything imaginable, but also to do anything physically possible. We are autonomous actors, freely forging our destinies.

Think tanks such as the Cato Institute and the Hoover Institution give pride of place to this extreme vision of self-determination. But real people, making real decisions, fall far short of this extreme. Unfortunately, think tanks that judge citizens by psychologically unrealistic standards also offer ineffective advice. One spokesman, for example, explained that "The rules for escaping from poverty in America are simple: 1) finish high school; 2) get a job, and stick with it; 3) do not have children outside of marriage. Those who abide by these rules of middle-class existence will not be chronically poor in the U.S."[45] The implication seems to be that these are rules that we can choose to accept or reject. We have free will. If we fail to follow those rules, we are responsible for our poverty.

In a free society like the United States, then, happiness and its pursuit is entirely up to us: "[E]veryone is the best and sole judge of his own private interest."[46] Diderot cheers on the person who "dares to think for himself, to ascend to the clearest general principles, to examine them, to discuss them, to admit nothing save on the testimony of his own reason and experience."[47] Kant entreats us: "Have courage to use your own understanding!"[48] In a free country, each adult person "is entitled to be the final judge of his or her own interests."[49] Americans are quick to assume that individual reason can trump our temptations, our habits, and our automatic decisions, however irrational. We even know when it is best to suppress these private urges and make decisions that are collectively binding. Political theorist Robert Dahl summarizes this view: "All are equally well-qualified to decide which matters do or do not require binding collective decisions."[50] These claims aren't exactly false. After all, we can often determine the course of our behavior. But given the unconscious shaping of it, these statements are recklessly unqualified.

As we've begun to see, our electoral decisions may be less free than our Enlightenment predecessors supposed, and less self-determined than we think. And it's not just the candidate's visage. It turns out that as we hand out ballots or roll out the voting machines, our political will may get a shove if the polling location makes the voting issue salient. In a recent study, Jonah Berger, Marc Meredith, and S. Christian Wheeler found that Arizona citizens in the 2000 general election were more likely to vote for an increase in the state sales tax to support education if the voting location were a school.[51] Does this voting outcome reflect the free will of voters? It wouldn't seem so. In every other respect—education, political preference, income level, etc.—those who voted at school locations were just like the people voting at churches, community centers, apartment complexes, and government buildings.

These research findings show that our surroundings unconsciously influence our behavior, and they are directly at odds with the venerated idea of a voluntary and fully deliberative democracy. This tension is dramatized when we find evidence of unconscious influences in the voting process itself. Voting effects, performance in the game of Trivial Pursuit, the aroma of fresh-baked bread, and lucky discovery-of-a-dime scenarios—all illustrate situational influences on individuals. These effects accumulate as situational influences spread throughout a population. Even mass hysteria begins with an individual. Sometimes an entire culture can produce the environment of unconscious influence. Culture-bound psychological syndromes are the best examples of these broad effects. For example, amok is a sudden, public, and violent attack on another person, designed to induce others to kill you. It is a characteristic form of suicide in Malaysia. Other syndromes are more generic. In Lahore, Pakistan, the most "Westernized" of girls—girls who speak English in their homes or who watch Western cable television—are at greatest risk of having an eating disorder. The same was found for South Asian girls in Bradford, England. In both studies, girls were asked to complete a variety of questionnaires yielding scores regarding issues of body image, attitudes and behavior regarding food and diet, degree of Westernization (expressed by consumption of Western food and English spoken in the home), and traditionality.[52] As predicted, girls with the highest Westernization scores were most prone to bulimia nervosa. This is an interesting finding because the influence of Westernization is likely more diffuse than the kinds of focused norms within a family thought to produce cultural syndromes in individual cultures—e.g., unquestioned obedience to parents under threat of severe punishment. Westernization is measured in these studies largely in terms of passive exposure, such as whether and how much Western television, Western advertising, English language exposure, and so on, is available to the person.

Two observations are crucial here. First, if the likelihood of bulimia varies as a function of cultural exposure, it is worth speculating just how potent these influences could be when you are actually steeped in the culture. Second, no girl made the choice to adopt a personal style or attitude of a Western person here; the effect is largely automatic and circumstantial. Distinguishable cultural syndromes are a dramatic testament to the power of circumstance.

And consider culture-driven habits. In *Mindless Eating*, Cornell marketing professor Brian Wansink has studied the different eating habits of the French and Americans. The contrast is instructive, because the French have significantly lower obesity rates (and live nearly two years longer, on average), but the items in their diet are fattier. Why don't the French get fat? To an American like me, the reason may sound strange and new: They stop eating when they feel full. As a result, they eat less. Americans ignore the internal cue of comfort, even fullness, and plan instead to eat until the bowl is empty, the plate is clean, or the staff stops bringing food. This effect was dramatized in Wansink's "bottomless soup experiment," in which half of the subjects ate soup from bowls to which a hidden hose was attached. The hose replenished those bowls with soup while the subjects ate. The other half of the subjects ate from normal bowls.[53]

Despite eating 73 percent more, the "bottomless bowl" subjects were no more likely to report that they were full than the "normal bowl" eaters. They literally didn't know they were filling up. Focusing as Americans do on external cues, they paid no attention to how they felt, even though all of the subjects, like the Americans and French, had the same biology. Instead, they continued to eat because they were fixed on their external cue: their bowl was half full.

This is as clear an instance of an automatic and thoughtless behavior as you will find. You don't explain a national difference in an area such as eating behavior simply by saying that millions of individuals are all making the same free choices about what and how they eat. Only the press of cultural environment can explain this difference. Now that almost everyone in the United States can enjoy gluttonous portions worthy of kings, "stuffed" is the new "satisfied." Now, if only we can make "gluttony" the new "healthy."

Environments matter to all forms of development, but some aspects of an environment matter more than others. Consider success in child-rearing. According to the best available evidence, what parents do or say doesn't much matter. But peer group does.[54] If parents want to influence their children, they should swallow their morality lectures and instead spend resources on living in a neighborhood where the kids do well in school and are not stigmatized by good performance and an interest in learning. Capturing the lesson of a number of studies, Judith Harris puts it this way:

> By living in one neighborhood rather than another, parents can raise or lower the chances that their children will commit crimes, drop out of school, use drugs, or get pregnant.
>
> If the kids in one neighborhood are generally sensible and law-abiding, and those in another neighborhood are not, it isn't just because the well-behaved kids have rich parents and the other ones do not. It isn't just because they have educated parents and the other ones do not. The financial status and educational level of *their neighbors* also has an effect on the kids. The fact that children are like their parents isn't informative: it could be heredity, it could be environment, who knows? But the fact that children are like their friends' parents is very informative; it can only be environment. And since kids don't spend a whole lot

of time with their friends' parents, the environmental influence must be coming to them by way of their friends. It is delivered, according to group socialization theory, by the peer group.[55]

Psychological science had to overcome decades of platitudes about the importance of character and its development through parental influence. Without question, this common prejudice of parental influence needlessly worries parents when good kids turn into bad ones despite endless parental sermons and expressions of love. But more important than a parent's anxious feeling of irrelevance is that science can help us to identify healthier environments for our children. Even parents with resources overestimate the direct influence they have on their children, but parental choices are not ineffective. It's more that the effective choices are made early on. If you want to avoid criminal influences on your child, don't rely on your best anti-crime sermon. Instead, you can make it unnecessary by simply choosing your neighborhood carefully—if you have that luxury. That is how we can exercise our free will, our power to determine our action—by selecting our environments. And we should choose carefully, because eventually, our environments control us.

The idea of environmental, unconscious priming of behavior gets little play in U.S. politics. Americans' confidence in their conscious self-determination can be seen in all sorts of attitude responses. For instance, only 30 percent of Americans believe that the poor are unlucky, whereas 54 percent of Europeans hold that view.[56] The rejection of luck as an explanation is the affirmation of self-determination. It must be a potent belief that leads 70 percent of Americans to believe that our share of the pie, our ultimate lot in life, is the result of our conscious control over decision and actions.

We may be boundlessly confident in our personal skills and intellectual power, but in the end it is circumstances, more than character or biology, that determine our behavior. Character is real enough; we doubtless have flexible traits that incline us to help strangers, or to be competitive or sarcastic. And this is why the different behaviors can come from the same circumstances. But character is not the firm plumbing that directs the inexorable flow of behavior; the environment directs the stream as well, even changing the course set by our character. Whether it is administering a shock to others, assuming the role of prison guard, or exhibiting greater willingness to help others when under the spell of fresh-baked bread, psychological science has shown that it is situations that tilt people toward their ultimate conduct. Character is a distant second. And this goes for both personal and social policy: what needs to be changed is the world beyond our skin. Outside strategies are the best de-biasers and problem solvers, and so situations of high fidelity are the better route to accurate judgment than a good heart or a focused mind.

THE TASTE FOR GNOCCHI AND
THE PRICE OF BASIC NEEDS

I love gnocchi. I know it, and now you do, too. You could argue that I am mistaken in believing that I love gnocchi, but you would lose. At the same time, I don't know *everything* about what I value. For the right trade (say, in exchange for a basic-needs policy in the United States), I am sure I would give up gnocchi, or even renounce the demon pasta entirely. When deciding which policy to support, often the decent thing to do is trade off certain things that feel valuable to you in exchange for things you believe others with more severe needs might value more. But our immediate reactions are powerful. We move very quickly to claims that certain values are beyond horse-trading. Some values are "hardened."

Granted, there is a reason to protect certain guarantees that a society makes to its citizens. However, that reason has nothing to do with the airy notion of rights, but with the fact that certain guarantees or priorities are central to people's well-being. For example, everyone knows that if Social Security weren't protected, we would be raiding it like drunken sailors. In fact, no one really thinks that the best way to achieve our goals is to make them subject to daily doubt and criticism. The reversal of poverty must be a protected priority. Its funding must be secure, insulated from change from administration to administration.

We imagine that we would sympathize with a child at our dinner table who was without food or health care coverage. From this introspective cinema, we infer that we must have fellow feeling—the right degree of empathy. So, not to worry. If we don't feel the same urgency to assist those farther from our dinner table, it must be because the problems are too complicated to understand or to manage. But the problem with an empathy-based method of moral evaluation may be simpler to understand than we imagine. Because we don't actually see the starving children, we don't think about them. And so we don't empathize with them, and don't act.

Another reason given for inaction is uncertainty. So it is no wonder that people don't assist when it isn't exactly clear how they should. If a child is drowning in front of you, it is clear what to do. If people are starving around the globe, it may be clear that you should do something, but difficult to formulate a specific intention or craft a plan that can be implemented. Do I work in a homeless shelter? Do I give money to UNICEF? Do I get involved in electoral politics to support policies that are most likely to help the afflicted group? Psychology doesn't answer those questions. But it does offer some clues about how we might respond to each of those courses of action.

When philosophers can't make any progress on a topic such as free will, which is right in their wheelhouse, and psychology has proven that the feeling of free action is routinely mistaken, it is time to draw a practical conclusion: We can't justify denying entitlements to the poor by an appeal to failures of free choice. There are many other legitimate reasons that those basic-needs policies could be rejected. Perhaps the market would provide more reliably for the poor. Perhaps charities do. These are questions for science, and they are answerable to the facts. Not so with the fanciful talk of free will. So you have to be willing to allow a lot of suffering in the name of a view as cryptic as alchemy.

People make choices to get what we want—few deny that. Many

choose a college, a job, a new car, a mate, hobbies, and favorite charities. Although these are different kinds of options, they are all real
ones. But people whose basic needs are threatened do not have many
effective options. They don't choose to live in a tenement in the way
that another might choose to rent rather than buy. And to claim that
impoverished people are responsible for the consequences of their
choices just because they could have chosen otherwise is an awfully
thin wedge with which to separate our resources and others' desperate need. When it comes to the requirements of happiness, effective
choice is choice enough. And sometimes, when we make poor choices,
it is not because we have neglected excellent alternatives, but because poor options are all we have.

If we are interested in improving human well-being, we should
set aside dithering controversy and mystification about free will—the
rhetoric of nation builders and ideologues—and cut quickly to
what we *do* know. For example, we know that when people have the
right options, they form habits, say, to save more money through
automatic-deduction plans, to eat healthier by controlling portion
size, and to stay sober by shifting social settings to patient but firm
supporters. But all of these habits are shaped passively, with changes
in people's circumstances and the crafting of institutions that enhance
their well-being.

The lessons of psychological research on automatic thoughts and
deeds—of systematic habit formation—extend far beyond the lab. If
properly handled, we can loosen the grip of undesirable habits, and
form new ones that will enhance our lives and the lives of others.

THE ROAD AHEAD

Identifying and correcting our biases begins with the personal and
social policies we adopt, not with spontaneous decisions we make.
Correction begins with a process in which we recognize our weak-
nesses and constraints, and so devise strategies to skirt them.[57]

But first we need to understand how the biases ravage our judgment, and how widely they have their effects. The normal reaction to the findings about automaticity is to insist that they have more to do with motivation than cognition, more with desire than thought. Whatever the misgiving, the biases are not themselves liberal or conservative. Instead, they are nonpartisan and obstructionist; they prevent us from doing what we want, from achieving our goals. Often we don't even estimate their costs because we don't know they exist. But they do, in damaging abundance.

Biases are also unyielding. When we *are* made aware of them, we don't have the ability or resolve to control them. But perhaps we can think around them—use our problem-solving powers as a means to correct them. In the end, the most effective strategies for de-biasing will contain all of the key features of effective personal and social policies.

The next chapter provides an applied primer of judgment and decision making. This primer is no drab catalog of cognitive inventory. It contains dramatic errors that will persuade us that the problems we face warrant attention. Cognitive biases have one property, in particular, that we need to take seriously if we are to pursue our well-being: they impose a weighty ceiling on our capabilities.

In breadth and scope, cognitive biases are at least as responsible for false beliefs as perceptual errors, and they are no more correctible. But knowing that they *are* illusions is a big step forward. Once we know they exist, we can then move on to develop remedies for them.

CHAPTER 3

Can We Rebuild This Mind?
A Tool Kit for Spotting Biases

Expensive Intuitions

B AD DECISIONS ARE COSTLY. THE PRICE CAN BE A SHORTER life, a larger debt, or a sadder existence. Everyone wants a longer life, and yet we take our health for granted and ignore warning signs. Nobody enjoys personal debt, and yet we spend money we don't have on items we don't need. No one hopes to be downhearted or to die alone, and yet many of our decisions destine us for more isolation and less joy. Our individual minds are fine for purchasing food, selecting a pet, and planning a career. We can also perform technical feats—calculate the pressure of a gas, match DNA profiles, and construct elaborate models. But there are many things we cannot do alone: construct a government, build nuclear theory, assemble a transit system, and eradicate famine. Now we can add a few things to the list, such as spotting and counteracting racism, controlling global warming, reducing traffic fatalities, and creating a social safety net for our impoverished neighbors.

It is worth remembering that a solitary mind is no match for the complexity of the natural and social world. But my point is additional. The examples here are complex in a special way: they involve delicately orchestrated group behavior, often coordinating many institutions in a combined effort. It can be mystifying when these efforts fail. For example, why can't some urban public schools achieve graduation rates above 50 percent? It can't simply be a money problem, because some schools with lower per capita expenditures perform better. Indeed, no single factor appears to prevent failure. To alleviate these problems, we need to carry out careful policy experiments, as we will see in chapter 6. But some failures are the combined effect of individual errors, and are predictable from what we already know about the limitations on human judgment. One overconfident person can be corrected, persuaded, or otherwise neutralized; a group of overconfident individuals, all with the same mistaken beliefs, can do some real damage, as we will see when we look at the planning fallacy. Consequently, at least some actions taken by groups can be improved by urging a *method* for making good decisions. Improvements in individual decision making can produce group benefits.

These social benefits are within reach, but the biases—our systematic cognitive tendencies toward error—are sturdy barriers. Biases persist even when people have the time and information to make a good decision possible.[1] We dramatically underestimate our health risks. We adapt easily to overeating and lack of exercise, and to a host of other maladies such as HIV, heart disease, and cancer that are not altogether self-inflicted. Inoculated with optimism, we don't take adequate precautions, in health or in wealth. Shifting from sickness to saving, people discount the future value of many resources, and so radically undersave for lots of important and foreseeable prospects, ranging from the costs of college education and health care to retirement. But these decisions are not just personally costly; they are socially costly as well. The total cost of optimistic bias and irrational discounting—what Adam Smith called "the contempt of risk and the presumptuous hope of success"[2]—is difficult to estimate. But in costs to our health care and social welfare systems alone it must surely run into billions of dollars annually in uninsured treatment and indigent services. People whose judgment leads them into poor health and poverty eventually become the responsibility of the state. And that is why social investment in a prepared and educated citizenry can more than pay for itself.

When people regularly make serious errors that have bad effects for themselves and others, and when they cannot control the processes that produce them, it becomes a matter of public concern. It is an open question whether, and to what extent, the government should step in, as it has in similar cases. Helmet laws are a case in point, and I take them up later. But first, we need to see the evidence of our global and systematic proneness to error. The case for institutional correction of cognitive biases grows stronger as the list of biases grows longer, and as their threats to well-being become clearer.

WOW! WHAT ARE THE CHANCES? BASE-RATE NEGLECT

People aren't very good at judging the probability of particular events—that a child will be injured in a school shooting, that we will get food poisoning at a restaurant, that a routine mammogram will produce a positive result for breast cancer, that a stranger on the train will commit a theft, or that someone will have a heart attack in your presence. We make our guesses, but what we really need to know is the base rate—the relative frequency with which an event occurs in the population. That information can be hard to get. As a result, we ignore base-rate information, and rely instead on intuition. We begin with a small number of familiar instances that come to mind, and assume they are representative.

Our intuitive biases are errant, stubborn, and systematic, so they often prevent us from using information correctly. And when two events happen close together in space or time, we look for stories that glue together bits of otherwise insignificant events. What we should instead be looking for are base rates—the frequency of different events in a population. It is our insensitivity to base rates, or "base-rate neglect," that is so often at the heart of our individual cognitive failures. Consider our investment failures. When we sit back and recall, with satisfaction, our investment successes, we seem to remember *only* our investment successes. Instead, we should calculate our successes divided by our total investment decisions. When we do that, the results look far more modest. Because we "see patterns" that aren't real, we fail to appreciate that, overall, while the market tends to move higher over long periods of time, in the short term, market movements are random. So people "trade on noise," thinking all along that they are acting on good information about the forces behind stock prices. They commit the base-rate fallacy when they suppose that their portfolio will outperform a randomly selected basket of stocks.[3] Writ personal, we think we are different. Other people aren't like I am, with my searing ability to peer into the universe of stocks and pick a winner. The same frailty causes us to plan for perfection, so that our projects end up late or poorly executed.

Of course, in some cases we do consider base rates, and we embrace or dismiss them at just the right times. Baseball managers match their left-handed batters against the opponent's right-handed pitchers, and vice versa. If you look at the data, this really is a better bet than ignoring match-ups. And following base rates, many of us have learned to dismiss the promises of even our favorite politicians, just going on the probabilities.

The best solution to base-rate neglect is to get the base-rate information and then to use it. But this advice can be like telling folks to buy low and sell high: difficult to argue with, and impossible to know when you are succeeding. In addition, base-rate information is often hard to get, and effortful to use. And even then, honoring base-rate information is only one of our values. Applying this information in a just and fair way matters, too. Courts often reject base-rate information about race or ethnicity that is diagnostic of crime when using that information might lead to unfair decisions. In other cases, the cost of getting base-rate information may be too great to be worth using it. But just as a person's biases can erode their individual well-being, collections of biased individuals, such as juries, citizen groups, and legislatures, can do some real damage when trafficking in policies about crime, hunger, illness, and public education. The value of base-rate information will typically swamp the cost of getting it.

THE WORST-LAID PLANS

The base-rate fallacy is at the bottom of many other fallacies, particularly self-flattering predictions about our own performance. It is too easy to forget our little embarrassments, and to look instead at an unrepresentative sample of complimentary performance. To reverse this trend, a little planning can make all the difference. Poor planning catches up with people in all endeavors. Most people adopt an "internal approach" to planning problems. Suppose we are planning to move to a new apartment, and we are trying to calculate how many days it will take to pack and move. When we think to ourselves about the necessary time, we think about each step in the process, rather than how badly we have underestimated in the past. We can complete the move on time only if: we have enough boxes, and people to pack them; if no friends or helpers back out; if we don't have many repairs to make on the apartment we are vacating, or too much to clean up afterward to get our security deposit. Be honest: When moving, how many times have you worked through the night, packing and cleaning before a big move? If it is more than you would have liked, it's because you have adopted an "internal" approach to the problem. The "outside" solution to the moving problem can take different forms. If you have enough money, you can just hire a mover. If you want to handle the move yourself, you need to follow a strict plan. The regimen we'll examine in a moment may seem sterile and effortful, but it beats failure.

Each "negative" is, by itself, unlikely. But when you add them all up, it is pretty likely that at least one of them will happen. Unfortunately, people don't find this point about combined probabilities intuitive. Planning for potential harm is like an insurance policy against risk. There were many unlikely events that might have caused the New Orleans levees to fail, but engineers and policymakers alike underestimated the combined probability that one or another of them would happen. Of course, too many assumed, inaccurately, that the levee construction was sound; they supposed that the only serious risks were external to the levee—such as the strength of the storm and depth of the water. But the levee was also poorly constructed. Policy is always subject to miscalculation of risk, but it is important that the calculation be made. The best we can do in these cases is to focus on base rates—the relative frequency at which some disaster or other will occur. This solution requires that you take an outside view of your goals and your ability to achieve them, looking at base-rate performance on similar problems. The same goes for policy.

Most of us have heard of the Denver airport not because it is a famous hub, but because its baggage delivery system was so bad it received national attention. The planners constructed a poor schedule. They didn't foresee that an untested and novel technology required more time for successful implementation. And the planners allowed the purpose of this complex luggage delivery system to constantly change. In order for the baggage system to work smoothly, there must be an empty cart lined up to receive the bags. But apparently installers didn't notice that the carts were either unavailable or poorly aligned, causing the luggage to get backed up or even damaged. Six months after the system's opening, a manager giving a tour described the luggage problem as a "novel phenomenon that they had just started to work on."[4] The resulting delays cost about $1.1 million a day.[5] The airport, owned and run by the City of Denver, was sixteen months late, and $2.8 billion over budget. The project was partially subsidized by $800 million in public funds.[6] The proportion of that $800 million devoted to cost overruns could have gone to the area's publicly funded universities, to Denver's homeless, to Denver's public schools, to meal programs, or to countless other causes that would have immediately and tangibly improved the lives of the people of Denver. But by the time the airport was under construction, it was already too late—psychologically—for any of that. Everyone was prepared to honor sunk costs, and hope for the project's redemption.[7]

Other cases of poor planning have been transformed into success stories. In the last few years researchers wondered why poor farmers in Africa failed to use fertilizer on their crops, which they knew would drastically improve their yield and wealth. The reason wasn't ignorance or naked irrationality, but poor planning. The fertilizer vendors traditionally approached the farmers of Western Kenya near the beginning of the growing season, when fertilizer would be most beneficial. Unfortunately, this is also when farmers have the least money, because they are farthest from the harvest payments. The chief barrier to fertilizer use, then, was low savings. Once they discovered this, researchers designed a prepayment plan and a timing plan that tied crop *sale* at the end of the season to fertilizer *purchase,* to be used in the spring. And with this modest plan, research activists helped people to substantially improve their crop yields.[8]

No one likes missing deadlines or losing sleep. Poor planning causes both, with all the stress that results. It is costly when it causes us to squander money or labor on a poorly implemented policy. A five-step procedure can correct the planning fallacy, but the steps require an external approach to the problem.[9] The trick is to assemble the track record for past projects. How is the current project different from the others? How often were you overcommitted in the past? Are your current obstacles greater or smaller?

We could try to reverse this costly error by using an internal correction factor that builds in extra time to complete the task. But our private calculations never seem to leave us enough of a buffer; we fix our sights on a deadline based on a best possible scenario, and don't adjust enough for the predictable problems, delays, and shortfalls.

SURE THING:
OVERCONFIDENCE AND THE PRICE OF CONCEIT

The "internal" approach to problem-solving is a kind of heuristic—a rule of thumb to solve a difficult problem. The overconfidence bias, so crippling to our finances, is the most widely documented frailty in the lab. But many others might be mentioned: the availability bias, base-rate fallacy, planning fallacy, and the status quo bias. Although many of these systematic cognitive errors were first demonstrated in the lab and not in the field, we can see how these biases give poor policy a foothold. Suppose, for example, you were trying to determine the greatest threats to people's health and safety. People have many anecdotal beliefs about the risk of AIDS, car accidents, terrorist attacks, food poisonings, and toy injuries. Our perception of risk drives our personal decisions about what to purchase and where to travel. But it also prompts our social decisions about worthy policies to fund. In one experiment, subjects were asked to indicate the most frequent cause of death in the United States, and to estimate their confidence that their choice was correct (in terms of "odds").[10] When subjects set the odds of their answer's correctness at 100:1, they were correct only 73 percent of the time. Remarkably, even when they were so certain as to set the odds between 10,000:1 and 1,000,000:1, they were correct only between 85 and 90 percent of the time, respectively. They would literally have bet the farm, and had a fair chance of being dead wrong. It might be easy to think that overconfident judgment is a problem only for callow laypeople, and that experienced executives and highly trained scientists are free from it. But these overconfident judgments are utterly representative of those made by professionals in medical care, financial services, and a host of other settings of "expert" decision making.[11] In fact, physicists, economists, and demographers all suffer from this bias, even when reasoning about their field of expertise.[12] When you have a good theory, overconfidence may do less damage. The problem is people usually believe they have a good theory. But this bravado simply masks ignorance or feeble intuition. And when that happens, we fail to take medical precautions or plan for financial safety. In short, we gamble with our happiness.

Why do people find it so difficult to learn from the lessons of overconfidence? First, individual cases typically don't give us systematic feedback about the quality of our judgments. How many people actually keep a diary of expectations for the day, log their confidence estimates that events will occur, and then later match those estimates with the actual facts of the day? We don't have the time—and anyway, such a diary would only tell us how overconfident we are. In order to know how overconfidence leads us astray, we would have to compare the long-term outcomes of our actual decisions against alternative decisions we didn't implement. You would need to be two identical individuals to bring off that experiment.

The cure for the overconfidence bias will instead have to work from the outside in: find the important life decisions that people are most overconfident about, and then give them choices in which their overconfidence will do no harm. In very special cases we may even identify tasks that will benefit from overconfidence. For example, overconfident company managers may budget capital in a way that is more responsible to shareholder interests. They save the company money precisely because they are overconfident in their personal ability to reduce risk. Less confident managers may pursue this goal less aggressively.[13] While promising, these cases of a fortuitous fit of bias to task success are rare. In the meantime, the examples on the other side of the ledger pile up, leading to the same lesson: don't count on your cognitive biases having beneficial effects, or on their proneness to willful control. Instead, render human discretion less necessary by elevating the quality of the options. Wherever possible, give people only good options, options that will serve their long-term, considered interests.

WHEN YOU PUT IT *THAT* WAY: FRAMING BIAS

Vocabulary, like comparison, is a powerful tool in the science of persuasion. A prosecuting attorney may say that the defendant's car "smashed" rather than "hit" the plaintiff's automobile.[14] Pundits may describe taxation as a "loss" rather than an investment for future benefit. The effect of such framing can prompt us to reason badly and ignore relevant information about the population, and focus instead on anecdotal impressions. Framing is, shall we say, prejudicially suggestive.

Not surprisingly, framing can cost reasoners their shirts. In a simple example advanced by leading judgment researchers, respondents in a telephone interview evaluated the fairness of an action described in the following vignette, which was presented in two versions that differed only in the bracketed clauses.

> A company is making a small profit. It is located in a community
> experiencing a recession with substantial unemployment [but
> no inflation/and inflation of 12 percent]. The company decides
> to [decrease wages and salaries 7 percent/increase salaries only
> 5 percent] this year.[15]

Although the loss of real income is effectively the same in the two versions, the proportion of respondents who judged the action of the company "unfair" or "very unfair" was 62 percent for a nominal reduction but only 22 percent for a nominal increase. The reason for this preference has been known for more than twenty years: We perceive the reduction of salary as a loss, but not the same increase in inflation. We hate the idea that our salary might be lowered—even if the reduction in pay is offset by deflation—and will do nearly anything to avoid this kind of loss. To use the language of bargaining, we see the reduction as a risk, and we are risk-averse.

Not all risks are financial. Consider how "message framing" can affect our health risks. Messages carrying the same statistical information can be cast in different ways, and will prompt different behavior. Policy makers can report to the public that people within a certain age range and illness stage who get tested for HIV or breast cancer and test positive have a 70 percent chance of living beyond seven years, or a 30 percent chance of dying in under seven years. These numerical messages have different impacts. In order to test the relative effectiveness of health messages, researchers at Yale and the University of Minnesota created either gain-framed or loss-framed videotapes.[16] The gain-framed videos explained the positive effects of healthy behavior and regular breast exams, and the loss-framed video attempted to frighten the viewer with the bad things that could happen if they didn't see a doctor. The subjects who viewed the loss-framed message were significantly more likely to enact detection behaviors, such as arranging for a mammogram. Message framing has improved motivation for HIV testing, too.[17]

Even if psychology won't tell us what we ought to do morally, we should admit its power to make us act more efficiently.

I'LL TELL YOU MY PREFERENCES AS SOON AS I CONSTRUCT THEM: PREFERENCE REVERSALS AND THE PROMINENCE EFFECT

Cognitive research sometimes begins with a few modest exercises in problem solving, and ends by raising some of the deepest issues in the study of the mind. The story behind preference reversals and the prominence effect is an example of this strange path. Economists predict that when people say that two goods, or two options, have equal value, they are prepared to buy and sell them under all the same circumstances. And it shouldn't matter what method you use to determine the value, an assumption economists make called procedure invariance. But it turns out that different decision procedures elicit different preferences. Early research showed that when people were deciding how *attractive* they found a bet ("making a choice"), they were influenced mainly by the probabilities of winning and losing. But when deciding on buying and selling prices on a ticket to make one of these bets ("setting a price"), people were influenced mainly by the dollar amounts to be won or lost. The researchers went a step further, however. They reasoned that if choice and price-setting could be made to conflict, people might suffer "preference reversals"—irrational on any account of decision making. Studying gamblers in a Las Vegas casino, researchers found exactly the same pattern of reversal. In the cases where people preferred the high-probability gamble to the high-payoff gamble, 81 percent placed a *higher* dollar price on the high-*payoff* gamble.

The immediate lessons are simple. Even though people may report valuing a particular option, choice and price-setting invoke different cognitive processes. When asked to *choose* between two gambles, they pay special attention to the probability that they will win. When asked to *set a price* on the value of the bet itself, they look at how large the potential payoffs are. And like nearly all of the biases, the effect is robust, and cannot be reduced by monetary incentives.

Real public choices usually involve the same tradeoffs between goods and money, and there are especially revealing results in public-choice settings where people address public concerns such as a clean environment or traffic safety. One experiment modeled a typical public-choice setting. Subjects were presented with the following scenario: Traffic accidents in Israel claim about six hundred lives per year. The Israeli Ministry of Transportation is considering one of two programs to reduce the number of traffic casualties. (Casualties, of course, are expected to be the prominent factor in evaluation.) Program X expects a fatality rate of 500 people per year at an annual cost of $55 million. Program Y expects a fatality rate of 570 people per year at an annual cost of $12 million. When people were given this information, 67 percent of the respondents chose Program X. Thirty-three percent chose Program Y. But when people were denied cost information for Program X and inserted a cost to match its attractiveness to Program Y, 96 percent of those respondents filled in a number smaller than $55 million. In other words, when matching, they preferred Program Y to Program X, even though it saved fewer lives.[18]

Sometimes a feature's prominence is a contextual affair, and can be boosted by what you'd think were irrelevant additions to a set of choices. For example, by simply introducing a low-quality pen into a choice set originally composed of just a high-quality pen and a specific amount of money, you could induce more people to ignore the money and select the high-quality pen. This is a classic preference reversal, provoked by the content of your available choices.

It is less important that people exhibit preference reversals than what this psychological fact shows about the nature of preference. Preferences are not monolithic, stable, and unchanging entities whose existence can be uncovered with the right equipment. Instead, they are works in progress, psychologically messy and complicated in all the ways classical economists sought to avoid. The discovery of a preference is, in part, a constructive process.

DO NO HARM: THE OMISSION BIAS

One of our most treasured intuitions is that it is worse to bring about harm than to let harm occur. There is a moral difference, we think, between *acts* and *omissions*. But these intuitions are feeble. Strain them a little, and we soon get confounded. For example, a large proportion of health care funding in the United States ends up being spent on patients whose life prospects are poor and life quality is low, for extravagant and expensive life-saving efforts. We focus on the treatment of disease far more than on the promotion of wellness. Wellness-promotion is an act; health neglect is an omission. The government heavily subsidizes this kind of emergency care not covered by third-party insurers. These federal resources are limited, and could be used to radically improve the prospects of a much larger portion of the U.S. population, who lack insurance but whose health would not require, say, extravagant efforts. As a result, people without health insurance die at higher rates for want of routine risk-reducing drugs such as cholesterol-lowering statins. It is not clear how we arrived at the current allocation of health care resources, but our system didn't fall from the bottoms of cherubs. We need to examine why a responsible allocation wouldn't move money away from late-stage care, perhaps leading to the death of some, and toward the maintenance of tens of millions uninsured, saving the lives of many more. When presented with this kind of choice, our moral certitude dissolves and we can do little more than reassert that the offending act is wrong.[19]

Getting to the bottom of the omission bias is not easy. What distinguishes an act from an omission may be little more than who happens to have the gunboats—in other words, whom the current, "default" policy already protects. At a minimum, people avoid costs of commission, but do much less to evade costs of omission, even when the latter are higher. If an inoculation against a childhood disease causes five deaths per hundred thousand children, parents prefer not approving the inoculation (that is, "doing nothing"), even when the disease itself kills uninoculated children at twice that rate. This is the omission bias.[20] From the parents' perspective of their own accountability, your child's death by inoculation is something you *did* (a commission); death without it was something that *happened to them* (an omission). The stress created by contemplating these high-conflict choices is heightened by the feeling that we are responsible for an unwelcome decision outcome.

There is something stilted and scholastic about this distinction, however. If you are clever enough to be contemplating the distinction between acts and omissions, you are also clever enough to know that you are exposing your uninoculated child to more risk by closing your eyes and hoping, itself a decision. As a result, the conclusion we should draw from the literature is not that some omissions are blameworthy, but rather that some patterns of conduct—such as not getting your child inoculated—can be positive decisions *not* to do something.

Understood as positive acts of omission, then, the omission bias may even partially explain one of the more stubborn questions of this book: Why has judgment and decision-making research been used so sparingly in policy analysis? The answer? Informing policy with experimental findings would require a change in the status quo, and this in turn requires a commission; you have to take positive action, and thus assume greater accountability. But we might approach this issue instead by asking: Why are researchers nervous about the consequences of *overapplying* their research on, for example, affective forecasting and happiness, but sanguine about the consequences of *underapplying* it?

Possible answers to this question are worth thinking through. They reveal the powerful influence of our psychological inertia—of what we get used to—on our apparent indifference to existing levels of human wealth, need, and suffering. After all, 10 percent of the U.S. population is impoverished. Nearly 20 percent is without health insurance. And there is no evidence that this tonic level of suffering and risk is inevitable in an affluent democracy. In order to create a more decent society, researchers (and everyone else, you might suppose) should be anxious for a social policy that incorporates our best psychological science into our social policies. The psychological evidence suggests that a basic-needs policy could plausibly increase the lower subjective well-being of the poor, while leaving largely unchanged the relatively higher subjective well-being of other groups.

The invisibility of omissions is a stubborn bias that dogs us in every area of life. In baseball, many a heroic diving catch in the outfield begins with laziness and indecision. Having broken for the ball so late, or having run it down with so leisurely a stride, the player can only compensate for his misjudgment with a dramatic final effort. People remember the dive and stretch, not the break for the ball or the loafing chase. So it goes for the invisibility of omissions. Some heroic efforts are required only because we are in the same breath responsible for a failed policy. Shouldn't we make the dive unnecessary?

It will be difficult and expensive to recover from our social welfare omissions. For example, by having no thought-out public health policy preventing poverty-related diseases, we have produced a tuberculosis problem, particularly among patients with HIV.[21] And when a poverty-related disease is allowed to flourish, it is tragic that the impulse to help is discouraged by the fact that the victims are now so ill that it takes extraordinary efforts to treat them. And we haven't even begun to catalog the overwrought aid organizations that arise simply because government allocations give institutional legitimacy to sorrowful neglect. Think of the volunteers who drive needy people to doctor's appointments, dispense meals to the homeless, or try to teach children material that they should be learning in their terribly underfunded schools. We are fortunate to have such gracious people in our society. But we have grown comfortable with this goodwill, and it now subsidizes an attitude of civic neglect. Indeed, would volunteers ironically be blamed if they withdrew their support?

Poor policy has produced a class of social heroes, selfless individuals who administer to the sick and needy, and another that advocates on their behalf. A decent society has a different take on these activities. It acknowledges the sacrifices and rewards the efforts, but doesn't see the problems they treat as inevitable. Instead, it tries to reduce the need for such heroism in the first place, by preparing for and treating the cognitive and empathic limitations that require it.

STEADY AS SHE SINKS: STATUS QUO BIAS

We all feel comfortable with what's familiar—our collection of music, our old pet, the soothing creaks of our trusty wooden floor. We even prefer the faces we see most often, especially our own. The status quo is comforting. So it is not surprising that we have a bias in favor of our existing environment. The status quo bias causes us to favor existing or entrenched courses of action, over alternatives that we would otherwise agree had greater value. In the original experiment on the "endowment effect" on which the status quo bias is based, mugs were given randomly to some people in a group. Those who now had them were asked to state a price to sell their mug; those without a mug were asked to name a price at which they would purchase one. Usually, the average *sales* price of a mug, a coat, a car, or a house, is substantially higher than the average *offer* price. Put in policy terms, people don't appreciate when an existing option is more costly than a new option, because people rate existing or "default" options more positively than alternatives. We may like sticking to the familiar, taking the path of least resistance, or just being lazy. Maybe we see the change as risky, or we fear the new effort will be too costly.[22] Whatever the reason, we favor the status quo.

And indulgence has a price. We have mortgages, credit arrangements, insurance premiums, and cell phone plans. These plans amount to our existing or default options, and psychological inertia often discourages us from pursuing better, more efficient options. Who can be bothered to hunt for a less expensive cell phone service contract or track changes in semiannual insurance premiums? But when we don't, we usually pay a price. This is not to say that we *should* spend more of our waking hours finding a better phone service deal, but rather that we should be clear that there is a real price for not doing so.

The status quo bias is at the root of many bad individual decisions, but in the end, our cell phone bill is our own business. Public policies, on the other hand, concern everyone, and sometimes status quo arrangements have effects that are widespread and fatal. This is the dark side of the status quo bias. Consider a specific and common effect of the status quo bias. Jennifer Jackson was a twenty-two-year-old from Canaan, Vermont, who liked riding horses, playing baseball, and practicing the clarinet. She also needed a lung transplant. On July 18, 2004, Jenny died while waiting for a donor lung.[23] And she is one of roughly five thousand who die every year while waiting for an organ. Yet this tragic event was not inevitable. In fact, she might have lived had she resided in Spain, Austria, Belgium, or Portugal, where there is one key difference in donor policy: everyone is automatically considered an organ donor and is put on the donor rolls unless he registers to "opt out." In other words, the status quo position is to donate your organs upon your death, because this increases the number of donors available. (In Spain, at most 15 percent have chosen not to be donors, leaving 85 percent available donors. But in the United States, less than half have even made a decision about whether to donate, and only 28 percent have actually signed a donor card.)[24] In most of Europe, laissez-faire—let the organ needy beware—is not the status quo.

It is not that Americans object to organ donation. Like the citizens of opt-out countries in Europe, Americans overwhelmingly *approve* of organ donation. But when it comes to doing something about it, we suffer from psychological inertia, or a status quo bias—we tend to prefer an existing state of affairs over alternative ones. The result: in the last ten years alone, the United States has seen in the neighborhood of sixty thousand of its citizens die while waiting for donor organs. Thanks to a cognitive bias that is part of our natural condition, we are unable to execute our desire to help others and ourselves.

Behavioral economics, a new field already recognized with at least one Nobel Prize, has uncovered yet another case of costly inefficiency, though this one is quite mundane. In the early 1990s, automobile insurance providers gave drivers in Pennsylvania and New Jersey a choice between two coverage options regarding the right to sue. In exchange for lower insurance rates, drivers in both states were given the choice of a reduced right to sue. But the default option was different for each state. In Pennsylvania, the default option was the full right to sue. That is, if they did nothing, they had the full right to sue. New Jersey drivers had to take action, by selecting the alternate option, in order to acquire this right at an additional cost.

Drivers in the two states are similar, so we should expect to see similar percentages in New Jersey and Pennsylvania. In fact, the results are startlingly different. Motorists' choices followed the default options in each state. In New Jersey, where you have to take action to secure your full rights to sue, 20 percent of the drivers opted for the full right to sue. In Pennsylvania, where the full right to sue was the default option, 75 percent of the drivers retained the full right to sue. If New Jerseyites and Pennsylvanians are demographically similar, then either Pennsylvanians paid $200 million more than they needed to or New Jerseyites paid $200 million less than they should have.[25]

U.S. representatives appreciate the lesson of the status quo bias without knowledge of the research. The pay raises on their $165,200 salary take effect without action on their part. By contrast, there is no such default cost-of-living adjustment made to the minimum wage, which, by the end of 2006, had remained at $5.15 since 1997.[26] Increasing the minimum wage would require congressional *action*, and that might spark controversy. But then again, so might a congressional pay raise held to the same standard of transparency.

READY TO MIND: THE AVAILABILITY BIAS

In commonsense reasoning, people have a knack for inferring representativeness from casually observable properties. Why do people generally suppose that they are safer in their cars than in a commercial jet? Are children today more likely to be snatched on their way to and from school, or are these events just better publicized? Are we more likely to die in a terrorist attack these days, or is our sense of unease just the result of overreporting?

This "availability heuristic" certainly works in special conditions, but it is not generally reliable. The availability bias is possible because memory does not merely record statistical information. In an effort to economize, it records jarring, unusual, and otherwise salient events as representative. According to the two pioneers of the biases in reasoning, Tversky and Kahneman, the availability bias occurs when we "assess the frequency of a class or the probability of an event by the ease with which instances or occurrences can be brought to mind."[27]

News and gossip items not only produce vivid images, but also keep them in public consciousness. Shark attacks are big news items, but more people die from falling airplane parts than from shark attacks. Diabetes and stomach cancer kill about twice as many people per year as car accidents and homicide, yet crashes and murders swamp the more frequent and quiet killers.

Media coverage trades on this tendency, keeping dramatic, even if unrepresentative, images in our minds. Consider sentiment about public aid revealed in standard "content analyses" of television and print media. To take just one example, while African Americans are only 29 percent of those falling beneath the poverty level, in the middle 1990s 65 percent of poor people on the networks were African American. The print media, too, portrayed the poor as African Americans. There, African Americans comprised 62 percent of the poor portrayed in *Newsweek, Time*, and *U.S. News & World Report.*[28]

The availability heuristic is the unconscious cognitive rule that helps us process this information. But it is not simply like a faster chip in our brain; it is one that buys speed at a price. It tells us that if an event is easy to recall or visualize, it must be representative. As a result, events whose instances are difficult to generate seem less available for consideration.

The availability bias can obscure the need for particular public remedy for a social problem. Police see intravenous drug users when they are dangerous criminals, needle-sharing addicts who commit battery when desperate and steal whenever possible to pay for their drug habit. Health care workers, however, see them much later, after they've contracted HIV or collapsed suddenly. By this time, they are helpless and pathetic. If you are a police officer, it may be hard to vote for funding to treat intravenous drug users, because it is difficult for police to generate in their minds instances of them as helpless and needy. And once again, separated from addicts by goals and roles, it is hard for police to span the empathy gap.

And so it goes for the weightier matters of terrorism, kidnapping, poverty, and public safety. Some events are made more accessible to thought by their jarring or unusual character. News and gossip items such as murder and celebrity arrests produce vivid images, and keep dramatic events in the public consciousness. Images of the welfare queen or the shifty panhandler preoccupy citizens far more than their actual frequency would warrant. School shootings are big news items, but more people died, for example, from lightning strikes in 1998—a representative year for lightning fatalities (the mean is about ninety fatalities per year in the United States between 1959 and 1994)—than from school shootings in any year in the United States (less than half that in any year from 1992 to 2005, years when school shootings received much press).[29] Worrying without cause is a real cost. Before embarking on a public campaign that scares rather than informs, policymakers need to be sure that scaring people actually motivates them to take evasive action, and that they have the means to take that action. Otherwise, the public push to fret is a dead loss.

I KNEW IT ALL ALONG: HINDSIGHT BIAS

Although our experiences present a skewed sample of all events, we still try to learn from those experiences and use them when we make decisions about what policies to support. We appeal to our personal exchanges with strangers, our memories of good intentions executed badly, and job hopes dashed. And we construct stories that make sense of them all, no matter how inaccurate.

As events unfold, people are already trying to make sense of them so that—no matter what happens—they are less surprised by outcomes than they might have been. Hindsight bias is our tendency to find past events more predictable than they in fact are. Traditionally, the phenomenon of hindsight bias is established by asking subjects to estimate the likelihood of various outcomes of an upcoming event, and then retesting them after asking them to recall how likely they had found each of the possible outcomes before they happened. Fischhoff and Beyth[30] did just this in an early study. Before President Nixon's trip to China and the Soviet Union in 1972, a group of people were asked how likely they found a variety of possible outcomes (for example, Nixon meeting Mao, the Soviet Union and United States establishing a joint space program). Two weeks to six months after the trip, those same people were asked to fill out the same questionnaire. But there were a few additional questions. They were asked to recall the probabilities they assigned initially to the same events and, if they couldn't recall them, to assign the probability they would have assigned immediately before Nixon's trip. They were also asked if each of the listed outcomes had, in fact, occurred. For the events that subjects thought had occurred, they remembered their estimates as more accurate than they in fact were. For the events thought not to have occurred, subjects recalled their estimates as having been lower than they in fact were. The effect not only has staying power; it seems to strengthen with the passage of time. After three to six months, more than eight out of ten people displayed hindsight biases. Therefore, after learning the results of Nixon's trip, subjects believed the outcomes were more predictable that they actually had been.

The results dramatize how hindsight distorts our judgments of predictability. Once we know that an event has occurred, we rewrite history. We conceptualize the event as having been inevitable, and conclude that it was fairly predictable all along. And while you are already changing history, you may as well make your predictive skills look good.

At first, it might be hard to see the harm in claiming that we knew it all along. Isn't this just a little conceit in which we can indulge? Perhaps. But conceit breeds complacency, and the main cost of the hindsight bias may lie in failing to pursue superior courses of action because we don't see how truly superior they are. Without proper acknowledgment of our initial errors, the hindsight bias blinds us to the mistakes, and removes the incentive to respond to the data with care and modesty.

With our confidence brimming, then, scientific research on the frailties of human judgment has not yet had influence on those aspects of policies made by the judicial and legislative branches of the U.S. government designed to improve human welfare. These plans include shaping attitudes toward poverty, encouraging saving among lower- and middle-income people, and the threat of racism.

Not every arm of government has been indifferent to judgment research, however. The CIA was quick to see its importance. The most obvious application concerns the value of propaganda, persuasion, and managing public backlash against bad policy. Each of these features can be advanced by judgment research. Suppose a country's leaders have an agenda that doesn't enjoy broad support among citizens. Suppose, further, that these leaders have decided to go to war against a country to establish control over an area of the world they think would be of strategic importance. Research on the hindsight bias might hold clues to the shaping of public opinion and deflection of blame for poor intelligence. In recently published internal papers, a 1978 document analyzes the first studies on the hindsight bias (which received funding from the Defense Department):

> These results indicate that overseers conducting postmortem evaluations of what analysts should have been able to foresee, given the available information, will tend to perceive the outcome of that situation as having been more predictable than was, in fact, the case. Because they are unable to reconstruct a state of mind that views the situation only with foresight, not hindsight, overseers will tend to be more critical of intelligence performance than is warranted.[31]

The CIA may have been interested in the hindsight bias, but the U.S. court system has been far less vigilant. More than twenty years on, there is still no systematic response to it by the courts.

This is unfortunate, not least because hindsight studies leave little doubt that jurors, like other people, confuse hindsight and predictability.[32] And this leads to huge awards based on misunderstanding. In one case, a radiologist was sued for malpractice for failing to notice the radiographic signs of a three-centimeter tumor, which, three and a half years later, was diagnosed as a malignant thymoma, from which the patient ultimately died. The defense had an argument, of course: The plaintiff's expert witnesses were committing the hindsight bias. They had the benefit of having radiographs taken more than three years later, so they knew how the story turned out: "The defendant radiologist was being accused of negligence because of an alleged misinterpretation of chest radiographs that had been rendered prospectively and without any knowledge of what future radiographs would disclose, and yet he was being judged by radiology experts who had full knowledge of what the future radiographs actually did disclose."[33] The error rates for a radiologist dealing with this sort of data hover around 30 percent. Was the jury moved by this evidence of hindsight bias? Did they appreciate the fact that knowing the outcome made it seem more foreseeable, or that a substantial minority of radiologists would have missed the same tumor at that stage? They were given plenty of time to consider the evidence, but in the end it was a simple and rather obvious bias that led them to assign blame. It took just three hours for the jury to find the radiologist liable for malpractice by a 10-to-2 vote; they awarded $872,000 to the family of the deceased patient.

START THE BIDDING: ANCHORING AND ADJUSTMENT

Whenever we make a decision based on incomplete information—setting the price of a used car, estimating how many people at brokerages are involved in fraud, or weighing the seriousness of a spreading flu virus—we have to start the estimation process somewhere. More than you might imagine, however, it matters where you start.

In an experiment by Tversky and Kahneman,[34] a wheel is spun and, when the arrow stops on the number sixty-five, participants are asked if the percentage of African countries in the United Nations is greater than or less than 65 percent. For another group of participants, the wheel is spun and stops at ten, at which time they are asked if the percentage of African countries in the United Nations is greater or less than 10 percent. Surely people's final estimates could not reflect influences that are so obviously irrelevant? After all, the process of spinning a wheel could not have anything to do with the percentage of African countries in the United Nations. But this irrelevant information has a shockingly potent effect: in the 65 percent condition, the median estimate of African countries in the United Nations was 45 percent; in the 10 percent condition, the median estimate was 25 percent. This is what psychologists call anchoring. It sounds rather comforting, but anchoring is a disquieting effect. It begins with a value that can be arbitrarily chosen, and this random number may set the range of the entire decision-making process.

Anchors are everywhere. They also influence the home-pricing decisions of real estate agents. In one field study, a group of real estate agents (along with novices) were shown the listing price and other information about a house. They were then asked to estimate the value of the house. The agents had all of the usual information available for pricing: property characteristics, prices of neighboring properties, and the chance to see and inspect the house. The findings are sobering. Under the circumstances of free and lazily available information, not to mention real estate expertise, listing price acted as a powerful anchor on their estimate.[35] Bias isn't just for novices. Even the experts get anchored.

Anchoring could be lucrative for legal practitioners—personal injury and real estate attorneys (not to mention their clients), for example—who may be able to elevate the payoff of a client's claim by fixing the opposition on a higher starting bid. But it can also provoke judgments that violate standards of truth and justice. It turns out, for example, that judges who have an average of more than fifteen years of experience in deciding criminal sentences are influenced by *what they themselves identify in other contexts as an irrelevant sentencing demand*. In a series of experiments in the field run by Birte Englich and Thomas Mussweiler,[36] a nonexpert advised an expert on the proper solution to a problem. The layperson's relatively low credibility was acknowledged by all; it was, after all, a layperson making a judgment about an arcane matter of sentencing. Yet the mere suggestion was enough to anchor judges' sentencing decisions. Indeed, anchoring effects may explain why nearly identical crimes can get such different sentences. Jurors may assign responsibility, but judges typically handle sentencing. In order to do so, they rely on a recommended or required sentence. As it turns out, judges' decisions are anchored by the sentence demanded by the prosecutor. This happens even when the judge acknowledges that the sentence demand is irrelevant, and it happens even for judges of different levels of experience.

INTERVIEWS IN LAKE WOBEGON

We are naturally disposed to exaggerate the powers of our intuitive assessments of evidence. And for the same reason, people find the truth about our inaccuracy quite incredible. This is why the internal perspective does not motivate us to change:

> A large majority of the general public thinks that they are more intelligent, more fair-minded, less prejudiced, and more skilled behind the wheel of an automobile than the average person . . . A survey of one million high school seniors found that 70% thought they were above average in leadership ability, and only 2% thought they were below average. In terms of ability to get along with others, *all* students thought they were above average, 60% thought they were in the top 10%, and 25% thought they were in the top 1%! Lest one think that such inflated self-assessments occur only in the minds of callow high-school students, it should be pointed out that a survey of university professors found that 94% thought they were better at their jobs than their average colleague.[37]

And yet we don't see the irony in our conceit. Of course we *feel* competent; that's why we find it so easy to reject evidence that conflicts with our perceived competence. But we pay the price. As one example, millions of dollars are spent on interviewing that would be better spent on other activities, or on nothing. When "experts" on hiring and admissions committees and parole boards perform personal interviews, they are outperformed by simple prediction rules that take no account of the interviews. In fact, unstructured interviews may even *degrade* the reliability of human prediction.[38] That is, evaluators cripple their predictions by participating in unstructured interviews; the interview information used is irrelevant to (and so dilutes) accurate prediction about the candidate's future performance. Although the interview effect is a well-known finding, highly educated people ignore its obvious practical implications.

At the University of Texas Medical School in Houston, a team of researchers had an unusual opportunity to study just this question regarding the contribution of interviews. They compared the medical school and postgraduate performance of two groups: 50 students initially rejected on the basis of their interviews, and 150 who had been accepted through the traditional interview process. Both groups had been interviewed by the same admissions committee. In three areas of evaluation—attrition and preclinical and clinical performance through medical school and one year of postgraduate training—there was no difference between the initially accepted and initially rejected students. It doesn't appear that the interview process improves the ability to predict performance of medical school applicants.[39]

Still, if interviewing makes us comfortable, what's the harm in it? Can't interviewing be our little indulgence? Well, it turns out that interviewing is a bit like putting vintage Bollinger on your breakfast Wheaties. For a midsize organization, the interviewing process for a single position with an annual salary of $50,000 will cost the organization $7,500 to $10,000.[40]

Why doesn't interviewing beat a simple formula? There is a battery of reasons. Interviewers don't agree about what questions to ask job candidates or how they should be evaluated. The rest of the inaccuracy comes from paying attention to things that don't matter— so-called nondiagnostic cues such as physical attractiveness (including a candidate's weight), the candidate's nonverbal cues (including posture), and overweighting information from the first four minutes.

Interviewers also have a nasty habit of preferring candidates of the same race and gender as they, even when they protest that they have no such preference. No surprise that the substantive stuff gets missed along the way: when asked twenty questions about what happened in a twenty-minute interview, interviewers averaged only ten right.[41]

It seems we don't really know what the interview is supposed to tell us, and when we can agree, we don't really know whether it predicts success. Should it tell us how friendly the candidate is, how he performs under pressure, or how smart he is? If all three, how should each be weighted? Even more careful, structured interviews still offer no advantage over a simple paper-and-pencil cognitive aptitude test.[42] There could hardly be better evidence that as a way of selecting successful job candidates, graduate students, professional students, and potential parolees, overall, interviews are a flop.

What do people say when faced with the evidence? The shouts of outrage commence: Interviews register important "intangibles" that couldn't possibly be captured by a quantitative record. After all, there is a "human dimension" to an interview lost by the heartless crunching of performance numbers. And in any case, not all valuable information can be measured.

These complaints are common, but the lesson demonstrated by the interview effect isn't that complicated. If you have a clear standard of success—passing your first-year medical school exams, completing college in under five years, not committing a related crime after release from prison—then an interview simply adds cost. It does nothing to make your prediction more accurate. The interview is simply not diagnostic. It may be true that some information is not measurable, but interviewing for medical school is not a case in point. We resist the conclusion that interviews don't matter not because the argument outstrips our tiny brains, but because we find the lesson insulting to what the French call our *amour propre*—our smug sense of how clever and perceptive we are about people.

Self-serving biases are at the root of this seduction.[43] The interview effect occurs because we have unwarranted confidence in our subjective ability to "read" people. We suppose that our insight into human nature is so powerful that we can plumb the depths of a human being in a forty-five-minute interview—unlike the dimmer bulbs who were conned by the attraction of a (reliable) formula. By telling ourselves that no formula is a match for our wits, we quietly defect from the better strategy. We make no grand pronouncement, and no overt defense of our intellectual authority. Instead, we experience what George Eliot once called, "that pleasureless yielding to the small solicitations of circumstance, which is a commoner history of perdition than any single momentous bargain."[44]

Our need to pump up our self-image must be powerful if it is causing us to dismiss such convincing evidence that we are not up to the task. But the drive for a positive self-image is not simply an emotional reaction; we also lack the information to contain it. Our overconfidence survives because we typically don't get complete feedback on the quality of our judgments. It is a regrettable, but certain, fact of life that we can't compare the long-term outcomes of our actual decisions with the decisions we would have made if we hadn't interviewed the candidates. And that is why it is so easy for the interviewers to conclude that they chose wisely.

By now, you should be impressed by the sheer weight and variety of the cognitive biases—and by the fact that they are equal-opportunity offenders, suffered by the smartest, the most experienced, and the best informed. But resilient characters don't marinate in bad news; they transform the message into a new challenge. How can we reason better? What steps can we take to discipline our biased brain, this electrically charged gray mass between our ears?

SELF-HELP: THE PROMISE OF EDUCATION AND EFFORT

Scratch any pedestrian, professional, or pundit, and just beneath the surface you will find someone who believes he is better than others on challenging tasks. That is, after all the motor-driving self-serving biases. But if the research contradicts this conceit, the next self-flattering belief is that you can learn to eliminate your own biases by a sheer act of will; you are the master of your own decision-making domain. This is an inside strategy for de-biasing.[45] An inside strategy is a process of individual reflection, a little mental exercise, in which we try to reverse the effect of our biased reasoning. If you have a bias, hey, think it through! Gather more information! Concentrate, focus, imagine! Inside strategies have two distinct features: they are adopted voluntarily, and carried out with self-control.

The effects of cognitive bias are not simple mistakes, correctible by simple exposure to the facts. Biases are systematic, and the errors they produce are more like perceptual illusions than factual blunders. Knowing that it happens, or how it works, still doesn't make it go away. Endorsing inside strategies, then, is risky. We get to fully choose our own course of action, but we are also held fully responsible. And like all voluntary choices we make, they reflect well or poorly on our personal virtue.

The most prominent inside strategy, applied to fix overconfidence and hindsight biases, is called the "consider the opposite" strategy. According to one of the groundbreaking studies on de-biasing, people "have a blind spot for opposite possibilities" when making social and policy judgments.[46] So this "inside" strategy urges people to consider alternative hypotheses for the occurrence of events they believe they understand. For any of the beliefs that we hold with undue certainty (e.g., "New York State is the largest state on the eastern seaboard," "Los Angeles is west of Reno," or, more important, "the defendant is guilty beyond a reasonable doubt"), we can follow a simple rule: "Stop to consider why your judgment might be wrong."[47] For example, ask yourself whether, respectively, you have considered South Atlantic states that get less press, the orientation of the United States, and your confusion over the DNA evidence. When asked to generate pros and cons for a judgment made, Koriat, Lichtenstein, and Fischhoff showed that people's overconfidence was reduced.[48] A variant of this strategy, sometimes called *perspective taking*, may also reduce gender and racial bias. Perspective taking proceeds by attempting to assume the point of view of another person. "Consider the opposite" is a portable inside strategy that is unusual in that it is at least marginally effective. But performing even this exercise on the fly is an awful lot of work—if we even remember, after saying what a good idea it is, to actually do the work.

Yet the groundless optimism persists that we can be educated to correct bias. Some of the best books on cognitive bias trade on this hope, and say that being aware of our proneness to bias is the first step in correcting it: "They [the biases] are hard to correct spontaneously, but they can, with a little steady work, be put right by anyone who becomes aware of them."[49] The evidence demonstrates exactly the opposite. We happily defect from such voluntary prescriptions, despite offers of money, threats of accountability, and urging of concentration. Most adjustments, alas, don't work at all.[50]

The reasons for this are easy to imagine. To implement this self-improving strategy correctly, you need to envision the different ways in which you might be mistaken. But this exercise is extremely effortful and, as a result, it is probably unrealistic to suppose we can be so vigilant. Imagine constantly policing your thoughts whenever you make a decision—with friends, at work, or relaxing at home. Was I overconfident in the statement I just made? How might the situation have turned out differently? Like any kind of exercise, inside strategies require a serious commitment of energy, for what may be only modest rewards. Will people have the discipline, motivation, and concentration required to implement inside strategies?

Outside strategies may seem paternalistic, but inside strategies can be enormously intrusive as well. If implemented, they would slow ordinary conversations to an awkward tussle, rather than permitting the spontaneous and delicate choreography of social exchange. Like rumination, they would mask true emotion, by first prompting reflection on the "appropriateness" of one's emotional reactions on every exchange. These intrusive procedures of correction promise to keep us at arm's length from ourselves, and threaten natural social interaction. They are also effortful mental exercises, and sometimes we just don't want to get off the sofa.

These fixes are also unpromising because our biases are made of stronger stuff than meager contemplation and flaccid will. Self-control, after all, has its limits. People quickly move to more gripping tasks, or abandon their efforts when they feel they have satisfactorily concentrated, focused, and imagined. In the end, however, these biases arise because we are applying these errant strategies with greater focus.

Remember, we don't just like our impressions; our attachment to them is close to an *addiction*. We form them automatically, uncontrollably. Imagine if we offered an alcoholic money not to take the drink in front of him, or a heroin user money to not take the fix just waiting for him. He would jump over the money to get to the goods. His habit is too powerful to allow him to prefer the shadowy promise of later gratification of spending money. But now suppose we changed his environment, removing easy access to the drug of choice. This separation, as it happens, is the first move in the treatment of addiction.

A behavioral policy based on an outside strategy recommends eliminating the temptations to defect in the first place. One kind of outside strategy plans the set of choices available to the decision maker. A timely instance of this outside strategy is contained in the Sarbanes-Oxley Act, which is designed to stem corporate fraud. In principle, the act attempts to prevent "independent" auditors from working with a bank or brokerage firm for more than five consecutive years.[51] Of course, the details of its implementation may have rendered it a fig leaf for auditors continually to rotate back in and for firms to continue to run both sides of the regulatory aisle.[52] But the push toward an outside strategy for containing bias is the right one. An inside strategy advises the auditor to be impartial, as though this request would not strain the abilities of ordinary people with normal resolve. Another inside strategy might entreat her to choose a course of action that is professional and direct in delivering bad news to the very company responsible for her employer's financial growth. In either case, there is ample opportunity, and plenty of incentive, to ignore this honest advice, however naïve. The outside strategy limits the auditor's power to ignore this advice, by limiting her period of employment at a firm. In so doing, an outside strategy might require that you select a solution that is not intuitively satisfying. But it meets the long-term goals that the auditor wants to achieve. It increases the chances that an auditor will act honorably, and that she will report figures that are objectively correct. Auditors may protest that they could handle the temptation and be forthright and impartial, but this is just more self-serving bias.

Like addictions, the biases are systematic and psychologically incorrigible. We often blame the failures of our spontaneous individual decisions on limitations such as weakness of will. Like addictions, the biases have a fairly stable biological source, reinforced by habit, and so it is not surprising that they are very difficult to counteract. And like addictions, they are best treated by not tempting defection: never permitting a forbidden taste "just this once," and reducing exposure to environments that trigger the bias.

There is one way, however, that cognitive biases are distinctly *unlike* addictions: they are not restricted to a tiny, afflicted corner of humanity. Rather, they are the province of us all, part of our natural human condition. We can counteract the force of psychological habit only by an equally powerful intervention. Institutions provide the structure, and decades of research on the psychology of human judgment supply a lever with which we can truly improve human welfare. So, institutional solutions, instead of spontaneous individual efforts, offer the best hope for bringing our damaging tendencies into line with our objective interests and the common good.

Consider the example of auditors from Arthur Anderson who didn't do their mental exercises. They became too familiar with their clients to evaluate impartially the firm's financial health and deliver the bad news. Instead, when they found that their client's company was performing poorly, they discounted the firm's prospects for future failure, and got used to the firm's imperfections. This adaptation to client imperfection has been demonstrated by scholars at business schools throughout the country, and it shows just how difficult people find it to forego inside strategies.[53] It may be too much to expect an auditor to be professional and direct in delivering bad news to friends, to the company responsible for her employment, or to the company responsible for her employer's steady stream of income. In fact, even when we *try* to exercise a disciplined impartiality, we often fall short of our goal. And so we place restrictions on the kinds of employment relations we can enter into. For instance, there are many reasons that doctors do not treat themselves or their own relatives, but surely one of them is that their emotional and personal attachments compromise the impartiality of their judgments. (Should extraordinary efforts be applied to keep my wife/husband alive?) Conflicts in auditing raise health issues of a financial kind.

Although auditing fraud is in today's news, brokerage houses might take a page out of Homer's ancient epic of Ulysses. The self-binding strategies so effective against the siren songs have been applied in nonfictional settings. Missouri legislators, for example, were the first to provide a central registry that allows gambling addicts themselves to sign up for permanent exclusion from casinos in that state. The addict is flagged and ejected whenever he needs to present identification: when he enters the casino, withdraws money, or cashes in chips.[54] Many other states now have self-ejection programs, though Missouri's remains the most exacting and threatens violators with criminal sanctions. Even so, many addicts are relieved to have these programs. Said one grateful gambling addict, "Permanent ejection [from casinos] is my voluntary choice, and it is absolutely necessary on my behalf."[55]

There are even products and services that you can use to bind yourself to good behavior. If you know that you have the money to make timely automobile loan repayments, but are chronically late, an alarm placed on your car will remind you that a payment is due.[56] The device is a little black box. Its four-button keypad is mounted under the dash and connected to the car's ignition system. Once the dealer and the customer have agreed on a payment schedule, the schedule is loaded into the dealer's computer program. As long as payments are made on time, the light on the module displays green. On the first day a payment is delinquent, the light blinks red for twenty-four hours. On day two it flashes in pulses of two. On day three, there are three quick pulses. On day four it beeps all day long. On day five, the car won't start. The device will not shut a car down while it's operating, but once your payment is five days late, your car won't start again. When the customer does make the payment, a code resets the module. The dealer removes the module once the car is paid for.

Self-binding measures like these push judgments "upstream" and make willpower less necessary. A particularly interesting example is described by psychologist and economist George Loewenstein: a credit card addict made a personal contract to donate to a repellent cause (e.g., the American Nazi Party) in case he failed to meet his behavioral goals. Not everyone needs to takes such peculiar measures, but everyone needs outside strategies to reduce bias.

THE ROAD AHEAD

Outside strategies initially require personal resolve, too, but much less of it, and they can pay large benefits in good later judgment. In fact, many social institutions promote outside strategies for improving judgment, and these provide a key model of social change. The Securities and Exchange Commission prevents brokers and fund managers from making unwarranted guarantees that some people might believe. The Food and Drug Administration controls product labeling and promotion by people who sell food and drugs. The National Labor Relations Board imposes severe restrictions on what may be said by employees, union officials, and especially employers. And the Federal Trade Commission controls unfair and deceptive trade practices.[57] In each of these cases, the government has used an outside strategy to prevent individuals from committing errors in judgment. These regulations do not only target fraud; they also control product contents and descriptions so that a normal person does not need Ph.D.-level competence to make an informed decision. For example, the FDA restricts to 20 the number of maggots "per 100 g of drained mushrooms and the proportionate liquid."[58] This saves you a lot of research legwork, even if you would not have guessed that there was *any acceptable number* of maggots in your mushrooms. The SEC has ensured that consumers do not have to sift through false or complicated statements to determine the credibility of those statements. And in the most direct attack on bias, the Social Security Administration prevents individuals from "discounting the future"— undervaluing their future needs while overvaluing the tempting morsels of the moment—by mandating that a percentage of their salary be invested in a government account.

Research on judgment also shows that people fulfill their intentions best when they act automatically, and do so without the halting deliberation or indecision that often spells inaction. So, once we line up our social priorities, we should craft policies that make their funding automatic. If we want to ensure that children have adequate nutrition, health care, and shelter, for example, then we should cultivate an automatic route from our plan to our goal. Our good intentions may culminate in actions such as charitable giving or political support for effective government conduct. When we take aim at the right goals, happiness and the common good are by-products of our automatic minds.

Creating environments, then, holds great power for good *and* evil. Automaticity is good when it causes us the thoughtless click of the seat belt, the spontaneous gesture of help for a stranger, and unselfconscious absorption in pleasant activities. But automatic psychological processes are personally and socially harmful when they trigger repetitive worry, set off wasteful spending sprees, or make us prey to marketing strategies that distort our considered preferences. We can lubricate the path to virtue.

We want to improve human welfare on a budget. When it comes to inexpensive remedies, there is nothing better than institutions. The twin demands of efficiency and welfare, then, suggest institutional remedies. These remedies may, to some extent, limit the range of an individual's spontaneous choices, and so may be subject to the charge of paternalism. But I will argue that these remedies are not paternalistic in any substantial sense of the term.

The ravages of such biases as status quo and overconfidence are plain. We can't improve our well-being simply with a few more choices. Maybe it is one of our sweeter features that we think we are special. Our belief that we, above all others, could make sense of additional choices, or could willfully undo our biases, is our little gloss on the adage that each human is unique. But this adage has a rider, that "I am a little extra-special." If we want to base our personal and professional decisions on sounder footing, we should remember that we are only one in seven billion people in the world, and each of them is special, too. So you may as well pull up a chair under the fat part of the distribution.

One thing is certain, however. We can't reverse the biases by wishing them away. The will is a cheap umbrella in a stiff wind. Maybe it is easier to just control the weather.

| CHAPTER 4 |

Outside the Mind

Breaking Bad Biases

I N OUR QUEST FOR A BETTER LIFE, WE WANT NOT JUST TO avoid blunder but to perfect our condition. Our biases, however, stand in the way of improvement. Biases of availability, base rate, overconfidence, hindsight, anchoring, and status quo—these are all natural, spontaneous, and entrenched patterns of behavior. They are like bad habits with unwanted and damaging effects—but with one big difference: we usually know that we bite our nails or eat too many sweets. We recognize our bad habits; we don't recognize our biases. One we don't recognize is our undue optimism in our ability to exert self-control.

Biases require special attention. Now that we know the biases we face, we can begin to correct them the way we break bad habits, by using outside strategies. These can be small personal incentives, such as employer-subsidized interest rates for homes purchased near your work, or big policies, such as Social Security. They can be introduced with "gentle nudges" or "hard shoves."[1] But they all arrange a person's environment in a way that elevates the quality of his choices, and improves the chances that he will reach his goals. The standard economic dictum that choice promotes well-being equates the multiplication of choices with liberty. We are familiar with being offered choices merely for the sake of having them—sixteen brands of baked

beans, three thousand types of mutual funds, and constantly changing cell phone plans. These are options without much purpose,
the kind of choices that research has shown prevent some people
from making any decision at all and cause them to regret their choice
later on.[2]

The discipline imposed by choice structures is welcome, because
habits are difficult to break by an act of resolve. The confidence we
have in our self-control is heartfelt, no doubt. But the execution fails
more often than we admit. And when we do recognize the failures,
we still give ourselves reasons to backslide. Recovering smokers often think they've found a situation in which it is "safe" to lift their
tobacco moratorium. Reforming gamblers boast that they've discovered that roulette is less addictive than blackjack. Overeaters swear
that the next bear claw is their last one. We always seem to find
exceptions—excuses, really—that allow us to forsake a well-tested
rule, and instead follow an intuition that gratifies us now but pun-
ishes us later.

Now, suppose we took seriously the analogy between a cognitive
bias and a habit. Habits are compulsive, automatic, and normally invulnerable to efforts at willful control. So are biases. Once established, the analogy suggests some examples of institutional outside
strategies for the correction of biases, strategies such as those used to
control nailbiting, speeding, overeating, or shopping.

The dismissive reaction to outside strategies is itself automatic
and habitual. If it did any good, we would suggest a twelve-step program for poor reasoning: "Hello. I am Homo sapiens, and I am an intuition addict." The behavior gets triggered without intention, and it
continues with little effort. Our addiction to intuition, to subjective
impressions, comes from a familiar pattern of "repetitive satisfaction"
at the bottom of any habit. In this case, we rely on our intuitive
judgment, and enjoy the positive feeling that accompanies our overconfidence. These cues coalesce into a cozy pair, like tension and a
massage, or anxiety and a good laugh, and the repetition casts a firm
habit.

When poor reasoning strategies are as tempting as sex and candy, how can you abandon them, especially when the steps to do so seem counterintuitive? In order to crack this habit, you have to pry apart precisely those cues people cannot seem to separate. You might try convincing yourself that alternative strategies are effective, as so many educated investors have. You might use your willpower to override the automatic cuing from the environment that causes you to use the old habitual, but less effective, strategy. When excited about a big purchase, take twenty-four hours before making any commitment. Or, finally, you might change the circumstance or environment, so you can interrupt the repetition that produces the habit. If you are trying to quit smoking and are sorely tempted to smoke in bars, then avoid bars.

These steps might not seem like self-help strategies to break bad habits, but they are. But it is difficult to apply institutional procedures in the service of personal and societal reforms. This approach offers no road map, and that is a problem. Having the facts couldn't hurt. Persuasion is important, but it is often not enough to change minds. It is for reasons like this that David Hume observed that reason alone does not move man to action, and Aristotle complained that some people, once in the grips of a theory, don't need education; they need discipline. I couldn't agree more. The strategies that follow in this chapter and the next call on that discipline. So advice that merely calls for attention to the evidence is unrealistically hopeful. As we have seen, plenty of people have all of the existing evidence for the superiority of a reasoning strategy, and yet they will not listen to the data.

Rather than highlight evidence, we might try to override the habitual response. It isn't easy to override an ingrained, automatic response. And, as always, we are on the watch for effective advice useful to real people, not descriptions of how computers or pathological people might behave. As a result, this bland advice to override entrenched patterns of conduct faces the same charge of undue optimism. Specific advice to competent adults, though, could help, particularly when they are far enough away from the object tempting them. For example, long before the hook is sunk deep, it might help a home buyer to be told that a mortgage over 40 percent of their income places them at serious risk of default, and even greater risk of dissatisfaction with their purchasing decision. Borrow more than that, and you are at much greater risk that the normal winds of fortune—job loss or unforeseen expenses—will force you to abandon your mortgage, or live on a shoestring, bitterly begrudging a punishing monthly payment. With this advance knowledge, a hopeful home buyer might avoid a purchase he would come to regret.

Finally, we might try changing the environment—and this strategy of reform is the most promising. According to the psychological research, taking the boy out of the country *will* eventually take the country out of the boy. Even without the help of a scientific theory, Alcoholics Anonymous had the right idea. If you change the person's environment, you can break the connection between a potent cue and an entrenched response. Change the environment in the right way, and you can break the bond between the bar and the bourbon, the corral and the cussing, the oven and the overeating.

It certainly worked on college students. A Duke study looked at the habitual behaviors of transfer students as they moved to a new university.[3] Their habits of exercising, reading the paper, and watching TV—even when strong—did not survive the transfer when the move destabilized or disrupted the living circumstances that supported their habits. The disruption in their behavioral surroundings apparently blocked automatic cues, which then required intention to carry the action through.

Because people are most likely to break habits when they are in new environments or situations, institutions (such as local governments) can use smart policies to influence people who are, say, moving to a new home, city, or job. For example, it is a lot easier to convert new residents of a community into habitual users of public transit than long-time residents. And this is why some communities offer new residents free passes on public transportation.[4]

The psychology of habit change, then, may carry unexpected but lucrative lessons for public policy. After all, so many costly behaviors stem from habits. In public health, for example, at least four of the leading health risks in the United States emerge from everyday repetition of action, eased by contingencies of the environment— substance abuse, obesity, tobacco use, and inadequate exercise. The ultimate costs of these health risks are enormous. Substance abuse alone cost the United States more than $180 billion in 2002, and the cost is steeply increasing.[5] In that same year, medical expenditures for conditions attributable to overweight and obesity were $92.6 billion.[6] Tobacco use is a similar bane. In the United States alone, excess medical expenditures owing to tobacco use averaged $75.5 billion from 1995 to 1999, and if we add that to the death-related losses in productivity, the figure increases to more than $150 billion.[7] Inadequate exercise, or "lack of leisure-time physical activity," as a habitual part of daily life, cost $24 billion in 1995.[8] Its health effects amounted to about 2.4 percent of all U.S. health care expenditures. In today's dollars, these four habit-based health risks together amount to about $0.5 trillion annually. And none of these costs is decreasing. It's not that willful intention is a weakling; it's just that habit is bigger, quicker, has a longer reach, and finishes strong.

PSYCHOLOGICAL JUJITSU

Breaking habits needn't mean focusing on behavioral triggers or defanging automatic psychological processes. It can mean *balancing* bad habits, such as biases, against one another. Take a classic case of long-term planning. Most adults aren't saving nearly enough to retire comfortably. We are going to live longer than we expect, and it will be more expensive than we suppose. What's more, by the time we actually face the decision to take a hundred dollars out of this month's paycheck and place it in our retirement account, it is already too late. We perceive this allocation as a loss. The only remedy is to move the allocation decision upstream, earlier in the judgment process, diving into a current that leads inevitably to the destination we most desire.

A particularly dramatic and recent success in bias-harnessing re-search comes from behavioral finance. At the end of 2003, employ-ees of many U.S. companies were able to use a plan called Save More Tomorrow when they made contributions to their retirement plans. The plan allows employees to direct a portion of their future salary increases toward retirement savings. Everyone believes you have to start saving sometime, but that now is not the best time to start. So it is difficult to get people to sign up for savings plans. SMT is different from a standard savings plan in that it uses psychological research in behavioral economics to design a plan that employees will join and then not defect from, using people's inertia and procrastination to their advantage. We say we want to save more but don't take the nec-essary steps. We procrastinate. So the plan application asks prospec-tive participants if they would like to start three months from now, and commits them to doing so at the time of enrollment. This allows them to experience the deferral of commitment to an unfamiliar or effortful change in a course of action, and so to experience whatever they find attractive about procrastination. But once in the plan, iner-tia takes over (as predicted by the status quo bias),[9] and people tend not to opt out. In addition, judgment research shows that peo-ple are loss-averse, weighing losses far more heavily than gains, and this prevents them from enrolling in a program in which they can witness the decrease in their paycheck. So loss aversion is built into the plan, taking the increased contribution out of the participant's pay raise, so that the participant does not experience it as a loss or reduction. The results were almost immediate. By predicting and an-ticipating the pitfalls of procrastination and defection, saving rates more than tripled over twenty-eight months, from 3.5 percent to 11.6 percent.

Millions of people are enrolled in self-directed pension plans. If they all signed onto an automatic investment plan like this—putting judgments, especially about future increases, in the hands of a remote-control system—they would greatly increase their probability of fi-nancial security. SMT is now a favorite choice of investors at the two mutual fund behemoths, Fidelity and Vanguard.

This effect reaches far beyond the moribund province of financial accounting, into the morbid topic of organ donation. It appears that people in the United States who fail to enroll in organ donation do so because they do not want to think about such a loss, or their deaths. And families who must make this decision quickly on behalf of a deceased loved one often face regret. Both of these circumstances combine to cinch inaction.[10]

When a reasoning strategy brings nothing but benefits, it is easy to get on board. And the best way to determine what makes such strategies successful is to look at thriving examples now and then, and do a little "reverse engineering" on the process.

TRUTH ON A BUDGET

If all it takes for people to fund their retirement better is a little balancing of loss aversion and procrastination, it looks like people are for it. After all, everyone likes a bargain, and there is no better deal than getting something for nothing. Few changes are literally free, but some can make people better off without making anyone worse off. History has been witness to many simple solutions to big problems. Fluoridation of water has massively reduced tooth decay,[11] and inoculation has wiped out measles and pertussis in treated populations.[12] The seat belt law has, by some reputable estimates, reduced auto fatalities for front seat occupants by 45 percent in passenger cars and by 60 percent in light trucks.[13] A single feature of these successes is noteworthy: the intervention was mandated by law. Individuals had no effective choice whether to subscribe to the interventions; even if they wanted to avoid fluoridation, it is impractical to cook with and bathe in bottled water. Dispensing fluoride in the public water source makes the decision easier for the public. In fact, it makes the decision *for* us, though we do make decisions about which measures to support. When we support the right policies, we can even choose the way we bend our bad habits. In fact, policies regularly improve lives without introducing moral hazards. We know what we want; it is only a matter of getting there. Now let's watch some habits bend before our eyes.

"Rub Hands Together to Produce Copious Foam"
(sign in truck stop bathroom)

There is a surprising amount of money to be saved by making dull activities more efficient. Hand washing is a good example. Nobody wants to do it because it is time-consuming and boring. But unwashed hands are carriers of invisible and beastly bacteria and viruses. Over 150 years after the great Hungarian physician Ignaz Semmelweis learned that he could eradicate childbed fever by implementing a staff hand-washing routine—and endured years of ridicule from the medical community for his pains—the problem remains. You just can't get as many professionals as you'd like to practice good hand hygiene. In hospitals, where the staff wants to avoid giving patients illnesses they didn't have when they arrived, the numbers are as jarring as the solution is tedious. The most comprehensive study of hand hygiene concludes:

> The excess hospital costs associated with only four or five health-care associated infections of average severity may equal the entire annual budget for hand-hygiene products used in in-patient care areas. Just one severe surgical site infection, or bloodstream infection may cost the hospital more than the entire annual budget for antiseptic agents used for hand hygiene.[14]

A study conducted by researchers at the University of Geneva showed that patient care workers complied with standards of hand hygiene only after a long time of shaping their behavior.[15] They were monitored by officials of the hospital. Wash basins were moved to public locations, so failure to comply could be easily observed. They were issued bottles of antiseptic. Most of these are outside strategies,

changes in the environment to produce behavior most apt to achieve
our goal of clean hands.

The ways in which people tend to reason ineptly about costs and
benefits are well understood. In general, people notice low benefits
and high risks. Contingencies producing high benefits and low risks,
such as placement of fluoride in drinking water, are "offscreen."[16]

How should hospital employers and public officials secure compliance? A threat is easier to appreciate if it is on-screen. And nothing
is so persistently on-screen as a screen saver. So hospital officials at
Cedars-Sinai Medical Center in Los Angeles installed on computers
on the ward photographs of doctors' own germy hands super-
imposed with images of cultures from a Petri dish.

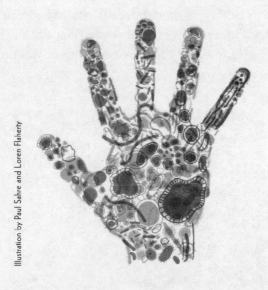

Illustration by Paul Sahre and Loren Flaherty

Compliance shot up to nearly 100 percent. The screen savers
worked better than the Starbucks cards worth ten dollars provided as
an incentive or the free Purell bottles handed out at the hospital's
front door and parking lot entrance.[17] If normal people suffer the
"Lady Macbeth Effect," automatically responding to feelings of moral
guilt by washing their hands,[18] just imagine the strength of that

cleansing impulse when your screensaver tells you that your hands are really dirty.

The Power of the Fly

If you are trying to get your toddler to brush her teeth, a toothbrush with flashing lights will do the trick. To get people to wash their hands, you make it easy to do, and you make it difficult to neglect, by monitoring the behavior and by making the performance public. The secret to gaining compliance is process control: channeling risk aversion with a disgusting screen saver featuring germy hands. These techniques deliver control over the processes of decision and action. They also delivered control efficiently. We don't like spending too much effort to begin our thoughtful activity. When you find a process that is easy and rewarding to follow, you can cultivate thought and action that has real follow-through. Speaking of washing your hands . . .

ACTUAL URINAL IN SCHIPHOL AIRPORT

The Schiphol airport in Amsterdam has the cleanest men's rooms around—no sticky floors or discolored tile beneath the urinals. Maybe you wouldn't want to stitch up a knife wound in there, but you could certainly eat a sandwich. What is the secret behind this spectacle of lavatory cleanliness? You need to look closely at the urinals. Inside each, strategically positioned and embossed in the porcelain, is the image of a fly. An economist responsible for Schiphol's airport expansion explains the strange power of the fly: "It improves the aim," and "If a man sees a fly, he aims at it." You may not have guessed that there are people who conduct "fly-in-urinal" research, but there are, and the Schiphol research staff revealed that the etchings reduce urine spillage by 80 percent. One of the Dutch general managers has a more probing, cognitive explanation for the fly's effectiveness: "It gives a guy something to think about. That's the perfect example of process control."[19]

Thoughtlessly, seamlessly, automatically, and even a little gleefully, male travelers do what is best to maintain a clean bathroom. Men don't think, "Hey, here's a fly, and I am going to aim at it." They just do it. And doing it is so popular that fly decals are now available for use in the home.[20]

These are impressive channels to good behavior. But not all of them need to originate from individual choice to be effective, or even fair. Some are the result of governmental intervention, and are as welcome as if we had chosen them ourselves.

Chevrons on the Road

Perceptual cases of bias are well known and understood.[21] Perception is a rigid and fast process, and perceptual illusions are notoriously incorrigible. The Department of Transportation has run experiments using optical illusions to get speeders to slow down. According to a research study by the American Automobile Association, chevron markings, distance cues that make the road appear to be narrowing, "convince drivers that they are traveling faster than they really are." This design has been implemented with palpable effect. In Japan, chevrons reduced by an average of 40 percent vehicular crashes in six locations. Though there is some evidence of adaptation to chevrons for repeat drivers, the design has clear applications.

Department of Transportation commissioner Christopher Lynn announced that "this is a proven, simple and inexpensive way to slow
down drivers who are approaching dangerous intersections or resi-
dential neighborhoods at high speeds."[22]

A DRIVER'S VIEW OF THE ROAD,
OUTFITTED WITH A CHEVRON.

In the Netherlands, researchers addressed the problem of slowing
down drivers on roads with eighty-kilometer-per-hour speed limits,
particularly near village entry points. They settled on creating a rippled surface near the shoulder, which gave the illusion of making the
lane narrower. A narrower lane would make it more difficult to drive,
and consequently cause drivers to slow their vehicles. However, the
shoulder rippling, researchers feared, might cause drivers to edge
toward oncoming traffic. In fact, it did have this effect, so researchers
counteracted this tendency by widening the center line and narrowing the rippling on the shoulder. A simulation of this new configuration demonstrated a significant effect in speed reductions.[23] When
used on a real road in a before-after study, the configuration led to a
20 percent decrease in accidents after two years.

Outside strategies in these cases can promote, rather than undermine, a person's individual autonomy or sense of contentment. Such
interventions are not coercive or paternalistic.[24] Is it wrong for a governmental agency, such as the Department of Transportation, to use

an optical illusion to secure compliance? Since the driver is not aware he is reacting to the illusion by feeling he is driving faster than he in fact is, he is not choosing to slow down on the basis of the responsible use of information. Instead, he is, in effect, being tricked. But because this trick has consequences of which everyone would approve, it is benign.

Of course, one objection to outside strategies comes from sensitivity to government intrusion into matters of personal choice. It is realistic to worry that these strategies open the door to government abuse. Should a mental alarm go off when an office of the government, such as the Department of Transportation, tricks you into compliance with the law? The automatic perceptual response bypasses the process of deliberation. But it does secure compliance and save lives. What is the price of this trick? Well, in general, people don't like to be deceived, especially by an arm of the government. Suppose the driver could make a choice? Suppose he were informed that he was objectively safer in contexts in which chevrons and other engineered precautions extracted compliance? There is a test to decide whether an outside strategy for de-biasing is coercive. We ask: Is this circumvention of deliberate choice one that a reasonable person would reject? If so, why would a reasonable person choose a riskier option when there was no cost associated with a safer one? And what is the basis of the more general concern about institutional prosthetics for human judgment—particularly when the success of the outcome is not only measurable but striking?

The examples we have contemplated illustrate the power of outside strategies to correct harmful tendencies in behavior. We now have a way of testing whether this controlling option offends a person's desire for choice. Answers to these de-biasing questions provide a way of thinking about whether an occupational requirement is unduly imposing, or a governmental provision paternalistic. Many other countries have already made their choice. Chevrons and rippled road surfaces can be seen on Google Earth in Paris, Stockholm, London, Hong Kong, and New York.[25] Intervention is seen to be warranted in these places because, at negligible cost, this passive, outside strategy serves the driver's, and the pedestrian's, goal of living a longer life.

Words That Hurt: Prescription-Related Death and Injury

Medication error ends lives with startling frequency, in the hundreds of thousands every year. Of the many deaths, the National Institutes of Health estimates as many as six hundred a year are caused by pharmacists' phonological errors when saying, writing, or keying in drug names.[26] A pharmacist is most likely to confuse the initial sound of a drug name, especially if it is stressed. And the error is more likely if the words share a succeeding vowel. Below are just three small samples of the many reasons to worry:

Patanol, Paxil, Pepcid, Phenergan, Plavix, Plendil, Prandin, Pravachol, Premarin, Prempro, Prevacid, Prevpac, Prilosec, Prinivil, Procardia, Procrit, Prograf, Propulsid, Proscar, Proventil, Prozac, Pulmicort

Xalatan, Xanax, Xenical

Zerit, Zestoretic, Zestril, Ziac, Ziagen, Zithromax, Zocor, Zofran, Zoloft, Zomig, Zyban, Zyprexa, Zyrtec

Sound-alike drug names are not a disaster *waiting* to happen: the tragedy is already unfolding. You need the heart medication Procardia? Sorry, you just got Proscar, which has shrunk your prostate (if you're a man, anyway) and left your heart problem untreated. Or perhaps you need the anti-HIV drug Ziagen? Don't worry: before you die from untreated AIDS, your blood pressure may improve because what you got was Ziac. A recent study of 130,000 patients who died from prescription drug poisoning found that these events were clustered at the beginning of the month, when pharmacy traffic was high due to the receipt of government checks.[27] Increase pressure in a brittle pipe and, lo and behold, it bursts.

Can we reduce the occurrence of prescription errors by asking pharmacists to pay closer attention to what they are doing? Pharmacists are, after all, trained professionals, urged to give the most careful attention to the transmission of information. Shall we tell them to ignore all noise in the pharmacy? Read prescriptions more carefully? This is the counsel of inside strategies, but such advice is a waste of time. Massaging the messenger doesn't make the news any better. Changing the message, on the other hand, does. Prescriptions are filled too frequently for the feeble reach of attention and resolve to efficiently avoid fatal error. Effective solutions require social engineering, not psychological massage. What we need is a *system* that rejects drug names that are phonologically similar to the names of existing drugs, uses short names instead of long names, maintains a quiet environment, does not allow drugs to be stored in alphabetical order, eliminates handwritten prescriptions, and uses barcodes, and specifically barcodes that include the dose and contraindication on new drugs.

With the help of the most theoretical areas of language research,[28] things are finally moving in this direction. The U.S. Adopted Name Council and the Institute for Safe Medication Practices have tested a computer program to regulate proposed drug names and flag the ones that are at high risk for confusion.[29]

EXPANDING THE ERROR-CATCHING NET

Passive strategies in health care are already on the rise. Following the lessons of this prescription-safety measure, soon medical malpractice may also be treated with outside strategies in an attempt to create an error-reducing system in hospital settings. The humane way to reduce the number of medical liability lawsuits is to improve patient safety—then people will not only receive the care they deserve but also have no reason to file.

As a recent summary of malpractice and patient-safety research shows,[30] when fewer patients are injured, fewer patients sue. In an enormous Harvard study involving 31,000 medical records, 1 in 25 patients was harmed and only 4 percent of those harmed actually sued. If we focus just on lawsuits, very few are meritless. (Moreover, meritless cases are quickly thrown out of the courts.) In another study by researchers at Harvard and Brigham Young examining 1,452 lawsuits, evidence of medical injury was found in 90 percent of the cases.[31] And these aren't infected hangnails. In 25 percent of the cases, the patient died.

With the evidence that the vast majority of patients suing genuinely are injured, the reasonable thing to do is compensate the victim and improve patient safety so the mistake doesn't get repeated. The savings in reduced judgments and legal costs can then be used to fund new patient-safety measures. The point is not to limit awards in deserving cases, but to reduce error.

The examples canvassed in this chapter—such as the road chevrons and the improved prescription drug measures—provide clear improvements in quality of life. They are achieved by outside strategies, relying on the environment, rather than the conviction of the actor, to improve performance. All of these improvements are, by any measure of lives or resources saved, ludicrously cheap. And there are more to follow as this chapter continues. At the same time, none of these life-improving measures breed moral hazards. People whose lives are saved from enhanced prescription safety measures do not suddenly start experimenting with drugs or petting unfamiliar animals.

There are many coercive measures that would improve some aspects of your well-being, such as your physical health. A government might, for example, mandate a morning exercise period. The question is: is such a measure unacceptably coercive, incompatible with the liberal ideal of pursuing our own conception of a good life and living a life of moral integrity? To answer this, you need to find a principle. So far, we have seen that any such ideal is compromised by the many threats to truly free choice.

Consider the recent "wellness movement" among companies to prohibit things such as tobacco use of any kind at any time among employees,[32] or to encourage exercise. There is little question that the existing body of law permits a company to decide whether it will employ tobacco users. It is not so much that you don't have a right to abuse your own health. You can always find legal ways to do that, such as skydiving, stock car racing, or overeating.

It is not too cynical to suppose that companies have purely economic motives for their wellness programs. Wrapping this motive in the compassionate talk of employee wellness would imply paternalism: that the company knows what is best for the well-being of its employees. And when the measure prohibits behavior you exhibit on your off-hours, it looks like a privacy issue. The employer will then point out that the bad health effects of smoking are not restricted to the off-hours. In the end, then, unless smoking makes you a member of a protected group, there is no issue here; companies can fire smokers as they see fit. Offended smokers can band together, or can simply leave for other, less meddlesome employers.

But it is easier to find a new job than a new country. Employees can quit if they don't like their employer's legal regulation—if they find it coercive. More problematic is the *government's* efforts to control conduct such as smoking. It is not paternalistic, for example, for the government to curb smoking, even if the smoker reports he would happily assume all risks himself. In order for an intervention to be paternalistic, the behavior it curtails must be purely self-regarding, behavior that affects only the actor. But as difficult as it might be to be stranded at O'Hare airport for six hours or more without a cigarette, others are badly affected by secondhand smoke. Therefore, the decision to smoke is not purely self-regarding.

If there is anything undesirable about policies that restrict our current choices, it is not simply that they might shape our preferences. After all, sometimes we choose the instruments of shaping, and in other cases we accept the ones imposed by the government. The private sector has plenty of horses in that race as well. We identify the unwelcome cases when the tools are selected by companies and agents who we believe are not first interested in our well-being—or, even worse, who might have an economic motive for deception.

The simplest case is when esoteric products of science such as pharmaceuticals—whose development requires arcane training and whose safe use must be regulated by scientific offices of the government—are advertised directly to the public. In light of the competitive market and the volume of money to be made through market share, the temptation must be great for a company to influence an untrained and vulnerable public. Magazine and television scripts read as vaguely as a horoscope: "Tired? Not enough sleep? Distracted? You may be depressed." It is possible for anyone to see himself in such a description.

The threat of shaping our preferences or judgments—without our consent—is an obvious worry about the media. And the consequences of doing so are not always aligned with the public's best interests. Continue further the pharmaceutical example. There is a serious need to address the widespread and costly health problem of depression. Depression is a real disorder, but it is also big business. Millions of people in the United States are treated annually for mild depression or generalized anxiety. Since the inception of SSRIs (a popular class of antidepressants), once the market share settled out, there were a handful of medications that dominated the industry: for example, Lexapro, Zoloft, and Paxil. But now there is a new market to conquer. People who are depressed or anxious are also prone to excessive rumination; they are preoccupied with negative thoughts, and play them over and over in their heads. Pain is a recurring theme in these downbeat meditations. Depressives report having all sorts of pain, much of it nonspecific and not responsive to treatment.[33] But now there is a drug, Cymbalta, advertised late at night, for the pain that accompanies depression. Rather than leave the causes of prescription to doctors, drug companies bring news of their pharmaceuticals directly to the people. This direct marketing is an effective way to increase the use of their drug, because doctors respond compliantly to patient requests for the kind of medication they see advertised on TV. A recent study published in the *Journal of the American Medical Association* showed that doctors were five times as likely to prescribe a depression drug (Paxil) if the patient mentioned having seen an advertisement for it.[34] This finding represents the incentive that pharmaceutical companies have for "direct-to-consumer" advertising, where the "consumer" who responds to the ad is likely to be compromised by an illness.

This is not a prelude to a rant against drug advertising. The same concerns about targeting a vulnerable population with ads could be raised for many industries, such as plastic surgery. The lesson I urge is more focused: Opponents of *government* policies that shape choices must object to more than just the government's power to control our preferences. After all, *private* industry can do that without our consent as well, albeit in a much more clandestine way, through advertising and other marketing measures that sneak beneath our conscious radar. In short, we shouldn't naïvely believe that, without government, there would be no coercive, shaping influence on our choices and preferences.

Why should Lunesta and Zoloft and Flomax be able to advertise on TV, but not Marlboro or, say, Bacardi? If the government's message to private industries such as pharmaceutical companies were clearer, it would be easier to find a principle distinguishing acceptable and unacceptable intervention on behalf of a person's well-being. Whatever that principle may be, one lesson is unmistakable: If you oppose government regulation because you believe it illicitly shapes our choices, you need a special reason for giving a pass to private sources of choice shaping.

LEARNING TO LOVE GOOD REASONING

How can we persuade people to use the superior, institutional solution, the solution they themselves agree is best? How can we get people to aim at the psychic fly in their mental urinal? Members of Congress, policy makers, businesses, and professional associations—individuals and groups that forge policy—must be persuaded that effective policies and good decisions vault the bad influences such as weakness of will, procrastination, crippling doubt, chronic overconfidence, and gut reactions. In consumer and media areas, there are federal offices that could provide institutional solutions to judgment problems, organizations such as the FDA and the FCC. In all of these cases, the policies would, wherever possible, use the tricks of outside strategies. They would halt the environmental hair triggers responsible for poor judgment, and introduce distance between the conditions that create a desire and the object of that desire. If alcohol compromises your judgment, keep it out of the house. If people reason better using some mathematical techniques rather than others, then use the more effective ones. Policies should allow consumers to cool down, making sure that the all-important life decisions are made in a cold state, impose a waiting period on them. No car purchase, no job acceptance, no major elective surgery, and no home mortgage should be allowed without the psychological distance that time provides. Policies could allow us to perform psychological jujitsu, leaving the bias in place, but balancing it against opposing biases that counteract it. Chevrons produce the illusion that we are traveling faster than the desired speed, which balances the bias toward speeding. The Save More Tomorrow plan uses our psychological inertia and procrastination to offset our loss aversion and tendency to maximize disposable income. Finally, good policies would create reasoning habits designed to eradicate the kind of rumination that makes us freeze or withdraw from decisions.

It is difficult to fill all of these desiderata at once. But policies often navigate a complicated consensus.

POLICY PROPOSALS

The examples of drug naming, road chevrons, and automatic investing illustrate efficient ways to improve human performance. How should an affluent society respond to this new-found efficiency? How should it react to this institutional tool to do more good with mini-

mal costs? It is tempting to make a grand call for a national evaluation of our priorities, one that recalibrates our values so that we can
place basic needs for children somewhere above, say, mosquito abate-
ment. But such calls are mere publicity stunts when they come without plans for implementation.

Why not just raise taxes to fund basic-needs policies? We are,
after all, an exceedingly rich nation. This is a pragmatic proposal,
and would often be morally justified. But taxation needn't be the first
line of defense against social injustices. In fact, many people openly
oppose taxation to fund basic needs, even when it is the only certain
method for putting food into children's mouths. The easy response to
that opposition is to concede that few people actually like taxes. But
that is barely an explanation, and no justification at all. In any case,
it isn't really relevant. Nobody likes inoculations, either, but the
short-run pain gets compensated come flu season. The problem is we
don't feel the *absence* of flu like we feel its effects, so we never come
to appreciate it when we *don't* come down with it. Taxation is really
just a way of trading money for services. The question then becomes,
is it a good trade? If people feel it is a good trade and they have
the money, they will make the payment. And they certainly don't
like paying for headaches. Most countries in Europe have higher effective tax rates than the United States, but the benefits of taxation—
longevity, personal security, child welfare, employment programs,
no-worry pensions, and health care—are ever in the minds of the
recipients. So people complain less about taxation, even when paying more.

Public policy has to take people as it finds them—their preferences, capabilities, talents, and warts. This doesn't mean that policy
makers must pander to our taste for fad and impulse. But it does
mean that they shouldn't be guided by psychologically unrealistic
goals.

From personal to policy decisions, incentives and sanctions act as
outside strategies that align our behavior with rewarding outcomes,
all without draining our attention away from other enjoyable activities. With intelligent policies in place, our nation can better fund the

priorities we say we value, such as adequate public education, health care, and humane treatment for the impoverished. But we fall short. With high-school graduation rates at about 70 percent over the last decade, and below 50 percent in some of the nation's largest urban centers, such as New York and Los Angeles[35]; major health indices (e.g., infant mortality) lagging those of some third world countries; and more than thirty million people in poverty, these declarations seem empty. But low-cost, low-sacrifice policies might prime our commitment. Without resolve on the horizon, the only hope is to make outside strategies easy and inexpensive to adopt.

I am not proposing that we fire senators and hire psychologists. Instead, we should place elected officials in the best position to understand that they are unconsciously influenced by multiple, misleading sources of information. Whether or not elected officials heed this finding, the government can still play its information-disseminating role. A government budget office should track net savings and costs from results of federally funded research, such as that performed at the National Institutes of Health and the National Science Foundation. In 2005, funding for the psychological and social sciences from all federal sources was $2.3 billion, about 4.2 percent of all science funding, or just about 7.7 percent of the funding for life sciences.[36] This record would allow us to assess whether federal investment in psychological and social science research met our expectations.

Once we resign ourselves to the bad news about intuitive judgment, a flood of policy proposals break loose for public consideration. Because knowledge of human affairs requires arcane scientific information, good policies and procedures will enlighten, of course. But they will also control the hasty and overconfident judgments of novices. Though difficult to implement, all bills designed to bring about any social change could reasonably be expected to be peer reviewed, and so produce a prediction before they proceed to a vote in the House. In keeping with this proposal, procedural rules in Congress should prohibit members of Congress from posing as scientific experts on factual matters pertaining to policy.

An efficiency panel at the Office of Management and Budget should be established on which social scientists and statisticians could evaluate features of social policies and propose alternatives that would be cheaper *and* at least as accurate in achieving the proposed policies' goals. There is no reason to think that our first effort at an improvement in well-being is the cheapest, and an efficiency panel is an obvious way to recover excess costs and put that money to work. But there are many ways to improve efficiency. Congress should learn from the mistakes and successes of more efficient countries. Its committees could engage in a careful analysis of the costs, structures, and effectiveness of social safety nets in Europe and Canada. Examining nationalized health care, state pensions, legalized and decriminalized drug use and prostitution, and other social programs, U.S. government offices could then determine the feasibility of enacting these programs in the United States.

These suggestions are obviously underdeveloped, but at this moment they fill a vacuum in the public conversation about the social improvements made possible through science. We needn't push forward, full of wide-eyed naïveté about the steady march of science. In the hands of political administration, the use of science is thoroughly politicized. But science itself is not. When making judgments about complex social matters, policy makers should tie the long-term fate of these judgments to the balance of scientific findings. And where a public official chooses to trust his untutored, anecdotal judgment over the balance of scientific evidence, he must be held accountable, as should any defector. Policy makers must prove, by scientific means, that either the evidence is unreliable or their judgment is correct.

WHEN PSYCHOLOGISTS DISAGREE

You can find disagreement in every major advance in science. Like those in the physical and biological sciences, the disagreements in psychology occur against a background of agreement about central topics and questions. Here are just a few core sources of agreement in the cognitive science of judgment: Humans tend to irrationally discount the future. They are misled by the psychological salience of an event and tend to ignore the important issue of its frequency. They are sensitive to the way options are framed and often not their actual value. They place more confidence in their judgments than is warranted by their track record. They do all these things worse than they might. And they don't know it. And when they do, it doesn't change anything.

Few cognitive psychologists doubt the very *existence* of cognitive bias, the antiseptic term for the effects just discussed. A minority voice disputes our *understanding* of its causes, but not the effects. Few psychologists think that people will save better for retirement if they first receive the earmarked money and then place it into a retirement account themselves than if they use a system that automatically deducts a prearranged amount from their paycheck. Suppose we reject the option of automatic deduction. We should at least know what consequences to expect. There is no alternative theory that predicts that people can overcome the desire to spend their entire paycheck, adapting to its total. There is no theory of motivation that indicates that, if we want, we can cash the check, judiciously remove a self-prescribed amount, and deposit it into a retirement fund. This feat is humanly possible, of course. But there are wiser bets.

Psychologists agree, further, that the plan is more likely to be successful if there is a penalty for withdrawing the money early than if there is no penalty. According to a scheme of citizens' choice, psychologists don't decide what measures will be too paternalistic. Citizens decide that, when they clarify their values, or when, on a citizens' panel or in a voting booth, they are given a wide range of policy choices. Instead, psychologists answer broad questions about how various envisioned policy outcomes will affect ordinary citizens, citizens who fall within the normal range for intelligence, emotion, and motivation. They may also assist in the construction of policies that will be the least psychologically disruptive.

Some policy improvements are special-purpose, tied to the settings in the courtroom, the doctor's office, or at a parole hearing, where a cognitive bias may do its most potent damage. So it was a great advance when researchers revealed the tragic effects of the overconfidence bias on eyewitness identification, and offered methods to reduce the number of false identifications.[37]

The research psychologist Elizabeth Loftus has done more than anyone else to help juries understand the implications of the research on eyewitness testimony.[38] In her expert testimony, she explains to juries that eyewitness testimony can be very unreliable, that recalling is not like playing back a videotape, and that we fill in many of the missing details without knowing it—a process called confabulation. It is common for prosecuting attorneys to call upon other expert witnesses in an attempt to rebut Loftus's testimony. But such rebuttals don't deny, or present evidence against, the existence of confabulation. Instead, they usually raise the possibility that the eyewitness testimony is accurate. Confabulation is one of the best established effects in cognitive psychology, so the concept itself is hard to rebut. It is less difficult to assert exceptions to scientific generalizations. The prosecution expert might report having known someone with uncanny recall, or having had occasional research subjects with that ability. This fact, of course, would in no way compromise the findings on memory, nor would you need an expert to make the observation.

On a policy committee handling the government's role in financing retirement, imagine the corollary testimony of a behavioral economist: "I met a guy once who saved like there were *only* tomorrows." That may be; it *is* possible to oversave. But the existence of that exceptional human is utterly compatible with the overwhelming research finding that people, in the main, steeply discount the future.

Any scientist called to advise must be able to comment on the weight of the observational evidence, and this is not a wholly subjective affair. Most sciences have their own ways of quantifying the balance of evidence. Meta-analyses, for example, summarize the literature and estimate the size and direction of experimental effects on topics such as unreliability of eyewitness testimony. In addition, according to my scheme, some psychologists will be excluded from this consulting process. For example, clinical psychologists and psychotherapists without a scientific research background should not be called in that capacity by the House Committee on Science and Technology, as a consultant on any citizens' panel, or on any policy body. For policy issues involving serious and somatic psychological illness, such as schizophrenia or manic depression, there is an existing body of experimental science. A wing of clinical psychology performs empirical studies that conform to recognized scientific canons. Gratefully, researchers in that field can testify about the credibility of particular clinical hypotheses. But the scientific status of other areas of psychology—physiological, sensory, perceptual, cognitive, and social—is less contentious, and would find a legitimate voice on the House Committee on Science and Technology.

Feelings run high in policy matters, and you can never completely eliminate the possibility that a government office will cherry-pick advisors to predetermine an outcome, especially to ensure one an administration favors. The best you can do is make it difficult to bring off. When a mature area of inquiry agrees about the key findings, attempts to rig the process do stand out. These mature fields use impressive statistical tools that render verdicts outside of the frailties of cogitation and passion. These outside strategies are well understood and difficult to game. And as we will see next, these tools are already saving us precious resources.

THE ROAD AHEAD

This chapter opened with cracking examples of successful outside strategies, from Social Security to chevrons, from pharmacy environments to instructive screensavers. The story of outside strategies is uplifting, a vivid narrative detailing how psychological research has helped us to make better personal decisions and to promote the general welfare. Democracies ranging from England and the United States to Australia and France promote different visions of the common good. But none of them encourages squandering our material excess. When a country has some citizens who cannot meet their basic needs, decent societies try to allocate goods more efficiently, where they will supply more well-being for the buck; to start, those societies avoid wasting goods on higher-income portions of the population whose happiness and well-being are largely unaffected by more resources. You want to make sure everyone has adequate nutrition before you start throwing up from gluttony. Research on judgment and decision making leads us to a single, unmistakable conclusion: We should rely much more on well-tested choice structures, or systems of remote-control judgment. There is now solid scientific evidence that people, though not aware of it, undervalue many of the factors in life that are essential to their well-being. Science may not yet have the answers about how to live the *best* life humanly possible, but it can tell you, often precisely, how you can live *better than you do now*. And for less.

The superior accuracy and efficiency of forecasting customs would free up substantial funds to address persistent problems such as crime, poverty, and inadequate health care. Because people prefer to spend money on the same category of items they have saved on—an effect of what psychologists and economists call mental accounting—it would be most fitting to apply the savings from improved human judgment to initiatives for improved human well-being. The next chapter surveys this categorical effect in greater detail. The savings created by these simple solutions can then be used to address other personal and social priorities in a kind of targeted saving. But the cause is not lost if others lay claim to different priorities. If a government can impose its power on foreign populations, it can certainly find reason to oblige its own people to comply with its most civilized priorities. Ideologues can always throw tantrums. But there are pleasures unique to maturity. Real grown-ups can sustain the narcissistic injury of being made to do what we want to do anyway. And we do want to make sure that everyone in the world's most affluent society—children, above all—receive their basic needs with dignity and certainty. The problems our society faces are complex enough; we can be grateful that there are some simple rules to address them.

CHAPTER 5

Stat versus Gut

A Free Lunch

I HAVE ALWAYS LOVED THE IDEA THAT YOU COULD CATCH DE-licious crabs with a festering flounder carcass. Something for almost nothing: as bait, the ripe flounder works just as well as fresh salmon. Wouldn't it be great if decision making could be made more like crabbing? Then we would spend less on decisions that were more reliable. Of course, the act of crabbing is itself enjoyable, a value known in economics as a "process utility." But even if it weren't, the cost structure of recreational crabbing is irresistible. And it keeps you coming back. We might abandon reliable reasoning strategies less often if great gains cost so little.

Fortunately, some decisions are still cheap and effective. One ex-ample is close to the hearts of many parents. In maternity wards throughout the country, doctors have always done their best to assess the medical condition of newborns, looking intuitively at some com-bination of signs and judging the importance of each. Clinical expe-rience can be a hazy basis for such time-sensitive and high-stakes judgments. Decisions a doctor makes in the first five minutes of a newborn's life can permanently affect the child's prospects. But in 1952, an obstetrical anesthesiologist named Virginia Apgar imposed welcome discipline on this subjective process. The Apgar score, as it came to be known, provided a fast and reliable way of determining the clinical condition of a newborn one minute after birth. The score was the sum of five numbers, each based on a sign: heart rate, respiratory effort, reflex irritability, muscle tone, and color. Each factor was assigned a zero, one, or two. A score of ten indicated that the newborn was in the best condition possible. This fast and reliable diagnostic tool allowed doctors to snap into action if need be, beginning resuscitation or other immediate action. There is no way of knowing exactly how many newborn lives were saved by this modest score, and how many more were spared a diminished life. Now more than fifty years after its inception, nearly every neonate in the United States is still assigned an Apgar score shortly after birth. Some people may feel it is demeaning to assign a number to a human, but it is hard to know where this feeling comes from. Is it a visceral reaction? Is it a reasoned judgment? Whatever the source, this is one number that allows doctors and patients alike to be more human. It allows the doctor to deliver treatment tailored to the specific needs of the infant, and it can allow the infant to have, well, a life.[1]

Many people have a strong negative reaction to the use of numbers in human affairs. It invokes the image of an impersonal and uncaring bureaucracy, the faceless allocation of goods to citizens without names. And yet, here we have a newborn baby, treasured in every culture, the object of joyful tears and lavish attention, whose life and prospects are protected by a simple sum. This fact alone should help us set aside any knee-jerk reactions against the use of numbers in human dealings. We should instead find it easy to appreciate the power of mathematics to capture the subtle tissue of human affairs. The Apgar score will outperform the doctor in predicting the child's condition years from now, and that fact should make you trust and treasure the formula more, not less. Children should be able to count on adults to control their visceral reaction once they are aware of the formula's superior accuracy. If we can continue to love music after we know that octave structure conceals intricate mathematical proportions, we should, likewise, be able to love the numbers in forecasting customs, and use them to advance our well-being.

In the policy arena, however, the promise of these kinds of formulas seems harder to swallow. The Apgar score may not be strictly free, but it is as close as you get in a world where everything has a price; it has become a number cherished nearly as much as the newborn's length and weight, and arrived at almost as effortlessly. In the United States we are raised to believe that you don't get anything that valuable at so low a price, including an improvement in the quality of life. In fact, in economics a special name is reserved for no-cost improvements. Economists describe a policy as "Pareto optimal" if it creates more benefits relative to an alternative (usually the existing arrangement) and harms no one. Part of the attraction of something-for-nothing deals is that they improve conditions in this way.[2] Policies that are genuinely Pareto optimal are hard to come by, though; usually, the best we can hope for is near-Pareto-optimal improvements.

The question, then, is whether we are getting our policy results at the cheapest practical price. We know that we should take steps to improve our health, support quality education, and eliminate poverty and crime. Psychologists have devised a powerful set of techniques to do just this, by improving the accuracy of our beliefs at the lowest possible price. There is wisdom in psychology that we should take advantage of, and forecasting customs is part of that wisdom.

Of all the problems that plague human societies, poverty, famine, disease, and violence surely top the list. It may seem that some of these problems can't be solved. Some countries simply come to loggerheads, some tribes truly hate each other, some diseases just find ways to spread, and some people are simply too far away from food sources. When it comes to poverty, even Jesus punted, lamenting that the poor will always be with us.[3]

But there is reason for hope. Most complex problems can also have a hidden simplicity. The history of famine is a policy nightmare, claiming tens of millions of lives over the centuries and causing the needless suffering of millions more. We have been swamped by the traditional view of famine—that poor weather or other natural catastrophes cause famine, by wiping out a region's food supply. Drought, flood, blight, and pestilence have always been thought the chief causes of famine, and so eradicating those conditions has always been a priority of famine planning. The modern treatment of famine has been based on the traditional view. As each famine arose, it spawned a complicated network of donations from around the world. The United States and other nations would airlift food to the afflicted country, only to find no roads leading from the airport, no shelter for those waiting for food, and no real plan for food distribution. This "food availability and natural disaster" view never really explained glaring and puzzling facts about the onset of famine. Many famines, for example, run their course while the afflicted country exports food. During Ireland's tragic potato famine in the 1840s, and Russia's grain famines of 1891 and 1921, both countries shipped vast stores of crops to neighboring countries.[4] In addition, famines seem to be more closely related to economic factors such as inflation than to local food production. So if it isn't the destruction of a food supply by weather or natural disaster, what does cause famine?

Nobel Prize–winning economist Amartya Sen performed exhaustive historical research, and revealed the simple structure behind famine. Famine has little to do with the availability of food, and everything to do with political offices and institutions that are not accountable to the public.[5] In nations that have poor roads and airports, it is difficult for relief organizations to ship food. It is far better to give cash to the hungry so that they can purchase food locally—even if at inflated prices. This pattern of distribution reduces reliance on already overused infrastructure. But if the country's leaders control not only the nation's assets but also its elections, a starving population poses no threat of its leaders being deposed. That's why, Sen observed, you don't find famines in democracies. Famine is caused more often by acts of dictators than acts of God. The simple solution to famine, according to Sen's analysis, is not necessarily to grow more food. The solution is to make food an entitlement, easily available to all. Once it is an entitlement, the means for its distribution will follow.

How did the causes of famine resist understanding for so long? The answer is that we didn't feel the need to go beyond what we deemed obvious. Human intuition grasps at familiar causes, and gut reactions embrace falsehoods with confidence. The food availability view is so intuitive. Bad weather leads to a lack of food, and that means lots of starvation. Our reliance on intuitive judgment, like any addictive behavior, *feels* right when we do it. Not surprisingly, Sen's "entitlement" approach to famine management is institutional rather than intuitive; it is an outside strategy.

We make fast and intuitive judgments all of the time, and they are often wrong when it counts. The gut is a good guide when highly trained muscles remember their choreography. The mind of a chess expert can swallow the board layout whole, and art authenticators can spot a forgery at a glance. In fact, Malcolm Gladwell has written a lovely book about those "blink" moments.[6] However dramatic, these cases of lightning-fast accuracy are exceedingly rare. In their review of *Blink*, decision researchers Robin Hogarth and Paul Schoemaker analyze the twelve chief examples of successful blink judgments found in Gladwell's book, and find that the author uses mainly examples where performance is already good: the judges are experienced and the feedback is clear. In the real world, where most people make most of their blink judgments, performance is poor and feedback is bad. Genuine blink moments can be documented; it is much harder to say when and where blink judgments are accurate and useful. While it is possible to assemble a small number of fast and unconscious judgments, they are a weird motley of special-purpose tricks that fail "to establish representative sampling of judgmental tasks," leading us to "a thin and unrepresentative slice of life."[7]

Gladwell reveals one such trick when he tells the fascinating story of John Gottman's Love Lab at the University of Washington. One of its claims to fame is its reliability in predicting a divorce rate on the basis of only snatches of a couple's interactions. Behind this impressively speedy process are many hours of training, and painstaking coding of behavioral subtleties. But for judgments made at a distance, these fine points are unnecessary. An extremely reliable, low-cost reasoning strategy for predicting marital happiness already exists: the F-minus-F rule. Recorded daily over the course of thirty-five days, take the couple's rate of lovemaking and subtract it from their rate of fighting. If the couple makes love more often than they fight, then they'll probably report being happy; if they fight more often than they make love, then they'll probably report being unhappy. Judgment researchers Howard and Dawes tested their hypothesis on data from forty-two couples who "monitored when they made love, when they had fights, when they had social engagements (e.g., with in-laws), and so on. These subjects also offered subjective ratings about how happy they were in their marital or coupled situation."[8] The results were striking: "In the thirty happily married couples (as reported by the monitoring partner) only two argued more often than they had intercourse. All twelve of the unhappily married couples argued more often."[9] The F-minus-F rule even outperformed clinicians, who predicted what the couples would say about their marital satisfaction. Like any other successful diagnostic tool, this one identifies and sorts symptoms. But this impersonal judgment is far more efficient than Gottman's subjective blink judgment; it involves no laborious training, no slippery subjective convictions, no deceptive hunches, and no counterfeit "Aha" feelings.

Why do so many doctors, businesspeople, therapists, and parole commissioners, among many others, neglect these impressive results and persist in high-stakes gambling with people's lives? It seems to be nothing more complicated, and nothing more defensible, than a self-serving bias caused by pride. We cherish our intuitions. We are mesmerized by the dance of our own judgment—calculating, estimating, weighing the options, and the sense of understanding that washes over us when an explanation feels right.[10] We can't bear to believe that the subtle touch of human judgment—especially our own—is ham-handed. When we tell a story, we begin to feel we understand. Our muscles relax, and we let the sense of understanding wash over us. Unfortunately, stories are cheap, and even some of the most inaccurate are irresistible. (Think about the widespread but false belief that the majority of ulcers are caused by excess stomach acid, that the common cold is caused by cold air or, for that matter, that famine is caused by the unavailability of food.) And when we think we understand, we begin to think we know when to ignore the formula and believe the informal story, with serious, sometimes fatal, results. For more than twenty years we have known that simple formulas perform better than experts in medical, legal, occupational, and financial domains. No one has fully surveyed the damage. But it seems we want the human touch, even if it mangles us. This is a bad habit, worthy of being broken.

HUGGING BY NUMBERS

In order to act on our most humane instincts—to ensure equal effective opportunities, a healthy electorate, a well-educated and trained work force, and basic needs—it must be as easy as possible to pursue our personal and social priorities. We must either bridge or eliminate the barriers that stand between our desire to help and the tools that assist us. Our decision-making process must be streamlined and, as much as possible, automatic. Psychology and policy can combine to close this gap and to sweeten the sting of sacrifice, because there are few things easier and cheaper— and for some, scarier—than applying a forecasting custom.

When pitted against humans—experts or laypeople—forecasting customs have a stunning track record of success. In order to appreciate the promise they hold as policy tools, we should keep in mind their many applications. The examples developed here are just a few of the peaks on the landscape; they are not isolated, freakish effects.

Consider one simple rule that outperforms us, one we are free to use. Competitive colleges and universities may send out their acceptances first to valedictorians, but they also want to know when not to accept an applicant: when the applicant's past performance makes him a bad risk. To do this, they want to predict the applicant's undergraduate grade point average (GPA). Searching the records of recent high school graduates, admissions officers try to accept people who have the properties associated with a high GPA. What they find is counterintuitive. If you want to predict an applicant's success in college, you can outperform an admissions committee with only two pieces of information: high school rank and SAT (or ACT) score. This statistical prediction rule, a forecasting custom, can do a better job for less money.

This is how to predict academic success in college using a forecasting custom: You take high-school percentile rank and test score percentile, weigh them equally, add them together, and then predict that the students with the highest total scores will be those with the best undergraduate GPAs. Consider a concrete example: Suppose Smith's high-school rank is in the 91st percentile and her test score is at the 60th percentile. In that case, Smith gets a total score of 151. Now suppose that Jones's scores are 81 and 64, respectively. He gets a total score of 145. The rule then predicts that Smith will be more academically successful than Jones, at least as measured by undergraduate GPA.

What happens when we pit this formula against a college admissions committee? Which will be more successful at predicting the students' undergraduate success as indicated by their GPAs? The formula wins, hands down. Why? Because it *identifies* the relevant variables and *prevents* you from being swayed by irrelevant ones.

What could be simpler? So save the personnel salaries. Use a formula your child could solve. It is more accurate. It is fairer (or at least, less arbitrary). It is less time-consuming. And it is far cheaper to implement. People with poetic sensibilities can be dismissive of forecasting customs, worrying that the formula can't look into the applicant's soul. But then again, neither can the expert admissions officer. If what's in a person's soul hasn't shown up in their performance thus far, chances are it won't in college, either. So there is little reason for concern. Forecasting customs like this one end up selecting people from every group, from the math geek to the arts head. Some might complain that the focus on high-school rank and SAT score effectively excludes some demographic groups, or highlights only academic success in college. But that's not a gripe about the accuracy of forecasting customs. That's a disagreement about the goal of a college admissions committee. If you are concerned about an overlooked demographic group, you can formulate a forecasting custom to best select from that group as well.

Most forecasting customs work in this simple way, whether for credit rating, parole, mortgage approval, psychiatric disorder, heart attack prevention, or prostate cancer prognosis. Sure, smart statisticians can hand over forecasting customs that have more bells and whistles—with more, or more precisely weighted, variables. But even the no-frills forecasting customs typically trounce expert decision-makers, as we will appreciate in painful detail when we look at the application of those customs in parole judgments.

The secret to their success is that forecasting customs, like other outside strategies, place judgment beyond the reach of intuition. Outside strategies, especially models such as statistical prediction rules, should be used in every walk of life in which there are high-stakes judgments to be made. Is this proposal hopelessly naïve? Willfully unrealistic? After all, we can't even get people to do things that will save their lives—such as wear a motorcycle helmet. Why should we believe they will honor the cause of sound judgment by using a forecasting custom?

Well, it may be difficult for individuals to use such outside strategies on a daily basis, but they are already the obvious choice in the private sphere, where our intuitions dominate. Companies should encourage their employees to use outside strategies for their retirement investing. State regulations should make it easy for gambling addicts to self-evict. Once in the retirement plan, or on the gambling registry, people find it more difficult to defect. And so, after the initial commitment, achieving the planned goal doesn't require much effort. Automatic salary deduction and compulsory eviction from casinos imposes a cool distance between your present desire and the damaging act. You may still want the Twinkie, but now you've got to cross a psychological lava field to get it. An inside strategy offers no comparable resistance. Just ask yourself whether you are equally capable of putting a few dollars away "whenever you think of it," or watch a gambling addict to see whether he is capable of resisting by "keeping his mind off of black jack or roulette." Exercising will power is an inside strategy, and it doesn't work well when the desired object is within reach, or when the backsliding bite of the apple would go undetected.

It is fitting for employers and companies to promote outside strategies, because they use those strategies for their own benefit so often—for calculating a credit score or handling personnel issues. Which applicant will be the best teacher, student, salesperson? Will this applicant repay this loan? If this prisoner is paroled, will he commit a violent crime? Will this prostate cancer patient die within six months without immediate surgery? Of course, it is hard to overestimate the practical significance of these sorts of social judgments. People's lives depend on such decisions. We give all kinds of intuitive advice about how to make them, but as we have seen, most of that advice is worse than it might be. Forecasting customs are the outside strategies that outperform our intuitive strategies.

There are, of course, many other "gatekeeping" decisions on which it would be wonderful to save time and money: Which applicants should we admit to law school? Which prisoners should we place on parole? As long as we are clear about the desired outcome, we can craft a custom that will forecast it. But all of the challenges to prediction are problems because inaccurate or poor judgment in these cases threatens to treat people in ways that are unfair, arbitrary, or unsafe; it threatens their well-being. Forecasting customs can improve that judgment. Finally, even in those cases where humans are about as accurate as the forecasting custom, the custom's lower cost makes it the smart shopper's choice. Detecting brain impairment from psychological tests, determining personality characteristics, predicting length of treatment and hospitalization, and diagnosing— all are cheaper to do with a forecasting custom. The lesson, then, is clear: if you want to achieve your goal, use the forecasting custom over your subjective judgment.

No matter how overwhelming the evidence, though, we can't ignore the nagging feeling that a trained professional could outperform the formula if he just used his insight. Clinicians might be able to gain an advantage by recognizing rare events that (due to their infrequency) are not included in the actuarial formula and that countervail the actuarial conclusion. But how do we know when our own judgment should supersede the actuarial conclusion? In psychology this circumstance has come to be known as the "broken leg" problem, on the basis of an illustration in which a forecasting custom is highly successful in predicting an individual's weekly attendance at a movie but should be discarded upon discovering that the subject is in a cast with a fractured femur. The clinician may beat the actuarial method if he is able to detect the rare fact and decide accordingly. In theory, actuarial methods can accommodate rare occurrences, but the practical obstacles are daunting. For example, the possible range of intervening events is infinite.[11]

But there are difficult cases. The broken leg problem—the problem of deciding when to defect from a forecasting custom—occurs when the person comes to believe she has strong evidence for defection. And there is no question that sometimes people should do exactly that. But there is a good general rule of thumb. When there is no documented reason to suppose that the special "broken leg" property (usually one picked out by intuition) is a good predictor of the target property (e.g., recidivism), defection from the forecasting custom is usually a bad idea. We should all resist defecting well beyond what intuitively seems reasonable. As one of the fathers of forecasting customs, Paul Meehl, put the point, we should defect from a well-tested forecasting custom when the "situation is as clear as a broken leg; otherwise, very, *very* seldom."[12] This advice is based not on Meehl's intuition, but on the miserable history of defection from forecasting customs, documented in every study that pits forecasting customs against intuition. Intuition may not be accurate, but it *is* predictable. True to form, people are shockingly overconfident that their intuition can outperform forecasting customs, just as we have seen they are overconfident about their other skills.

Bad things start to happen when you defect from an otherwise reliable forecasting custom. From 1994 through 2005, the risky subprime loans leaped from 1 percent to 8 percent of the nation's total mortgage debt. When they were based on models at all, those models contained the rosiest of assumptions, so much like the undue optimism of the planning fallacy. With mortgages so easy to get, home ownership increased even as the poverty rate rose to 22 percent. Lending companies willfully chose to override the reliable outside strategy when approving mortgages. As one MIT economist mused prior to the subprime lending crisis of 2007, "People technically in poverty are owning homes."[13]

For a long time, mortgage loan and credit card companies had already gotten the message: they used simple prediction rules—almost exclusively—to evaluate the likelihood of an applicant's default. In these cases, government incentives were not needed; accuracy was its own reward when it saved companies large stores of cash. But slowly the companies defected from this strategy, convinced that there was money to be made by choosing to override the outside strategy in approving mortgages. The subprime market collapsed, the companies got spanked, and we will all suffer the economic fallout. But defection is seductive.

Counterintuitive as it might be, there is money to be made by *not* defecting. In the case of psychiatric diagnosis, the use of simple prediction rules would reduce the need for trained professionals. You still must treat sick people. But now they will be more accurately and quickly diagnosed. This translates to more humane treatment because it involves less suffering. And, if appropriate, the money saved can be spent on their treatment. At the moment, however, the use of forecasting customs is far too infrequent, and grudging when you do find it. Doctors, parole boards, therapists, and personnel committees say that their "trained judgment" is the most accurate available; we must rely on their "years of experience" and "expert intuition" to make successful decisions. Doctors tell us how many more years we can expect to live with an illness, parole boards tell us which criminals will become our neighbors (and tell criminals whether they will be released), therapists tell us whether a patient is neurotic or psychotic, and admissions committees tell us whether and what college or medical school we will attend. We will see the benefits of such decision procedures when we turn to a sustained examination of parole.

We also spend millions of dollars annually on the rehabilitation of young prisoners—with questionable success—and yet U.S. corrections policy pays billions of dollars to feed and house the nearly 97 percent of older inmates who will live peacefully until their deaths. Female prisoners have the same prognosis. Once again, simple equations are more accurate than the human experts: parole boards are worse than the available predictive tools—the forecasting customs—at identifying the dangerous 3.2 percent. The human touch may be costly after all.

GET OUT OF JAIL FREE

Some people who ignore forecasting customs, then, know better but do so anyway. One commissioner of the Maryland Board of Parole refuses to use forecasting customs. He explains his method for making parole decisions: "You look in their eyes; you can feel, you know, if they're being sincere or not. And you learn to sort of see right through them."[14] This strategy engages dimensions of judgment that may feel more human, and everyone is pretty much with the commissioner on this one. Like the parole commissioner, we imagine we can see the guilt in a convict's eyes, and are certain we can feel his sincerity. But remember, these impressionistic judgments are more unreliable than forecasting customs. So people seem unaware, or unconcerned, that they are trading familiarity for error. But you don't have to become ensnared in a web of error just to get the human feeling of concerned judgment. We are wrong to expect a feeling of warmth, a feeling of personal connection, from all of our judgments about people. Some of those good feelings come from knowing that the effects will help people, as with the Apgar scores assigned to newborns. But if the commissioner's error does not have exotic causes, it does impose exorbitant costs for the luxury of wanting a complicated judgment to feel familiar. The United States has an expensive parole system devoted to identifying prisoners who have served their time and deserve parole. And the U.S. Office of Corrections knows about the superiority of the VRAG (Violence Risk Appraisal Guide), and often uses it.[15] On the other hand, some behaviors resist prediction by forecasting customs *and* human intuition. Some state parole boards know that recidivism for sex offenders remains a stubborn problem for those formulating forecasting customs.[16] But even here, when human and forecasting custom are equally inaccurate, the custom may be preferable because it is cheaper. More preferable still might be not to parole sex offenders.

While judgments of criminal guilt must be "beyond a reasonable doubt," decisions about parole are not; instead, they are based on calculations of cost efficiency and guesses about reform. Statistical prediction rules are better at both tasks. When predicting violent recidivism, for example, there is a forecasting custom that correctly finds ninety more violent recidivists out of every one thousand predictions made, and at a fraction of the cost of a parole board.[17] States control parole boards, usually under a department of corrections. (Each state has a single parole board, along with a process of pre-parole screening by a special parole officer.) California has one board responsible for all parole hearings, and its seventeen members decide if any particular inmate will get parole. The parole board is split up into smaller groups that can visit inmates in prison. Much of the parole decision is based on the results of an interview and, as we have seen, interviews are repositories for the interviewer's ultimate inaccuracy.

The use of forecasting customs in many of these cases should be mandated by law, because pandering to the false pride of the "expert" may have too high a social cost. One cost is owed by corrections professionals, who keep harmless people in jail by deferring to their subjective judgment. In fact, more than twenty-five years ago researchers concluded that, when it comes to the difficult job of predicting recidivism, "actuarial predictions are more accurate, equitable, and consistent than intuitive judgments."[18] But because we fail to use risk assessment tools that are more accurate than humans in making such judgments, parole boards not only keep nonrecidivists in jail, but also free recidivists. The human and financial costs here are jarring, and so is the potential for savings. There are about 140,000 prisoners over the age of 55, and at $70,000 a year, it costs nearly three times as much to house them (for an annual total of nearly $10 billion) as it does prisoners aged 18 to 29. Only 3.2 percent of those paroled over 55 years of age return to crime, as opposed to 45 percent of those aged 18 to 29.

Mine is not a plea for leniency toward inmates, to give them early release because prison was a bad break. Instead, it is a caution about the bad effects of being mindlessly punitive. When prisoners serve their entire term—that is, they are not out on parole—they must be released with no strings attached, and thus no conditions that would edge them toward integration into the free community. Parole is really the only opportunity to smooth out this potentially rough transition. Leaving a prison setting from high levels of security, without any post-release supervision or support, is a recipe for recidivism.

While the general public has been waiting for more accuracy in parole decisions, we will have to wait a bit longer for the mandatory use of risk assessment tools. At the state level, parole boards are guided by statutes and administrative codes of that state, and at the moment, few states require the use of forecasting customs. Illinois's parole board *can* use available forecasting customs, but is not required to. Massachusetts is on the verge of requiring their use for parole-release decisions.

The introduction of forecasting customs would force no substantial change in the parole hearing procedure. In Illinois, for example, the parole process begins when the Prisoner Review Board notifies the inmate and interested parties about an upcoming hearing. One of the board members is assigned the inmate's case. In most situations, that board member hears the protest to parole and support for parole separately. Inmates, however, are not allowed to hear the protests. The inmate has his hearing and can hire an attorney. The inmate can present witnesses, testify himself, and present documents in support of his parole.

In making its decision, the board looks at criminal history, the facts of the crime, institutional adjustment, and outside parole plans. After the hearing, the board member comes to Springfield for a meeting before the entire board and presents the inmate's case. The board then votes, and the law requires that in order for a prisoner to win parole, a majority of members must vote yes. Currently, there are fourteen board members, thus at least eight members must vote for parole. All of the information required for a good forecasting tool is already in the inmate's file; it is the board's choice to use it or not.

"It is a subjective decision," said the general council of the Prisoner Review Board of Illinois, describing the judgment process of the board. Reasons to deny parole are that: it would depreciate the seriousness of the crime; it would have an adverse effect on institutional discipline; or the inmate cannot comply with the conditions of parole.[19] In Illinois, there is no risk assessment tool, no forecasting custom, used to determine the likelihood of recidivism.[20]

Parole board jobs are not low-level, functionary positions. In California, each member is appointed by the governor, requires confirmation by the Senate, and receives an annual compensation of $99,693. Obviously a good deal of money is invested in the parole system, but we have to add to that a sum more difficult to calculate: the cost of its radical incompetence.

Members of the Board of Parole Hearings in California come primarily from law enforcement and local government. But none appears to have a background in the sciences (social or otherwise) that would acquaint them with either the power of statistical prediction, or the frailty of intuitive judgment.[21] And as every summary of the forecasting custom literature has shown, people don't naturally use the statistical information, even when it is made available to them.[22] The only solution is to *make* them follow the numbers. But you can't do that, because then you might have to ask why we have parole board members, rather than computer programs, making the decisions in the first place.

Nearly everyone in a society benefits from the use of forecasting customs in parole. To convey some idea of the number of inmates these boards process, consider the practice in New Jersey that leads up to the parole board decision. Parole interviews are performed by one parole officer. Based on these initial interviews, the inmate may or may not go on to a parole board hearing. In 2005, 15,421 initial interviews were scheduled in New Jersey, and nearly 13,000 board hearings were scheduled. Most parole hearings are handled by two-member panels; a board hearing can also have a three-member panel or a full panel.[23]

In Texas, both a parole board and parole commissioners determine which inmates can be released on parole, depending on the case. The board has seven members; there are twelve commissioners. As in New Jersey, Texas parole officers may conduct assessments of the inmates to determine whether board or commissioners will review their case. In 2005, Texas considered 71,207 cases, and granted parole in 19,582 of these (27.5 percent). Hearings in Texas cost $5,606,811 in 2005, and board operations cost $2,698,113.[24] It is more difficult to calculate the cost of using an inferior method for evaluating dangerous people for release, or for continuing the incarceration of prisoners who would not commit a crime if released. This is an incredible workload, devoted to an extremely important constitutional value of human liberty. And forecasting customs are better than human intuitive judgment at discharging all of these tasks.

When I was in college, I regularly drove over to the Lewisburg Federal Penitentiary to tutor inmates as they prepared for their high-school equivalency exams. In Pennsylvania, the parole boards allowed an advocate to speak before the board on the inmate's behalf, and several times I served in that role. In one case, I recounted the inmate's dutiful study, his apparent sincerity, and his composure during our tutoring sessions. I hoped he would receive parole. He seemed like a pleasant enough person, as prison inmates go. He even passed the commissioner's test: I saw nothing sinister "when I looked into his eyes." I later found out that while I was tutoring this man, he was running a vicious protection ring in the prison, and he inflicted especially brutal rapes on anyone who opposed him. Somehow none of this came up when we were doing fractions.

So here we have a class of techniques—forecasting customs—that are cheap to develop and easy to use. They would save many millions of dollars in their many applications, and end much suffering. And they have the further advantage of blending with our natural tendency toward keeping a mental budget. This is a taste known as "mental accounting," in which people prefer, for example, to spend money on the same category they saved from,[25] and to earmark a bonus for spending and a rebate for saving.[26] We often group expenses into categories such as transportation, crime control, affordable housing, college costs, travel, and so on. In the case of parole decisions, whatever we save on parole boards and commissioners can go to crime measures such as rehabilitation, institutional job training, or more state troopers. Savings gleaned from the use of forecasting customs in law enforcement and corrections could fund related social goals—it could pay for any number of social programs documented to reduce crime or repair the damage it causes—which would be both effectively implemented and conducive to our well-being.

POLITICS BY ANECDOTE

Members of Congress are asked to do many things. They are asked to decide whether to go to war; which disease gets more research funding; how many schools, highways, and hospitals get built; how much to allocate to rehabilitation for drug use and HIV public health messages; at what rate to set the minimum wage; child health programs; and fossil fuel initiatives for global warming, to name just a few. Of course, members of Congress are inadequately prepared to pass judgment on such an array of technical issues. In fact, no one is an expert on all of these issues.

Because most congressional members lack the training and

knowledge to make substantial judgments about scientific matters, they need help in assessing social legislation based on technical theoretical information. As of June 2006, less than 5 percent of House members (20 out of 435) had Ph.D.s, and no senator had a Ph.D.[27] Less than 3 percent of House members (13 out of 435) and only 4 percent of Senators (4 out of 100) had medical degrees.[28] After the bachelor's degree, the most common degree held by members of Congress is the law degree, the J.D. Those members could tell you how to serve someone with legal documents, how to file an appeal, or what standard of proof is required in product-liability claims. But most could not tell you why the release of carbon warms the earth's lower atmosphere, or why stem cells could be used to reverse nerve degeneration. This is not a criticism of congresspeople; it is, rather, a description of the informational limits on ordinary legislators. And that is also the reason we need outside strategies to improve judgment.

Many issues that come before Congress have important scientific components that are too technical for direct consumption, and so Congress has its own way of screaming "Uncle." When they recognize they are out of their depth, members of Congress can select experts to act as advisors or consultants. Standing committees of the House—such as the House Committee on Science and Technology—also turn to experts, and hearings and meetings are held to examine, discuss, amend, and vote on pending legislation. Legislation is sent to committee before it is voted on in the House, and members often hear from experts and from one another in order to assess the pros and cons of a bill. But science would serve the purposes of democracy best without this system. Lobbyists, of course, have their influence, in a process that embodies the conflict between honest advice and a desire for profit. But unless you think that we should abandon the House Committee on Science and Technology, a committee that has faced concerns about conflict of interest since its formation in 1959, you need a special reason for pessimism about a proposed House Committee on *Social* Science.

Governmental committees could turn to the fields of cognitive

and social psychology to seek experts and advise legislative committees. Ideologues could politicize this selection process, of course, but
that worry is premature.[29] The more pressing issue is giving the science of decision and risk a seat at the congressional table in the first
place. While decision-making research now has a battery of promising fixes, there is virtually no way to get that message to Congress.
At the moment, experts in decision making who are on government boards often have little idea how they got there. The way in
which government offices contract decision-making experts is haphazard and unaccountable. And it is puzzling that a government
body charged with so many risky decisions has so little need for
expertise from decision scientists. Even one of the most prominent
psychologists of judgment and risk has appeared for congressional
testimony only once in his long and distinguished career, and in the
past few years, for only about one briefing per year.[30]

How is testimony and advice arranged? The House, for example,
has a list of committees and subcommittees that can commission testimony from experts or outside reports from research groups, and
then pass judgments on what they learn. But seating a committee is
not an antidote to bias and confusion. There is much politicking
about the composition of committees, and many ways to subvert the
goal of seating an impartial committee, as we have seen in the stem-
cell debate.

These inadequacies could be partly corrected by peer-reviewing
bills, wherever they draw on empirical research. Bills could be sent
out to dozens of experts, many more than the number on a committee. This procedure would ensure that the bill made scientifically
credible predictions, using methods widely accepted in the field.
Peer review of bills is desirable because there is no congressional rule
preventing members from rejecting scientific evidence, or just replac-
ing it with stuff they've made up. Bills for new military technology
require passing judgment on that technology's effectiveness. Antipoverty bills demand accurate predictions about how distributing
entitlements to the poor will affect their behavior.[31] Peer review of
bills may not yield perfect agreement about what the empirical ef-

fects mean, but at least any disagreements would be about the evidence rather than heartfelt intuition.

Legislative decision making can involve more effort than the rules require. But the habit of title reading and intuitive judgment rules the day. Some bills prompt elaborate and heated discussion, and it would be nice to know that this added energy produced light. This would go a long way toward showing that great minds at work can advance solutions to deep and important problems. But as long as decision-making procedures allow legislators to make intuitive assessments of the contents of scientific findings, that hope will never be vindicated. For example, in an effort to stem the spread of AIDS, in the summer of 1999 Congress considered a proposal to fund a program in Washington, D.C., that would provide intravenous drug users with sterilized needles. A March 1997 National Institutes of Health publication, *Consensus Development Statement on Interventions to Prevent HIV Risk Behaviors*, concluded that needle-exchange programs "show a reduction in risk behaviors as high as 80 percent in injecting drug users, with estimates of a 30 percent or greater reduction of HIV."[32] Another research project on needle-exchange programs from October 1997 in Baltimore demonstrated that "needle exchange programs that are closely linked to or integrated with drug treatment programs have high levels of retention in drug treatment."[33] In addition, a 1998 NIH Consensus Conference report on heroin addiction treatment "found that drug treatment programs can assist heroin users in halting their drug use."[34] In science, this is as good as it gets.[35] Perhaps some representatives find junkies detestable. Maybe they think addicts get what they deserve, or maybe they want to punish them. But if so, this must be argued and brought out into the open, so that we can identify our goals. As a matter of science, sterilized-needle intervention programs substantially reduce the incidence of HIV in intravenous drug–using populations, and together with drug-treatment programs, drastically reduces the risky addictive behavior that brings it about.

Intervention programs cost money, and it may be that lawmakers felt they couldn't justify a costly program when other good programs competed for funds. But this is not what was argued. Instead, a number of representatives assumed the role of scientific expert and, without proper training or background, announced that the consensus of the highest government-funded research body (the Department of Health and Human Services) was more flawed than their intuitive judgment. It takes a special kind of arrogance to fund the dominant research agency in the nation and then selectively reject its findings to favor judgments you have formed without any evidence whatsoever.

This special kind of arrogance is actually run-of-the-mill overconfidence, and it spans administrations; it is a separate question why overconfidence sometimes leads to corruption, secrecy, a sense of moral superiority, or criminal conduct in some politicians and not others. This may have more to do with a person's tendencies, such as paranoia, mistrust, greed, or spite. But everyone agrees that, in garden-variety factual matters, overconfidence is seldom good. In the 1990s, Bob Goodlatte (Sixth Congressional District of Virginia), who introduced legislation prohibiting federal funds from being used to develop a needle-exchange program in Washington, D.C., conjured a scientifically groundless prediction that participation in these programs "sends a terrible message to our children." He referred to "the damage that [such programs] do to our communities and our children." About the public health value of needle-exchange programs, Goodlatte just denied the evidence: "[T]he medical evidence is simply not there."[36]

Despite the overwhelming evidence that sterilized-needle programs work, other naysayers piled on. Dr. Ron Paul (OB/Gyn), representative from Texas, wore many expert hats while criticizing the idea of sterile-needle exchange, posing at once as an economist, psychologist, and moral guide. He represented himself as a scientific expert by making specific empirical claims about the influence that sterile-needle exchange would have on our children—he has, after all, delivered more than four thousand babies. And he commented on the economic and moral consequences of sterile-needle exchange as well.[37] Everyone, of course, thinks that he or she can deliver specific and confident advice about psychological matters. Step right up. No advanced degree required. Representative Fossella remarked, "Well, what kind of message are we sending to children? Is that the Good Humor van coming down the block? No, that is the needle giveaway van coming down the block. They are going to give needles away to drug addicts."[38] These peculiar House-floor fantasies are vivid and memorable, but there is no evidence that such programs damage children or anyone else.

It seems our ability to ignore evidence, however, is matched only by our power to fabricate evidence where there is none. In fact, if anecdote is our standard, anyone could make up dozens of other predictions about the *positive* effects of needle-exchange programs. But these are scientific questions, and it is better to let scientists answer them. Our tendency to pronounce overconfidently on the substance of scientific issues is no less damaging here than it is in the case of rejecting forecasting customs. Both reactions dismiss a superior judgment in favor of an inferior one. Both embrace anecdote and conceit over the evidence and respect for scientific expertise.

What kinds of questions require expert knowledge not enjoyed by members of Congress? There are many, but here are just a few. Will a helmet law reduce motorcycle fatalities? Will a reduction in fossil fuel consumption decrease the rate of global warming? What are the long-term effects of the HeadStart program, of handgun availability, of uninsured children? These are complicated questions, but with the right instruments, we can get straight and accurate answers. We just have to learn to listen to them.

THE ROAD AHEAD

By carving out a place for forecasting customs in policy, I am not suggesting a country on autopilot. Quite the opposite. A country that uses accurate forecasting customs cannot use them mindlessly. Its institutions must constantly update the information on which the customs are based. Otherwise, we couldn't capture new behaviors in the social community that altered the forecasting custom's predictive accuracy.[39] Society changes, and so do the people in it. But improving accuracy is only half the motive. The vigilant and aggressively humane society envisioned here doesn't just record those changes—it creates and nurtures them.

Human experience and judgment will retain a secure place in this picture of efficient and accurate decision making. We will use our intuitive judgment to identify our values, and to order our priorities. We can think about our values and priorities fully, and discuss them abundantly with others. Citizen panels, discussed later, can provide one path to comfortable deliberation. These values and priorities could be addressed in detail in a new political setting I've proposed—a social science panel of the House Committee on Science and Technology. This panel of psychologists could be devoted to identifying social problems treatable by forecasting customs and similar methods. And who knows? It may even be possible to train thought processes to be just a little bit more like forecasting customs.[40]

There may be a few remaining citizens who are unnerved by the use of forecasting customs. But it is important for them to remember that they are still in charge. It is likely that an enterprising statistician could create a forecasting custom that better predicted whether a particular citizen was likely to become a first-time offender, but no one is proposing to develop such a custom; the value of individual freedom is treasured by Americans, and this results in our opposition to incarceration for any reason other than actual conduct. Humans can always override the decision dictated by the best statistical model. But once we decide to use the forecasting custom, we should override it in favor of our intuitive judgment only in truly extenuating circumstances because, after all, we have already exercised our control by choosing to follow the rule. When we take measures to bind ourselves—Ulysses-style—to the proven strategy, this, too, is an exercise of human judgment. Introducing some element of remote control into our judgment and decision making could make these processes more accurate than ever before. In addition, as every retirement investor has noticed, by foregoing some idle freedom in the short term, we can gain more freedom in the long term. But just as important, by insulating yourself from the excesses of short-term spending and giving the proceeds to those in need, you allow others more freedom now.

Forecasting customs have immense promise to improve the quality of life at bargain-basement prices, but evidently that is not enough to win converts. We still need to create an environment in which devoted users will be able to persuade skeptics. Our intuitions are driven by present experience. We can overcome this powerful force if we make it easier to apply these proven strategies. These strategies get a fair shot when they are given the same kinds of support that businesses have to shield their products from competition. Drug companies receive protection from competition for their new drugs, even though generic suppliers could supply the drug for less money. Some building products are not available to anyone but licensed installers, even though many of these items can be installed by the handy homeowner. These regulations shape our choices. Once choice-shaping has increased the use of outside strategies, we can begin to appreciate their superior performance and recognize their benefits. Others recognize them, too. The challenge is to make their use more routine, more automatic. That's why, at least in some cases, using outside strategies isn't just a good idea; it's the law. Good institutional designs don't happen by accident. They require a New Republic.

CHAPTER 6

The New Republic

The Destination of Our Desires

A S THE TWENTIETH CENTURY OPENED, THE LIFE EXPEC-
tancy of a U.S. citizen was just over forty-seven years, and
as the century closed, it was seventy-seven years.[1] During
that time, individuals didn't become more responsible. Instead, they
were the lucky beneficiaries of social policies that improved their
well-being. Medical advances, retirement packages, welfare programs, inoculation campaigns, health care plans, and workplace safety
provisions have all extended life and its enjoyment. We should never
doubt the power of well-crafted policy to have far-reaching, positive
effects on citizens—far more than campaigns that appeal to individual
responsibility.

Contrast these social programs with individual pursuits. People
long for happiness, and yet, ironically, happiness abhors the chase.
Researchers in psychology have demonstrated that the direct pursuit
of happiness is futile, raising levels of frustration.[2] Planning for happiness, then, is like preparing for a solar eclipse: you can appreciate
it only if you are not looking directly at it.

Unlike individual happiness, the pursuit of societal well-being
must be faced head-on; it won't happen by accident, or as a fortunate
side effect of feverish personal acquisitiveness. Quality education

and health care for everyone, equal effective opportunity, personal security, and basic needs—all of these sources of well-being are supplied through planning.

There are plenty of examples of social plans for improvement. In the past, science has helped the government protect and improve human well-being. When Thomas Edison warned the public about the dangers of radiation, scientific societies throughout the world adopted resolutions that now protect people from overexposure. With a subtle twist, scientific findings from psychology can protect people from the punishing effects of poor decision making. The new psychology of judgment matches the old physics of radiation. Physics made it possible to develop more destructive bombs. Psychology can help us to improve the reasoning processes that lead to policy decisions. If we base policy recommendations on secure psychological findings, society can adopt measures that improve our lives while limiting risk, help the least fortunate without undue cost, and undercut the cost of temptation by cultivating virtuous habits. Every year spent dithering carries a price of unnecessary suffering and death.

If the task of psychological reform seems urgent, it's because these changes are within reach, and we may someday lament our costly hesitation. At life's end, people most regret missed opportunities, not pursuits that turned out badly.[3] Better to have loved and lost, and all that. People regret not having spent more time with their children, developed hobbies and talents, done enough for the people they cared about, and told their most cherished friends and relatives how much they were loved. These are personally costly omissions. But their damage might have been reversed, interestingly enough, by social policies—ones that might have made it easier for working parents to take more vacation or have more flexible work hours, for example. In the early 1930s, legislation on Social Security was delayed by pointless indecision, with nothing in its place, and during that delay millions of older people fell into poverty. Early opposition to inoculation, antibiotics, seat belt laws, and the chemical treatment of psychotic behavior all bore a tragic price in death, suffering, and lost opportunity. Government policy is not just a means of helping many people at once; it is also a kind of sentry that watches for the omissions we will come to regret in the psychological distance, shining a beacon on them so that our neglect doesn't kill people.

In order to make these changes, however, we must listen to science. Science-based policy changes are normally politicized and contested. But we should at least begin by acknowledging the findings. There is now a push for a national index for subjective well-being, one that constrains political institutions to future policies designed to bend our world toward happiness. And it is easy to find a place to start. Happiness and well-being are most easily damaged at or near the poverty level.[4] We might rely on our empathic faculty to guide us in deciding who needs assistance. But as we have seen, empathy is a blunt and fickle tool in social policy, nearsighted in both time and geography, and our policies should take account of that. We can celebrate that normal people empathize with those less fortunate, but acknowledge that fair and equal treatment requires that these policies reach all of those in need.

In order to honor this goal, we have to promote to government the insights about the nature of bias, and about the outside strategies to correct them that have been so celebrated in science. Until now, these insights about choice structure haven't had much effect on popular culture or policy. For the most part, U.S. citizens ignore, or have never learned, the lessons often grasped well by their creditors and insurers, by political operatives and advertisers.

When it comes to policy choice, then, we are little better off than those who, decades ago, ignored the advice about sterilizing their hands before performing medical procedures. In medicine, the consequence was palpable. People died. The neglect of these discoveries was a tragic error. The same delay in other areas of social policy produces death and suffering just as surely. If we want to correct bias, we will need a deliberate plan.

HAPPY ACCIDENTS AND DELIBERATE PLANS

We can even learn from accidents of planning. Nobody *planned* to make large areas of Chicago grocery-free zones; such a situation merely resulted from a mixture of uncoordinated incentives. In the predominantly black South and West sides of Chicago, residents are about twice as far from a grocery store than from a fast food place. In white, Hispanic, and diverse neighborhoods, however, fast food establishments and grocery stores are about equal in distance from residents. As the distance from grocery stores increases, so does obesity. In the "food deserts" in Chicago, about eleven out of every one thousand residents die of cardiovascular disease; the number is about half that in "food oases." The diabetes death rate in the areas with the worst access to grocery stores is more than twice that in the areas of best access. The correlation between food choice and heath is stable across differences in education, income, and race.[5] There is a lot more to this story, but its moral should be clear. We may want to leave urban design to market forces, but sometimes the invisible hand begins to tilt, and needs another to help deliver its goods. Should we let this imbalance persist interminably, along with the differential suffering it causes, or should we ask the government to help? Most of the time, we never ask, because we have a bias toward the status quo. We suppose these differences arise "naturally," or that they are inevitable. It is only when we compare neighborhoods that we learn that some imbalances are reversible.

Changes don't have to be big to be good, and they don't have to bind the entire public in order to be effective. Many small-scale, private changes can be made that will produce substantial improvements in your life—changes that don't require impositions by government.

In the beginning, there was tax withholding, a less painful way for citizens to pay the government for the costs of citizenship. Electronic banking allows consumers to pay themselves first. It has made it possible for a paycheck to pass directly from the employer's to the employee's bank; automatic deduction became an easy route to painless saving. From happiness research we know that humans adapt to nearly everything, including reductions in income, as long as their basic needs are met. So saving for retirement can feel effortless and habitual, and we can predict that people who do it in this way will forget about small monthly earmarkings for retirement accounts. At the same time, from judgment research we know that we are loss averse. So we can also predict that automatic deduction programs will work best when the redirection doesn't *feel* like a loss, like money has been "taken out" of the fixed paycheck, but rather is either "redirected" to another asset class or "set aside" from a raise.

Other small-scale policies combine incentives for individuals and employers. Some colleges and universities (and even some businesses) have "Walk-to-Work" programs that subsidize the purchase of a home within a mile or so of your job. These programs are generally underutilized, because people discount the nasty effects of commuting—in particular, they discount the stress it produces. They might choose differently if they knew the research that establishes just how bad a deal it really is to accept a longer commute along with that slightly larger home in the suburbs; long-distance commuters are significantly less happy. Kahneman and his colleagues showed that commuting is even *perceived at the time* as stressful. So, commuting is a generally unpleasant experience—so much so that, on a scale where lower rankings are negative, commuting ranks below "having lunch with your boss."[6] And yet people discount or underestimate this consideration when making the choice of a home. In a case like this, just knowing the research could persuade potential participants to sign on, or could prompt program administrators to highlight the benefits of not commuting when pitching the Walk-to-Work program. If it is the extra bedroom that drives the discounting bias here, ads could explain that what you saved through the program would allow you to add onto your house, and so on, making it easier for people to bind themselves to a better reasoning strategy.

Literally dozens of these small-scale, personalized strategies exist, some of them benefiting from the tiniest push of government incentives. Private landowners who want to manage their property in a

way that will benefit fish and wildlife habitats can secure federal incentives for a "Biodiversity Partnership."[7] Through another federal
incentive program, the National Park Service encourages people to
restore and renovate older buildings instead of tearing them down
and building new ones.[8]

In the private sphere as well, incentives are used to guide choice.
Credit card companies, for example, clearly trade on knowledge of
loss aversion when they offer the option of sweeping rebates or over-
payments into a savings account. And for those workers padded in
other ways, companies now use cash incentives to motivate overweight employees to drop pounds. It appears that the offer of as little
as seven dollars per 1 percent of their body weight significantly stim-
ulates weight loss.[9] These incentives give us a "gentle nudge" (to use
Dan Kahan's clever expression) in the direction of our own health.

In the United States, however, there is often entrenched political
opposition to structures that support the goals we all share. For example, the United States has no federal motorcycle helmet law, even
though skulls do not vary in hardness by state. Instead, the issue is
treated by many as one of rights rather than public health or safety,
as the seat belt issue is. And in many states, citizens won't adopt a
helmet law solely because it is deemed a government intrusion.[10] So
we can't expect citizens to embrace decision aids simply because the
government endorses them.

Fortunately, there are times when life improves without a determined plan, and we should be prepared to learn the lesson when it
happens. For example, in England and Wales in 1958, half of the
people who committed suicide did it by gassing themselves in their
homes. Starting in the 1960s, "domestic" gas—made from coal—was
replaced with natural gas, often located near oil deposits.[11] This
switch, driven by the cheaper price of natural gas near oil deposits,
amounted to the detoxification of gas used in the home. As it happens, gas from coal contains large amounts of carbon monoxide, and
natural gas has none. So from 1968 to 1975, the suicide rate fell from
almost 5,300 to nearly 3,700—a drop of one third—at a time when
suicide rates went up throughout the other countries of Europe. This

trend would be unremarkable if people had simply found other ways to commit suicide, displacing carbon monoxide with other methods. But this is not what happened. Over the years, thousands of lives have been saved due to an unwitting adjustment in the upstream environment.

These happy accidents are not rare, but because they are unexpected fallout and not the featured phenomenon, like a deliberate experiment, their lessons are often missed. Occasionally a few are unearthed. For instance, with nothing more behind them than the simple profit motive, global marketers introduced cable and satellite television into developing countries possessing promising economic profiles. India was one such nation. The introduction of rural Indian viewers to television elevated the status of women, increased women's reported autonomy, reduced tolerance for domestic abuse, and decreased the traditional preference for male children. All of these large effects on gender attitudes about women amount to about five years of education, and move rural attitudes closer to those found in urban areas.[12]

There is, after all, something to be learned from happy accidents, just as from deliberate experiments. But experiments have better defined goals and more carefully monitored conditions. Just think what a government could do if it made social goals—quality public education, safe shelter and adequate nutrition, effective opportunity and equal treatment, personal security, to name a few—the specific and intended result of policy.

FIDDLING WITH THE FUTURE

When addressing big policy issues, we face hefty challenges. The first is our empathy gap. Our empathy is stymied by our psychological distance from those in need. We care more for identifiable individuals than statistical ones. We think first of how people might be harmed by a new policy; those now harmed by an existing one are "off-screen" and therefore, out of mind. If the sheer number of deaths, or the utter magnitude of suffering, is demonstrably due to an existing policy, how do you propose to change it? The standard story is that citizens pressure their representatives, and the representatives vote in the interest of their constituencies. But this Pollyanna picture of democratic action is no longer credible, and the psychological research on the power of cultural orientation casts individuals as immobile on most of the big and controversial issues.

There is a better way. We need to remove some of the barriers to accepting new policies—mostly by lowering the stakes. We can do this by testing policies piecemeal, and by ensuring that they promise high-benefit, low-risk improvements. In some cases, the evidence either is already available or will be available soon.

It turns out that some policies are more tamper-proof than others. We can predict the effects they will and will not have. And when they are tamper-proof, our unwillingness to experiment with them cautiously is tragic, delivering, for example, thousands of people every year to death by handguns,[13] tens of thousands of victims to entirely avoidable vandalism and burglary, and millions every year to the hopelessness of poverty. These people deserve better. Intuition and arrogant overconfidence has had its run. Science deserves a fair crack at these problems.

Whenever discussing state intervention, people see Big Brother in any measure the State introduces to promote citizens' well-being. But this objection is more of a visceral reflex than a criticism. All around us are government-subsidized programs that secure and promote our well-being, yet few complain. We have the state to thank for a police department; a fire department; water services; a regulated investment system; an office that oversees, approves, and rejects drugs and their disbursement; and even a deed office to track and store property claims. We pay for these costly services in the form of taxation, for the purpose of serving the public good. And when it comes to taxation, the government doesn't allow citizens to pick their line items. The question is why don't people see Big Brother as clearly at work there? If someone with enough money wants to hire his own security service or fire fighters instead, doesn't the compulsory taxation interfere with his liberty? How about someone who would choose to keep that police and fire portion of their tax and risk victimization or fire? Should a decent society let him?

Of course, libertarians think they are decent people, and my examples aren't designed to show otherwise. Instead, they are crafted to illustrate that libertarian measures often cascade beyond their original purpose. Decent societies recognize that people take foolish risks, and that some are driven to those risks by arrogance, poverty, simple limitations on information, or, as in this case of neglecting government services, the discounting bias. Some citizens would take the gamble that they won't suffer a disastrous fire in their lifetime. But when they do, they will become the State's responsibility. They may be injured or killed in the fire. But so may their family and neighbors, who never chose to assume that risk. (After all, fires tend to spread.) Most of our actions ripple beyond our skin. Recognizing this, we must acknowledge that our own personal liberty is not an unconditional value, because exercising it poses risks to others that they would reject. In their wisdom, then, people crafted a society that thwarts a tyranny of reckless liberty.

If the agents are competent and otherwise rational, what is the warrant for intervention in cases of cognitive bias? The basis of the warrant can be expressed as a test: the intervention is warranted if, against a background of a fully informed decision maker and an unbiased standard, the decision maker would not have made the decision he or she did. In the present case, if the decision maker knew that he couldn't routinely calculate the risk, or couldn't resist taking the risk, he would have consented to any number of low-cost corrective measures.

De-biasing promotes rather than undermines autonomy. After all, biases threaten our ability to meet our considered and long-term interests. By recognizing the threat of biases, we give ourselves a better chance of meeting our long-term interests. At the same time, the approach I am suggesting does not impose a substantial conception of the good on individuals, such as compelling people to achieve better health through exercise. Rather, the bias-correcting procedures I have proposed enhance people's chances of effectuating their goals by enhancing their capabilities.

Mine is a plea for benign social experimentation. The phrase "social experimentation" conjures images of poking and prodding the citizenry with different policies to see how they respond. And this is indeed a cruel image. That's not what I'm talking about. I am proposing policies designed in consultation with decision scientists carefully selected for fairness and expertise according to guidelines set out by government offices.[14]

The first policies concern topics that are prudential rather than principled and hot-button: Let's tackle the issue of default rules in the insurance industry before we address gay marriage.

The rationale for careful social experimentation begins by admitting that we are already in the midst of many grand experiments. Social experimentation is not rare and underutilized. It is common, but often done poorly. Political administrations regularly run experiments of sorts that impose substantial burdens on the public, with little more than anecdotes and impressions to back them up. A multi-decade enterprise is now under way that provides evidence of a nation's well-being when a substantial minority goes without basic health coverage, or when a middle-class family can't afford to buy a home or send a child to college. At present, most policy proposals are ventures in social speculation of one sort or another. What we need is careful and responsible policy formation so that, when we find that the U.S. infant mortality rate is worse than Cuba's, we can trace the reasons why. The goal here is not necessarily to punish or reward but to learn. If it is a good idea for the U.S. Budget Office to track the effectiveness of financial outlays, it is also a good idea for a new government office, perhaps working together with other federal science agencies such as NSF and NIH, to trace the success of policy investments.

Whether successful or not, policy experiments are always under way. Another long-running grand experiment was the supply-side economics of the 1980s. The argument was that lower tax on the wealthy, and fewer governmental regulations on business, would fuel economic growth, and this benefit would "trickle down" to poor and lower- and middle-income Americans in the form of more employment. But there is a huge gulf between simple economic growth and any tangible benefit to the poor. For example, during the heyday of the supply-side approach, increased GNP never benefited the poor in a way that matched the efficacy of specially designed programs such as Social Security. In fact, during the 1980s, the poverty rate wandered aimlessly from 10 to 19 percent across administrations, while the GNP climbed along with all the other relevant measures. Judging by the poverty level, the poor benefited not at all, and may even have suffered more, if we look at real dollars. Contrasted with a dedicated entitlement program such as Social Security, whose increased funding reduced the elderly poverty rate from 35 percent in 1960 to 10 percent in 1995, current approaches that leave costly preparation to "individual responsibility" also leave vulnerable parts of the population unprotected.[15] More recently, the Treasury Department conducted an analysis of the economic consequences of new tax cuts, and concluded that the cuts made only a tiny contribution to economic growth.[16] Our government was clearly prepared to test out these policies on its people, but the experiments were not based on knowledge, and they were not designed so that we could learn from them. Because the government is running experiments all the time, under the name of "new policies," it would seem partisan, if not philistine, to object only to those policies that have the benefit of pilot experimentation or careful formulation.

It is time for new experiments in social policy, but this time done correctly. In particular, rather than recklessly denying so large a population their basic needs, while spending money on lower-priority, untested adventures, we should carefully experiment with a variety of redistribution and entitlement policies. We saw how experiments in the areas of investing and habit-control could help people make better decisions for themselves. Investment experiments produced the Save More Tomorrow Plan, and with it, higher savings rates for individual investors. Psycholinguistic experiments yielded models that reduced prescription-related errors, and so saved lives. Other applications await. A basic-needs program for the impoverished would cost many billions annually, depending on the coverage. Underfunded public education needs resources, among other things, to improve graduation rates, which have fallen below 50 percent in some high schools in our biggest cities. A fair policy of public schooling may require federal funding (perhaps allocated through the states) to subsidize schools poorly funded by the low property tax yield of impoverished neighborhoods. Ensuring the health prospects of forty-five million citizens without health insurance would likely cost billions as well. In short, even a start at handling these problems will be difficult and costly. But we are an extremely wealthy country, and our citizens, many of them children, are suffering. And while the initial costs would seem great, no one has done a serious accounting of the ultimate benefits. With problems this complicated and expensive, doesn't it make sense to use the tools of science to craft policies that will solve them more cheaply and securely?

Many people die, and others live in fear, when a simple policy would save them and harm almost no one else—a near-Pareto improvement with bells on. But you might have to experiment in order to know this. For example, the United States is virtually alone in the world in allowing the easy availability of handguns. We will see that every year that the United States fails to control availability, thousands of unnecessary homicides and suicides result—what I call "deaths due to delay."

How do you know when the balance of risk favors social experimentation over an existing or default policy? You don't. But you do know how many people will continue to die, or to suffer, if nothing is done. So you make a calculation, implement the policy, and then watch. And in order to arrive at an estimate, we must hunt for natural experiments that allow us to make fortuitous comparisons among governments on such issues as stem-cell research, immigration acts, and state-sponsored retirement pensions.

One kind of natural experiment examines a feature on which otherwise similar states differ, such as the state tax rate, the murder rate, or as we will see later in this chapter, the death rate from motor-cycle accidents. Economists and legal scholars have developed inge-nious methods for mining existing data that compare citizen behavior in demographically similar states with different laws. Economists Steven Levitt and John Donohue were able to conclude that access to lawful abortion following *Roe v. Wade* was a chief cause in the 30 to 40 percent reduction in crime beginning in the early 1990s.[17] And they were able to use this hypothesis to make finer-grained predic-tions that fortified the theory. For example, five states legalized abor-tion in 1970, and those states enjoyed a decrease in crime about three years before the rest of the nation did. In addition, states with high abortion rates during the mid-1970s had larger crime decreases in the 1990s when compared to states with low abortion rates in the mid-1970s. Control for whatever obvious factors you like. The rela-tionship holds up.

Government often tries to adjust the unwanted consequences of policies. But their clean-up operations are seldom called that. No-body ever devised a retirement plan thinking, "Let's make it psycho-logically impossible to fund." But that is what many people face when left to their own inside strategies of investing, like waiting until they feel they have some extra money, and then writing a check. If it weren't for Social Security or certain mandated pension plans, this ill-conceived plan would be the only one available. In that case, peo-ple would simply rely on their mistaken intuition that they valued all periods of their lives equally—or, if a bit more sophisticated, that they only discounted a later period to the extent that they were more certain to be alive in one year than in thirty. As a result, a much greater number would die impoverished.

When people dismiss promising new science-based policies, it is usually because they believe these policies are inconsistent with val-ues they regard as sacred. Typically, this unwillingness to assess the impact of these "sacred" or "protected" values is just an advocate's way of saying he holds the view dearly. But all values—even rights—are qualified. Free speech is not absolute; it is limited by agencies such as the FDA and the FCC. A ban on handguns and automatic rifles might be justified in the same way. This measure would not require taking away the right to bear arms. Law-abiding citizens would still be able to hunt with traditional rifles. But a vigorous effort must be made to remove prohibited guns currently on the streets. Only then could we assess whether any change in the loss of life made the limitations on handgun ownership desirable.

Some will remain unconvinced. There are at least two strategic ways to address resistance to these kinds of measures. The first is to emphasize how much is to be gained if the experiment is successful, and how little there is to lose if it isn't; in other words, highlight the policy's appealing cost-benefit profile. Another is to lower our psychological barriers to the new policy. One way to convey this message is to attach "sunset terms" to it. A driving force of procrastination and the status quo is the idea that a policy, once adopted, even an ineffective or harmful one, will be difficult to undo. This worry about the future introduces an imposing barrier, and eliminates the incentive for useful experimentation. But the concern could be removed by a clear qualification. A sunset term says that if the policy doesn't meet standards of success agreed upon prior to its implementation, we revert to the old policy by a designated date. In short, if the policy doesn't work, we end it. On the other hand, if we like the results, the policy can be extended or made permanent. This procedure, of course, won't lower the resistance on all issues, but it is promising for many workaday issues such as regulating insurance defaults and selecting a retirement plan.

Citizens and lawmakers nervous about intervention could place advance restrictions on the policy experiments so that they included sunset agreements, or success or failure agreements. Short-term sunset measures are not practical for all policies. A policy for energy independence, for example, would include provisions for solar and wind power, as well as for practical electric cars. These policies require an infrastructure built over many years. So it would be a waste of money to pay the start-up costs for a policy with such a short lifetime.

Administrative vacillation is not the only concern. People who see social well-being measures as paternalistic worry that policies, once adopted, would be nearly impossible to abandon; they take on a life of their own, and it then requires heroic efforts to wrest the provisions they offer from a public that has come to see them as entitlements. Just imagine what would be involved in eliminating Social Security or public education. Of course, perhaps these provisions persist because of psychological inertia. But maybe we are witnessing momentum: perhaps they continue because the public actually recognizes and values them. Seat belts, for example, are now widely viewed as part of a requirement that manufacturers provide a product that is safe.

We have to be sure that there is genuine evidence for this policy-inertia postulate, that it isn't just the time-worn complaint of "small government" partisans. The fact is, there are many well-known examples of government and lobbying groups easily undoing the policies supported and adopted by prior administrations. In 1954, the highest personal income tax rate was 91 percent. In 1964 it was 77 percent. In 1974 it was 70 percent. In 1984 it was 50 percent. In 1994 it was 39.6 percent, and has remained at roughly that level since then.[18] While this example demonstrates that some policies can be retired without sunset laws, unsuccessful policies might be easier to put down with sunset provisions in place. For example, an independent counsel statute has a five-year sunset term. As a result, Kenneth Starr's investigation of President Clinton lapsed in 1999, at a point when even Clinton's adversaries could think of little else to investigate. No matter what one thinks of the merits of that particular case, nearly all citizens believe that an independent counsel should have a special reason to investigate a president; few feel that counsels should be permanently assigned to investigate a president without reason or term limit.

Policies, once adopted, needn't enjoy a status quo bias characteristic of a permanent law. Sunset terms on selected policies are valuable because they prompt a close examination of whether a policy is working, and if so, how well.

SUICIDES AND SITUATIONS

The mantra about suicide—if you want to do it, you will find a way—gets repeated with every avoidable death. After two people jumped from the same university building at Arizona State University, one vice president at the university reportedly said that no change to the building was necessary: "The need is for psychological help rather than physical barriers." "What they really need is counseling and special attention," he said.[19] We all tend to believe this. We see suicide as an act of resolve—if you want to do it, you will find a way. But the scientific evidence suggests otherwise: suicide is not so much an act of character as an artifact of *opportunity*.

There are circumstances in which a suicidal reaction is hard to quarrel with. It is a reasonable reaction to the late stages of a painful terminal illness, for example. But aside from these special choices, suicide is nearly always a bad thing, both for the victim and the loved ones left behind. One tragically ironic feature of suicide—for those unable to resist the urge—is that the impulse passes quickly. In a study that followed 515 people who were prevented from jumping off the Golden Gate Bridge between 1937 and 1971, 94 percent were either still alive or had died of natural causes. These are people who, looking back, are glad their attempt failed. They went on to have children, satisfying careers, and full lives.[20] Alas, a huge number of people were not prevented from committing suicide. In 2002 alone, 31,655 people in the United States committed suicide.[21] Suicide is the eleventh leading cause of death, ahead of liver disease and cirrhosis, and ahead of homicide.[22]

What makes for a successful suicide attempt? The striking fact is that people who actually follow through with a suicide either use a means that is quick and irreversible once set in motion, such as a gunshot or a leap in front of a train; or a peaceful and slower method, such as gassing.

Guns are not likely to disappear from the American landscape anytime soon. People purchase them for many reasons: hunting, target practice, self-protection, and so on. But if they are a fixture of American life, we should make a sober assessment of the consequences. One consequence was examined in *The New England Journal of Medicine*. It studied the association between firearms in the home and suicides in the home in two U.S. counties between 1987 and 1990. It revealed that the availability of one or more guns in the home increased the risk of suicide in the home nearly fivefold.[23] Another study in the same journal followed 238,292 gun purchasers from 1991 through 1996. It established that new gun buyers were far more likely to commit suicide than the general population. Some of these first-time buyers, of course, may have purchased their first gun precisely to kill themselves. During the first week after purchase, handgun buyers had a suicide rate 57 times higher than the adjusted firearm suicide rate for the general population. Of course, this may well be evidence of suicidal opportunism if easy purchasing made possible what otherwise would not have been. In fact, an empathy gap may prevent us from tracking the number killed. But a focused determination to commit suicide cannot explain the array of findings. After all, handgun buyers were at an increased risk for suicide by firearm for the entire six-year study, and women who purchased handguns remained at elevated risk for both firearm suicide and firearm homicide during the course of the study.[24] People may attempt suicide when they want to kill themselves, but having a firearm at the ready makes them more tempted and more successful.

There may be no practical policy recommendation to make here, especially if gun control is an issue about which Americans have hardened attitudes. But there does seem to be a deep lesson about disagreement over well-being policies: when both sides are hardened, there is still a cost paid to sustain the existing policy.

ARCHITECTURES OF SAFETY

People have a mythical image of how the mind causes behavior, and this view makes policies, including anti-suicide measures, seem hopeless. They view the mind as a closed container, like a pliant balloon. Any outside influence gets displaced. Place one part under stress, and out pops psychic energy elsewhere. It is no wonder that ancient Roman doctors cut the veins beneath the paralyzed tongues of stroke victims: release a little blood, and the tongue should mobilize. Like all good Victorians, Freud also thought that our psychological mechanisms stored energies that would occasionally discharge, spilling out all sorts of socially unacceptable symptoms.[25] Freud was simply expressing the reigning wisdom about the mind.

This view explains our attitude toward suicide as an inevitable act of a troubled mind. Psychological energy needs to go someplace, we think, and if it is corralled by moral or social pressures of impending disappointment or hopelessness, it will cause trouble.

But this psychological "displacement" does not show up in the scientific evidence. We are much more like udders than containers, much more like ecosystems than cells. Our concrete environment draws out behaviors at least as much as any mysterious inner "character" produces them.

The myth of displacement underlies much of the public pessimism about the introduction of social policies. After all, what's the point of trying to control crime, suicide, or welfare fraud if it is inevitable? If people want to commit a crime, they will find a way to do it. If they want to commit suicide, they'll overcome any inconvenient obstacles. If they want to cheat on welfare, they will bring it off. But the displacement of human behavior—that you deter behavior in one domain and it will emerge in another area of life—is not a law of nature. And because it is not, there is a great chance that a well-conceived policy will improve human well-being with little downside.

Consider the situational causes of crime. Some buildings are easy marks, shrouded in trees and shrubs, with no porches, and having weak doors, poor locks, and lots of ground-level windows. At least as early as Jeremy Bentham's late-eighteenth-century prison design, architects have been interested in controlling crimes of opportunity, such as vandalism and theft, that poorly designed buildings make so easy to commit. Bentham wanted to control crime *within* a prison, though it turns out that the lessons extend beyond the bars. The best evidence indicates that you can reduce crime by adjusting four architectural concepts: increasing an area's natural surveillance, introducing territoriality, reducing social isolation, and protecting potential targets.[26] This includes more gates and other barriers that emphasize to *occupants* that this is their territory. Porches provide a place to relax and socialize, along the way increasing natural surveillance and publicizing one's territory. Aesthetically pleasing but crime-frustrating structures have been identified by convicted burglars as unappealing targets. And the numbers back up the reports. Buildings constructed for security are sites of fewer burglaries and assaults.

One social experiment with little downside risk began with the construction of crime-resistant buildings. In Brooklyn, two adjacent high-rise buildings prompted classic research on crime-resistant architecture. These two buildings had the same clientele but different architectures. One (Brownsville) dissuaded crime and reduced situations for committing crime. Brownsville had barriers marking private space, like lawns and gates, and offered residents natural opportunities for surveillance. The other (Van Dyke) did not: "Van Dyke Homes was found to have 66 percent more total crime incidents, with over two and one-half times as many robberies (264 percent), and 60 percent more felonies, misdemeanors, and offenses than Brownsville."[27] In another high-crime community, Clason Point Gardens, architectural improvements such as growing lawns, increasing visibility of common space, and designating space through landscaping, substantially reduced crime. In the two decades following the completion of Clason Point Gardens, "[t]he overall crime rate dropped by more than 50 percent, from 83 to 38 incidents per 1,000 residents per year, and the burglary rate declined by more than 25 percent.

The percentage of tenants feeling that they had a right to question strangers on the project grounds jumped from 27 to 50 percent."[28]

These numbers are surprising, but even more startling is the story behind them. Architectures reduce crime simply by eliminating opportunity. Ordinarily we explain crime, as we do suicide, as the result of a specific effort. But this picture is undermined by the observation that crime, like suicide and addiction, can be reduced best by adjusting *situations* rather than characters, alleviating temptations from the environment. Admittedly, the implications are rather embarrassing: I would like to think that, if I were a vandal, I would show more initiative than to be dissuaded by a lawn. But the evidence shows that things like lawns—which underline ownership and territory by the care they require—act as a restraint.

And it shows something else. When a beat cop "takes back a street corner" where drugs are being sold, dealers just move to another corner; crime is not reduced, but simply displaced. That is what makes drug dealing so difficult to foil; there are lots of street corners, lots of alternative opportunities. But not all behavior is like drug dealing, and not all contexts have easy alternatives. Like architectural barriers designed to prevent suicide, architecture can reduce crime without just displacing it. The effect can be established by tracking crime in the area upon introduction of this architecture. The surprising fact is that it does not simply send criminals elsewhere. Remember, when there is the possibility for easy money, opportunity itself may be sufficient for crime. Architectural crime control reduces crime by eliminating opportunity.

So, anti-crime efforts don't necessarily displace crime to another location. In fact, out of fifty-five displacement studies examining a variety of crimes, such as vandalism and burglary, twenty-two of them provided no evidence of displacement at all. In the other thirty-three, displacement was minimal. But in none of the cases was the crime displaced elsewhere equal to the crime prevented by the architectural measure.[29] What's more, we are now seeing evidence of "reverse displacement," where situation prevention reduces crime beyond the target area. In one example, video cameras in a parking garage reduced car thefts in that structure, but also in other nearby parking garages in the area.[30]

Crime-reducing architecture has a number of advantages over alternatives of increased policing or unaesthetic, barricaded residences. These buildings are not especially costly; the necessary materials are no more expensive than less secure designs. The structures are not intrusive. They can be pleasingly designed. They do not compromise privacy. They do not require more police presence. And, architecture can increase the chance of unplanned social exchange, making for familiarity with one's neighbors.

One proposal allows the government to use the ideas of crime-control architecture when it develops public lands, zones new construction, or builds public housing. At first, this policy looks like a no-brainer: save money and human lives by using architecture and psychology. But this social control by the government may worry some otherwise enthusiastic adherents. The first concern is the preconscious nature of the influence of architecture on our behavior. We are not given the opportunity to decide how to react to our surroundings. Surveillance cameras may reduce crime, but they may also heighten the anxiety of law-abiding citizens. So, architectural measures are a balancing act between harm and benefit.

We do have a choice about whether to adopt these measures. We can create either a policy that reduces the number of crime victims and prison inmates, or one that produces victims and inmates at existing levels. You might think the choice would be easy. But people sometimes object because the social control explicitly targets a social effect, as opposed to being a consequence, desirable or undesirable, of a policy introduced for another reason. Thus, those with libertarian leanings feel that our faculty of choice is being supplanted by government control.

It is worth noting, however, that the government has already made a decision with policy consequences: the decision to pursue alternatives to architectural crime control. But it has not avoided influencing crime by the architectural choices it *does* make, each time its zoning regulations allow the construction of office buildings, housing projects, and schools, or distribute police, funding, and so on. The crime initiatives selected by the government have opportunity costs, the price of gains foregone. They also crowd out other prospects for crime control. If you are going to wage a "war on drugs" largely by incarcerating nonviolent possession offenders, you will have to build more prisons, or else release violent offenders at risk of repeat offenses.

Murderers are a whole other story, and new research in criminology is aimed at not only identifying those prone to committing murder, but also stopping them before they try. In 2005, Philadelphia experienced 380 murders. In recent years about 80 percent of these deaths result from bullets delivered by handguns.[31] Imagine the cost of incarcerating murderers, restoring the lives of the victims' families, and of living in fear. Spotting future murderers is like prospecting for subterranean water from aerial photos. You look at the contours of a life to see what lies beneath. If you start with a large enough population of murderers, you can begin to zero in on the factors that place individuals at risk for committing such a crime. First, murderers are almost always men. Second, murderers have a history of crime against people rather than property. And third, the earlier in life these crimes occur, the greater the risk that the person will murder. Teaming up with parole officers and scouring records, criminologists and statisticians at the University of Pennsylvania have produced computer software that will make it far easier to narrow the pool of potential murderers.[32] But these research activists are also trying to change the life situations of those most at risk, providing for them all of the goods and services thought to counteract the predictable murderer's criminal trajectory—counseling for social isolation, heavily involving parole officers, and after-school programs. This is a completely novel approach to controlling situations, and an interesting alternative to another experiment that would involve simply controlling access to handguns, the implement of choice for the vast majority of homicides.

A FUTURE TO ENJOY

If we turn to motorcycle helmet laws, the fatality figures make a powerful case against dithering. In 2004, a total of 1,316 motorcyclists in
the United States suffered fatal crashes. Had all of them worn helmets, 671 of them would have been saved.[33] States without laws
could then calculate the number of lives that could be saved by passing a federal helmet law. In order to advance the case for a federal
helmet law, then, advocates for helmet laws should advertise the "invisible deaths," that is, those deaths that didn't have to happen. They
should also report deaths due to delay.

The numbers are pretty compelling. A motorcyclist is twenty-
seven times more likely to die in an accident than a person riding in
a car, with head injury as the leading cause of death in motorcycle accidents. Head protection makes motorcyclists more death-resistant.
Since 1989, six states enacted universal helmet laws, reducing fatalities by 15 percent in Washington and by 37 percent in California.
But not all states are trending toward helmets. A crash without a helmet does not mean certain death, and one with a helmet does not
guarantee survival. But overall, when involved in a crash, an unhelmeted motorcyclist is 40 percent more likely to die from a fatal head
injury and 15 percent more likely to receive a nonfatal injury than a
helmeted motorcyclist.[34]

We can easily count deaths that occur under existing policies, but
we don't count and publicize how many people *would have lived* if
some trivial law had been implemented. After all, how do you count
invisible deaths? We often track the bad effects of a policy once it is
introduced. And we commonly hear doomsday predictions about
the results of a policy if adopted. But it is much harder to chart the
bad effects of *not* implementing a different policy. It would be nice to
know, for example, how many people are dead because we don't
erect suicide barriers, don't reasonably regulate gun sales, and don't
have a federal helmet law. We are not like Jacob Marley's ghost. We
don't have the privilege of showing people the different paths their

lives might have taken. But Marley was, after all, an actuary. He dealt in forecasting customs.

There is a simple way to tell, with reasonable assurance, how many fewer people will die if a policy is adopted. Take the lives saved by wearing motorcycle helmets. Ideally, you could compare the fatality rate for a state before and after a change in a helmet law. In 1989, Texas adopted a helmet law, and motorcycle fatalities dropped by 23 percent. Since 1997, Texas weakened its helmet law, resulting in a reduction in helmet use. Motorcycle fatalities rose by 31 percent. The following graph tells the Texas story in simple terms.[35]

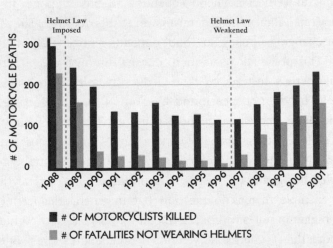

TEXAS MOTORCYCLE FATALITIES
1988–2001

Texas Department of Public Safety, 1999 and 2004.

Statistics can be tricky. But sometimes simple statistics tell the plain truth. Barring a miraculous conspiracy of numbers, you don't need to be an oracle to divine the gross forces behind them.[36] The ebb and flow of the numbers follow the presence of a helmet law. When the law gets weakened again, the fatality figures (and fatality

percentages) increase. And when the death count increases, it is not
simply because more motorcyclists are taking to the road. No matter
how many motorcyclists are registered, the unhelmeted dead in any
given year is always a larger fraction of the total when there is no helmet law. The reduction in fatality rate, then, establishes the importance of helmets for motorcycle safety. But in addition to rates, we
can look at counts. For example, how many people per year die in
Texas because the state doesn't have a mandatory helmet law? Assuming a relatively stable number of motorcyclists, the annual figure
exceeds one hundred. The sheer number of deaths exposes the effects of dithering and protracted controversy. Computed nationally,
for every one hundred motorcyclists killed in a crash while not wearing a helmet, thirty-seven would have survived had all of them worn
a helmet.

How do we decide when to abandon an existing policy in favor
of a new one? There is no general answer to this question. The threshold for changing a policy no doubt depends on one's political orientation. This pragmatic assessment doesn't diminish the importance
of civil liberties. Instead, it acknowledges that all civil liberties—for
example, freedom of speech and freedom of assembly—come with
qualifications. Those qualifications stand between speech and threat
or deception, between assembly and a mob. Only the most extreme
advocate is insensitive to factors such as a behavior's centrality to human well-being, and the cost-benefit profile of the policy regulating
it. For example, there is no question that, in general, the death rate is
much higher in states without helmet laws.[37] In fact, few even doubt
the more direct claim that wearing helmets saves lives. But that
doesn't necessarily lead to action. This is not an easy calculation, but
something like a dithering index must play a role in it. In the case of
helmet laws, we have to calculate how many more people die over
time than would survive if the new policy were in force. These numbers would allow us to determine whether the value we place on saving this many lives outweighs the value we place on allowing people
to make this particular choice of helmet-free transportation.

Different people discount or undervalue their futures in different ways. Some don't save enough, others abuse their health. Unhelmeted motorcyclists say they are willing to take the increased risk, but they probably fail to appreciate the pain, suffering, and financial hardship their death might cause to others, or the cost of treating their predeath injuries. But more than that, anti-helmet riders overstate the importance of the wind in their hair, and the feeling of freedom that conveys, precisely because they underestimate their ability to adapt to a helmet. A libertarian practice might underline the importance of individual responsibility and full disclosure by allowing people to ride helmetless if they sign a form setting out the risks, acknowledging that they understand and accept those risks. But the idea that this ceremonial acknowledgment of risk exhausts the requirements of sound decision making reflects a naïve and thin psychology of human motivation. Those same people may also report that they value a long life, time with their friends and loved ones, and living to ride again, values that conflict with helmetless riding.

It is important for a government to educate the public about these risks. But it is also important to recognize when individuals are beyond the pull of evidence. Such individuals irrationally discount the loss resulting from a helmetless accident, and vastly exaggerate the marginal gain in happiness from riding without a helmet.

This case for regulation will not convince everyone. But whatever headway we make in this case is significant for controversies about paternalism. The decision to shun a motorcycle helmet is, after all, about as self-regarding a choice as we will find. If you can make a case for regulation there, you can make it far more easily in other cases. Antismoking laws, for example, have been successful because regulators can point to the damaging effects of secondhand smoke. It doesn't matter that the smoker may have a right to harm herself, or at least risk it, because it is so easy to point to the likelihood of her harming someone else. But who else is made worse by a person's decision not to wear a helmet, even if that decision turns out badly? The argument I have offered focuses not on harm to other parties—which actually occurs in most of these cases—but on whether the individual is acting on good and consistent information. Regulations attempt to safeguard "other selves," even "future states" of the same person. This safeguarding reverses the tendency to discount the future, in much the same way Social Security is designed to blunt that tendency.

This safeguarding stems the costs of dithering in other cases as well. There is no telling how many children have died unnecessarily from childhood diseases as people have sat on their hands, and even opposed, inoculation. But they've died just the same. The same goes for helmet laws, Social Security, and the use of forecasting customs in the prevention of recidivism. To put it crudely, once the scientific evidence establishes a safer alternative (at costs that don't outweigh the improved benefits), then death and suffering beyond the status quo is a result of dithering—death and suffering due to delay.

It is worth thinking about this index when critics ridicule basic-needs policies, or well-being provisions, based on some generic speculation that a negative effect looms. This vocabulary of dithering tracks the suffering and death that occurs because we have no adequate basic-needs policy or universal health care program, suicide barriers or crime-resistant architectures. For the period from first proposal to persuasion, we should evaluate people's performance—both citizens and lawmakers—in terms of the death and suffering that their anti-scientific arguments have allowed through delay.

When scientific testing is the standard for drafting and adopting a policy, it is easier to hold lawmakers accountable for the tragic effects of their dithering. As we saw in the earlier case of a sterile-needle policy, the congresspeople attempting to block that policy made factual assertions—such as how needle-exchange programs would negatively affect children—that were straightforwardly empirical. In order to do so, they had to pose as scientific experts in front of their colleagues. If they were wrong, and the consequence is delay, we can estimate the deaths and suffering that delay caused.

The same could be said for other policies, such as seat belt laws. Once implemented in 1986 in nine of the ten most populous states, the seat belt law saved tens of thousands of lives in just a handful of years.[38] Since 1986, car fatalities ranged between thirty thousand and thirty-five thousand per year. Slightly more than half of the fatalities were passengers not wearing seat belts, and the National Highway Traffic Safety Administration showed that about 45 percent of these would have been avoided had the people been wearing seat belts—that is, about eight thousand avoidable fatalities per year. But to critics of this federal regulation, the benefit of the survival of eight thousand people is invisible; only the restrictions on one's liberty not to wear a seat belt, or not to pay for a seat belt, matter.

According to the NHTSA estimate, between 1977 and 1985 alone, the seat belt law probably saved as many U.S. citizens as the Vietnam War killed. The NHTSA numbers may be a bit inflated,[39] but not enough to blunt the effect. The sparing of life and avoidance of injury is stunning. Yet, rather than herald the results as a major policy victory—a policy innovation that keeps on giving—people forget the blessing, as well as the peculiar fight to get the law enacted.

Let's fold in the complication of moral hazards, the idea that people compensate for specific safeguards with risky behavior elsewhere. People love this kind of contention, which seems to reveal the futility, even the damage, of government intervention. In 1975, the economist Sam Peltzman published a classic study reporting that automobile safety laws—like seat belt laws—make people *feel* safer. Feeling safer, people believe they can "afford" to drive more recklessly (the so-called Peltzman effect). Of course, applying a scientist's name to a finding conveys the impression that it has the status of a natural law, à la Boyle's Law. But it turns out the Peltzman effect isn't a law. It isn't even an effect. A host of studies followed that either didn't find an effect, or found the opposite of Peltzman. Yet the conjecture has survived. The peculiar resilience of the thesis of offsetting behavior has not gone unnoticed. It took a careful analysis by Steven Levitt and Jack Porter to quash this conjecture. In it, they report that "wearing a seat belt reduces the likelihood of death by roughly 60%," and in 1997 alone, "roughly 15,000 lives were saved by seatbelt usage . . ."[40] Using a different analysis, a more recent article finds the same life-saving effect for seat belts, and makes the further discovery that the seat-belted driver is not more reckless. Comparing states with seat belt laws to those without, rather than fatalities before and after a particular time, they conclude:

> In contrast to the predictions of the [Peltzman] theory, we do not find any evidence that higher seat belt usage has a significant effect on driving behavior. Our results indicate that, overall, mandatory seat belt laws unambiguously reduce traffic fatalities.[41]

The original conjecture was that people not in the car were at greater risk when drivers and their passengers buckled up, because a seat-belted driver was more reckless. But there is no such self-defeating effect. The news is nothing but good for seat belt advocates: "Our findings indicate that seat belt use significantly reduces fatalities among car occupants, but does not appear to have any statistically significant effect on fatalities among nonoccupants. Thus, we do not find significant evidence for compensating behavior."[42]

The next battles on this front will be on the topics of health care and the safety of children's car seats. And we can count on the same ironic claim being made by proponents of compensating behavior: drivers with kids in car seats are more reckless than those without children in car seats. Arguments insinuating the futility of regulating behavior harbor the same basic assumption: restrain behavior in one place, and it will pop out somewhere else. But there has to be *evidence* for this compensating behavior. In its absence, you would need the arrogance of a god to simply dismiss passive strategies for cultivating valuable behavior, or avoiding damaging behavior, when government regulations such as seat belt laws have saved so many lives. Some critics of government regulation come dangerously close, but usually they simply treat existing conditions as inevitable. As we saw in the case of suicides and seat belts, the status quo is not unchangeable and the arrangements it dictates are not inevitable—a few tweaks to the environment could substantially reduce suicides and deaths from not wearing seat belts. The fact is a society can reduce murders, assaults, and burglaries, without thereby producing more elsewhere. The vague sentiment that situational controls are in some way re-

strictive is an awfully expensive feeling if it interferes with the implementation of these damage-reducing controls. So is the generic
charge that corrective or welfare-enhancing policies are moral hazards, and therefore, self-defeating and a wasteful imposition. Yet
these vague sentiments are behind much dithering. We need specific
evidence.

There is little danger in finding a few cases of compensating behavior peppering the vast landscape of human conduct. Maybe people who have their computers insured handle them more recklessly,
simply because having insurance reduces the incentive to be careful.
Or it may be that, as economists have claimed, increased health care
coverage produces eating habits that produce risks to health. For example, having health insurance that covers elective mole removal
might cause more people to have that procedure, costing the health
care system more.

But for all their publicity, moral hazards are a small fraction of
our total behavior. No law of nature states that risky behavior suppressed in one area of life must pop out elsewhere in one's conduct.
When homeless people begin accepting nutritious soup kitchen
meals over risky refuse, they do not begin to run with sticks or scis-
sors, introducing a new risk to compensate for their newfound well-
being. People in countries with fluoridated water systems don't offset
the good effects by flossing or brushing less or eating more sugar;
they aren't driven to reach any "natural" level of tooth decay.

The presentation of government regulation as futile and self-
defeating in this way is a dangerous game. Low-cost quality-of-life
improvements such as fluoridated water achieve their ends without
any compensating, damaging behavior. And this is the rule, not the
exception. In fact, habitual use of antiseptics, pharmacy safety measures, and speed-control provisions overwhelmingly belong in the plus
column.

At the same time, there is no evidence that helmets make accidents *more* likely. Researchers have taken seriously this possibility,
and have ruled it out. The engine sound alone swamps the muffling
effect of the helmet, and helmeted motorcyclists compensate for the

3 percent reduction in peripheral vision by turning their heads just a little more.[43]

In order to reduce thoughtless or unintended hardships, documented deadly policies could be described and discussed on the Internet. Public service announcements—much like the "Buckle Up" campaign—could inform the public about the steep benefits of wearing helmets. At the same time, helmet advocates must respond to claims of no-helmet groups by explaining that avoidable deaths like these are not purely private choices; the harm is not restricted to the motorcyclist when the cost is passed on to the state or the taxpayer to keep a brain-injured motorcyclist alive.

Successful policies liberate at a distance. They engage the person in activities that minimize rumination and temptation, while maintaining the prospects of choice and satisfaction. Prohibition of alcohol failed in part because it forced stunning changes in normal lifestyles. The measure was imposed with little public discussion, and no disciplined examination of the costs and benefits of alcohol. By contrast, antismoking legislation has proceeded piecemeal, not by making smoking illegal, but by making documented health risks introduced by smokers the force behind the regulation. Of course, people can make fun of targeted applications of a policy, but making fun is all it is.

We can expect that in a complex and multicultural society such as the United States there are many issues we will never get people to agree about—especially those regarding personal behavior. Our first job is to locate those issues about which citizens are open to persuasion, and then proceed on the basis of science and reason.

Issues of common agreement may provide a foothold. But even then, citizens seldom engage in the kind of public dialogue designed to locate and build upon whatever common values exist. So debates immediately escalate to angry accusations, or descend to mindless name-calling. We are witnesses to disappointing dialogue in political campaigns, television, and print coverage. The structure of this dialogue matters because the preferences people express depend heavily on the method used to assess them. In an atmosphere of calm conversation, available technical advice, and shared purpose in resolving an issue, citizen panels could be an ideal setting in which to plan policies and discuss hardened values. This does not mean that an opponent of abortion will announce that he now sees the force of reason, and wishes that all women might decide whether to take a fetus to term, or an opponent of capital punishment will declare that she now appreciates that retribution is the only way to fully respect a murderer's autonomy. These are polarizing issues for Americans, but not all issues facing us are so divisive. People are more likely to change their minds, or respond to evidence, on issues of public education, health care, and poverty—topics that have more of a foothold in their daily lives—even if they don't yield on gay marriage and gun control.

WASTED RICHES

American lore cherishes the idea that reward depends on hard work. This connection is what makes the resolution of Horatio Alger stories so satisfying. And this modest idea has a powerful reach. This homey American vision anchors financial reward in hard work, and even motivates abstract philosophical justifications of desert: people deserve to be compensated for projects to which they have made a contribution, or on which they have expended effort.

Many people have noticed that inherited wealth does not reward contribution and effort. Instead, it rewards legacies and lineage, the very aristocratic ills that early Americans were keen to stamp out. This battle continues. Concerned with the ideals that link reward to work, famous billionaires such as Warren Buffett and Bill Gates, Sr., have loudly criticized entitlement legacies. And they act on that principle. Buffett has set his children's inheritance at a quarter of a million, deciding that this amount is "enough to do something, but not enough to do nothing." The remaining wealth will be distributed to those in serious need.

Not everyone sees it this way. Critics of redistribution at death have a battery of complaints against estate taxation, a form of regular wealth adjustment designed to spread the effects of the chance accrual of wealth. Their claim is that an estate tax harms the economy. It removes the incentive to save, because you can't pass on your savings to beneficiaries of your choosing. And once there is no reason to save an "excess," you have less incentive to work as hard as you might. But there are also issues of justice. It is often argued that an estate tax is unfair to the wealthy because it disproportionately taxes them, and because it denies them their right to determine the destination of the wealth they have accumulated.

This opposition is initially understandable. It is natural for all people to want to help their children from beyond the grave. They may want to leave their children a financial legacy that will insulate them from the ordinary risks of life, and give them the leisure and resources to develop their talents. Poor people—in fact, most people—want this for their children. But what is natural to want and what is good or fair to want are often two different things.

Rather than discount what we already know about poverty, happiness, and adaptation to financial loss, in favor of sheer speculation and diffuse angst about government regulation, we should base our policy proposals on the actual findings of psychological science. If we want a rebalancing of wealth to boost citizen well-being, poor people are the most apt targets to receive the redistribution. Remember what we *do* know about happiness. We know that in Western democracies, people significantly above the poverty level adapt to all but a few life events. Apart from losing a child or spouse, we adapt quickly (if not completely) to ill fortunes as severe as serious spinal cord injury. Poor people, however, do not adapt to poverty. Since they could be raised out of poverty, their happiness is needlessly suppressed. Raising them out of poverty improves their happiness, without any known effect on those taxed.[44]

Ideally, of course, it would be better to use that money to create structures that would sustain for decades that portion of a nation chronically exposed to poverty—the undereducated, undertrained, socially isolated, sick, and mentally ill, or the just plain unlucky. And while some long-term strategies have been tried, such as job training programs, in the short term, people are suffering. Estate redistribution—or at least estate taxation—has promise as a low-risk policy to improve the well-being of those in need. And because there is a higher tax on income than on capital, estate taxation is one good way to rebalance or equalize the differences that emerge between the wealthy and the working poor. By leveling this region of the playing field, millions of people in conditions that cripple well-being would be made better off, at the cost of irritating the relatively tiny number of individuals who are wealthy enough to meet the redistribution criteria. Some who are subject to estate taxes will not be peeved, such as Buffett and Gates. The rest will fully adapt. So will their children.

If we do decide to tax de facto aristocracies, we should make it part of a policy experiment. Can we raise half of the people who are beneath the poverty level above it by distributing estate taxes to them? If aristocracies benefit the economy, that evidence is open to review. And if we fear that an airtight estate tax will cause the wealthy to flee to lower-tax countries, let's see if that fear is well founded. Policies needn't last forever, especially when the data show they don't work. That's what sunset provisions are for.

PATERNALISM AND HARDENED VALUES

It would be positively Big Brotherish for a government to tell you that you will be an engineer, or that you will drive a Ford. No one who sees a larger role for government in improving people's lives believes that government should supplant individual choice. In fact, no institution by itself can make better choices about an individual's interests than that individual, as long as that person is given an effective opportunity to do so. But in a complex society whose options often require technical knowledge, we cannot make better choices unless our institutions make our choices better.

In chapter 2, I illustrate the many ways our choices are shaped in everyday settings. In chapter 4, I punctuate this lesson by looking at the life-saving policies that would be blocked by loose talk of "social engineering" or "paternalism." The Department of Transportation "tricks" us into driving more safely by using chevron markings on the road. The FDA prevents us from the temptation of eating unsafe food just to save a few pennies. The SEC protects our future selves from our present appetites by blocking investment options whose risks are too complicated to understand for busy nonexperts. In all of these cases, what makes these forms of institutional assistance acceptable is that an average informed person opts for such assistance.

The proposals I have made to improve individual and social judgment place clear limits on government intrusion in the lives of citizens. No one is being made to think anything in particular as a result of these proposals. Paternalism isn't, after all, just any governmental involvement in our lives. It is involvement that amounts to *coercion*. But most measures prevent nonvoluntary choices that are driven by biases, such as racism and sexism. Still others, such as Social Security, enhance our autonomy by freeing us from poverty in old age. In order for a governmental measure to be paternalistic, it must be introduced against a person's will and justified solely by a claim that the person interfered with will be better off or protected from harm. But the solutions I have proposed can't be painted as paternalistic—not when the institutional assistance makes you *freer, happier,* and *more* informed, and, knowing this, you would have chosen it.

Some unusual personalities go beyond the simple desire for autonomy and free choice; they elevate their personal tastes to inalienable rights. These personalities may claim the right to gamble with their own futures, and report their willingness to pay the price should they end their days destitute. But we have now seen how unreliable these predictions are. And when their costs to society are so great, there is no reason to reward that errant overconfidence.

Consider another example of paternalism that never was. It may be that a seventeen-year-old has the intelligence and maturity to vote responsibly in the general election. But for the purposes of voting, we have to draw the line somewhere between a minor and an adult. The exclusion of seventeen-year-olds as voters in general elections isn't paternalistic. It is a rule justified by a concern for everyone's well-being, not just the voter's. Are governments any more paternalistic for regulating other kinds of behaviors that also affect the general well-being, such as compulsory retirement savings? Not if the word *paternalism* is to have any meaning at all. In the first place, many of these proposals are not paternalistic at all; they just involve government regulation. So antipaternalistic arguments are often just codes for "I don't see how I benefit from that regulation."

Is it paternalistic for a government to require inoculations? The Amish may believe so, but the rest of us look on in horror as their children die, just one inoculation away from a long and healthy life. When the idea first received serious discussion in policy circles and the media, inoculation proposals met with alarm. We first asked, "Should the government be allowed to compel people to get inoculated?" But the distress was quieted once the scientific results spread from the media to the public: childhood and adult inoculations easily and cheaply prevent death.

We can always ask where medical intervention ends, but there may be no single answer. An ordinarily competent adult may be depressed after a spinal cord injury or a sudden heart attack, and may resist treatments designed for his recovery. This behavior is unsurprising to physicians, who are used to steering a patient's behavior toward recovery.

The principle that treated inoculation as paternalistic interference vanished not because people were bamboozled by the success of inoculation, but because they began to appreciate that inoculation, even if coordinated by the government, helped people to exercise their freedom. And its benefits soon became an imperceptible part of the social landscape. The same power of top-down governmental measures can be claimed for Social Security. The compulsory nature of Social Security makes it a near certainty that forty-year-olds will have basic needs in their twilight years, and so make their decisions as freely and effectively as possible. And they will be free to make a wider range of positive choices because of it. In both of these cases, their freedom is enhanced by a top-down government measure that responds to what real people need and want—such as having water come out of their tap, and their garbage picked up.

Even private institutions could enact compulsory savings plans, though there is little wisdom in this measure if the job's wages are in the vicinity of subsistence-level. Such employment provides no cushion to allow the earner to adapt to the reduced income. Institutions, whether private or public, stand outside of us, beyond the lure of our impressions, intuitions, and biases. Because they can gather and coordinate information better than individuals, and are immune to personal temptation, institutions are ideal mechanisms for improving decision making. The job of the House Committee on Science and Technology, for example, is to address, generate, and evaluate proposals to improve citizens' well-being, and there is no reason that durable findings in psychology couldn't also play a role. But this committee is almost entirely occupied with the policy impact of the physical and biological sciences. The House needs either to add a committee on the behavioral sciences, or to be required to address behavioral evidence when considering related policy issues, empanelling a subcommittee accordingly.

I don't doubt that the U.S. electorate is unusually quick to perceive certain government initiatives as intrusive—I rode a Yamaha 400 in California and was often the only one on my stretch of road wearing a helmet—but there are frequent surprises. After all, in 2005, virtually everyone believed that Social Security was on its way out. But it turns out that people actually appreciate a program that mandates a secure retirement.

Some programs spawned by decision research meet less resistance because they are not enacted by the government. Instead, they are deployed in the private sector. Thaler and Benartzi's Save More Tomorrow plan uses one bias (the status quo bias) to correct another (the discounting bias) in retirement investing. But even people who deny that the cognitive biases are costly agree that because our brains have limits, we could sometimes use a hand in decision making.

Maybe normal citizens could calculate the rate at which we devalue something over time. Should we spend our time or effort in this way? Should I calculate the benefits of a blood-thinning drug prescribed for a heart condition against its costs if that drug cannot be taken with nonprescription triglyceride-lowering remedies, such as fish oil? Half a century ago, the calculation concerned water fluoridation. Maybe there is a hazard in allowing institutional judgments like those of the FDA to substitute for an individual's own calculations. Perhaps the hazard is that we will grow lazy, and stop learning about discounting or about the biochemistry of drug interaction. I have even heard that if government regulations attempt to streamline otherwise dizzying choice sets presented to consumers and overly steep discounting by retirement investors, our minds will soon atrophy. In time, we'll be unable even to formulate preferences or choose among them.[45] These antipaternalistic concerns seem ironically paternalistic. The suggestion seems to be that we should not assist people in deferring to expert or institutional judgment because such dependence will make them less cognitively able. This would be an interesting position if there were any evidence supporting it. But there isn't any; the scary vision is fabricated. On the other hand, there is a lot of evidence that our minds don't fall idle just because we aren't making economic decisions. We plan our meals, pay our bills, juggle our chores, manage our children, and coordinate with friends. Our minds don't wither once free from the maximizing impulse. Reducing the noise in consumers' environment frees them up to make other decisions, and to engage in other activities.

Some worry that government mandates send the signal to citizens that they can't be trusted or aren't competent to make judgments about their interests. But there are two sides to every signal. By not making opposing governmental decision aids available, isn't the government sending the message that we need no assistance; we are competent decision makers when it comes to retirement, health, and so on? Before Social Security, the impression was conveyed that individuals could do all the necessary financial planning. This impression is generally false.

Political opposition to specific institutional solutions to poor judgment is usually partisan, from quarters unshakably attached to the idea that all regulation is unjust. People who oppose Social Security, gun-control laws, seat belt and helmet laws, and antipoverty (or well-being) measures treat freedom from institutional solutions as a protected value, beyond the reach of pragmatic appraisals that tally the death and suffering caused by the status quo.

Perhaps the publicity principle mentioned in chapter 2—the prescription that policies and laws be open to public scrutiny—could protect citizens from manipulation in democratic decision making. But it might not. Useful versions of the publicity principle are difficult to state. For example, while Rawls supposes that "as members of society they will also know the general facts," we often fall short of that standard for innocent reasons. Ignorance resulting from natural cognitive barriers is not the same as ignorance resulting from secrecy. And cognitive biases *are* barriers. But more than that, Rawls says that our decisions about appropriate laws and policies "must rely upon current knowledge as recognized by common sense and the existing scientific consensus."[46] But this expectation falls somewhere between innocently hopeful and wildly optimistic. As this book has so often shown, common sense and scientific consensus routinely conflict.

In a time of megademocracy and technical development, citizens will always need to farm out decisions and defer to experts about the conditions that produce greater equality, opportunity, and overall well-being. There is nothing about the publicity principle that demands each individual understand the details of the processes by which decisions are made. Citizens don't need to become experts in nuclear physics to contend that nuclear bombs are a threat, nor does the government need to see to it that every individual has that expertise. You don't have to be an MD to responsibly take prescription medication. Normally, you can just defer to one.

It is better to think of the publicity requirement as demanding that governments be publicly answerable to citizens. Citizens can expect government accountability without falsely supposing that people can overcome their biases by sheer acts of the will. At the same time, in order to correct our biases, a government needn't be secretive or coercive. If citizens feel that their government is unresponsive, voters can elect representatives or a president they deem more responsive, or they may exert public pressure via their local representatives. In fact, a government that could not make arcane judgments without the specific and updated consent would grind to a halt.

Partisans of "small government" dismiss these institutional solutions as social engineering. The popular view is that these policies are carried out by a liberal state. The liberal state is an administrative state. Somehow, the managerial or administrative state is now associated with the left. The much-publicized proposals of progressive New Deal social planners gave this impression life, but surely the Progressive Era shares responsibility with socially conservative proposals that had an equally specific idea of how entitlements could lead to a better life. Over the years, social and economic conservatives have supported massive government interventions that wasted billions of dollars on ventures such as Star Wars technology, and enacted elaborate legislative protection for the inheritance of idle wealth, in direct contradiction to their avowals that contribution and effort were a necessary condition of success. Critics of the liberal state's managerial function decry its engineering role, when in fact it is the liberal ends they oppose. After all, if managerial function is the real target, then there are plenty of targets in each political party's role for the state. People with a lot of property endorse subsidies for the protection of property, yet oppose taxes that provide those services. The list of ironies is long.[47]

Social planning is neither desirable nor undesirable; it is unavoidable. The question is simply how to do it correctly. The FDA regulates many dangerous drugs. Suppose a mature and competent adult wants to take an unregulated drug (or even a regulated drug without a doctor's prescription). It is, after all, his health and his life. Shouldn't we allow him?

Of course we shouldn't; neither should any free society. One reason we shouldn't is that competence in these cases requires arcane technical knowledge,[48] much like the knowledge that psychological science delivers about the biases of judgment. Most people are unaware of these scientific findings, and as those very discoveries predict, many who learn about them still resist their lessons.

In the end, we have to decide what we care most about—to set our priorities and estimate the costs and benefits of particular kinds of conduct. Throwing money at the poor may be less efficient than trying to stimulate economic growth and produce higher employment; but after thirty years of attachment to supply-side economics and nothing but short-term oscillation in the poverty rate to show for it, we have permitted a generation of misery, of suffering and death, by any application of the dithering index. These are real, estimable losses. People who care about the poor—particularly about poor children—are ready to abandon the hope of a perfectly efficient solution, and try for one that raises people above poverty, even if less efficiently than we once fondly hoped.

RAISING THE FLOOR OF HUMAN WELL-BEING

The most robust finding in behavioral medicine is the socioeconomic status gradient: the increased risk of disease and chronic ailment as patients approach poverty. Stress is one cause of this risk, exactly the kind of stress induced by poverty. Other primates can compensate for stress, and find activities to distract them. But not so for humans. Robert Sapolsky points out: "[W]hen humans invented poverty, they came up with a way of subjugating the low-ranking like nothing ever before seen in the primate world."[49]

Many who oppose projects of social justice do so in the name of principles of classical liberalism, standards widely identified as foundational in a free society. For example: How much can a liberal society expect a citizen to sacrifice for the good of others? We would not expect a young adult in perfect health to give his life so that his heart might be donated to an aging person with heart disease. Yet we *would* regard it as callous to grab the last bite of food from an impoverished old person sitting at our dinner table. So we do expect some natural sympathy from others. But not as much as you might think, and probably not as much as we ought to. In our society, we do not expect the healthy person to give blood. How can we expect people to risk their income being redistributed to others who might need it more?

A House Committee on *Social* Science would go a long way toward explaining well-tested theories of human behavior to lawmakers and the public. However, federal funding for this advancement of knowledge is precarious. Even for the most durable mysteries of the universe, the public funding of basic science faces such trenchant opposition that funding agencies are driven to near-comical efforts at self-promotion. In order to capture public support, NASA has a publicity page that assures us that space research is not a waste of money. Its innovations have thrown off indirect, unexpected benefits, such as enriched baby food, scratch-resistant lenses, and better golf balls and portable coolers.[50] Imagine, by contrast, the direct social benefits that could be enjoyed if the pent-up talents of brilliant scholars from academic institutions were unleashed throughout the United States. It is amazing the work that has already been done with the relatively small social science funding allotted to the NSF and NIH. If our blinding biases were disabled, these offices would be massively funded, perhaps on the order found in Europe.

In the same way, psychological science can help us to eliminate the damage and waste of arrogant inaccuracy, to identify what costly options can be trimmed back without loss of liberty, what courses of action will promote and sustain expressed social commitment, and how goods irrelevant to happiness can be earmarked for more important causes without the feeling of sacrifice. This would complete Hume's vision of a social science "which will not be inferior in certainty, and will be much superior in utility to any other of human comprehension."[51] But more important, it would complete the arc of moral virtue, ensuring that human capabilities were developed as much as possible, and human needs were satisfied to the greatest extent possible. Children would rest with their bellies full, beneath safe shelter.

There are, of course, many challenges. Our sympathetic feelings are variable, while the object of our sympathy is stable. To be durable, humane goals must be achieved through policies that bind. Using social policy to correct our biases is like the experience of flying a plane by instruments. Without the instruments, we may feel like everything is fine even though we are actually upside down. When we fly by instruments, it takes some experience to get comfortable with them, and we don't always see the destination, but we know what it is, and we know that the instruments will get us there. A policy based firmly on science will focus our instruments on the destination, not on the ultimately sentimental, and routinely inaccurate, feeling that we are going in the right direction.

I first suggest the right direction at the close of chapter 1. The territory we have covered since that chapter was designed to remove the psychological obstacles to more humane policies. The best hope of eradicating poverty in the United States is amending the Constitution to guarantee an above-poverty income to all citizens. Only a constitutional amendment has the properties that make outside strategies effective in securing human well-being. Over the last thirty years, the U.S. government has had many chances to step in and safeguard the poor.[52] The most obvious lifeline would tether the fate of the poor to the advances of the rich. The percentage of national income represented by the bottom 40 percent of the population decreased by about one fifth between 1973 and 2001. At the same time, the percentage going to the top 5 percent increased by more than a third. Between 1970 and 1998, the portion of national income going to the top one tenth of 1 percent quadrupled, with the thirteen thousand richest families in the United States enjoying nearly the same income as the twenty million poorest.[53]

Remember, poverty is an enemy of happiness and well-being,

and fluctuations in circumstance prevent people from adapting to their situations. Post-war U.S. elections have produced both problems. For families in the 95th percentile of the income distribution, their income growth has been the same under Democratic and Republican administrations. Rich families have fared far better under Republicans than Democrats, while families at the 20th percentile have had more than four times as much income growth under Democratic versus Republican presidents.[54] These partisan effects never let the poor adapt and, under Republican presidents, never let them rest. A rational antipoverty policy would be nonpartisan, because the ills of poverty don't change with administrative control. A constitutional amendment would span administrations, and so stabilize the poor's treatment.

European nations have crafted policies that feed and support impoverished children without creating incentives for people to free-ride. Finland's child allowance is about one hundred euros per month for the first child, but the second and third bring in a total of only about thirty euros per month more,[55] hardly enough for a calculating person to regard having children as a sweet deal on the state's dime. Furthermore, in order to receive social-protection benefits, recipients must meet employment requirements. There, the government is the employer of last resort, meaning that the government expects its people to contribute to the society from which they benefit.

Unlike in the United States, qualifying individuals in most of the European nations are lifted out of poverty once they have made full use of all of the government programs available to them. In 2005, the U.S. poverty level was at 12.6 percent (or 37 million people) *after* qualified individuals made full use of all monetary aid, such as supplemental security income (SSI is provided by general tax revenues for aged, blind, or disabled people whose income is below a certain threshold), Social Security (funded by Social Security taxes), and Temporary Assistance for Needy Families (TANF). For children in the United States, the poverty rate in 2006 was 17.6 percent.[56] Contrast this with the governmental commitment of the European Economic Community. In Section 75 of Denmark's Constitution, for example, citizens are guaranteed either employment or above-poverty-level public assistance:

1. In order to advance the public interest, efforts shall be made to guarantee work for every able-bodied citizen on terms that will secure his existence.

2. Any person unable to support himself or his dependents shall, where no other person is responsible for his or their mainte-nance, be entitled to receive public assistance, provided that he shall comply with the obligations imposed by statute in such respect.[57]

In providing this assurance, the Danish Constitution is not un-usual. Many in the United States oppose the idea of a government that finances full employment. Opponents foresee inflation, claiming that the government would be "printing money" to subsidize another government program. Rather than using the image of "printing money" to preempt the serious discussion that the idea deserves, an open-minded person might ask whether the risk of guaranteeing income is worth saving millions of children from a life of poverty.

But the specter of inflation is a red herring anyway. After all, the U.S. government regularly prints money, as it is doing now to finance a colossal national debt, a direct result of a huge tax cut and a disas-trous war.[58] This is not a partisan contention; it is a condition decried by liberals and conservatives alike. Our children will pay for these decisions, and poor children will pay twice. By comparison, the inef-ficiencies of a basic-needs program are far less costly.

So we are left with the fact of need, on the order of a billion peo-ple in the world and millions in our own country, at or below subsis-tence level. For those who are able, the virtuous thing to do is give voluntarily. But weakness of will and the variable and capricious in-fluence of circumstance make this difficult. So the decent thing to do is craft a policy that is secure and durable. In order to overcome bias, we need to help people make their vulnerable virtues more robust and automatic. And you can do this only with the help of institutions. It is easy to keep our eye on the target, because there are people in need everywhere. It is harder to appreciate that our dinner table stretches to homes far away.

In the politicized atmosphere of science in the United States, it may seem irresponsibly naïve, even utopian, to envision a science of judgment and decision making elevated to the status of a precision tool in the practice of policy making. A decent society would order national priorities. It would make explicit decisions, in diverse contexts and formats, about national security, economic growth and employment, caring for the poor and sick, and the environment. Once these priorities are identified, we can listen to science for the most effective ways to serve them. Bills that depend on scientific expertise should be peer-reviewed. The House should use the proposed Committee on Social Science to make policy recommendations that depend on specialized knowledge in the social sciences.

When a forward-looking policy proposal is especially controversial, the government should sponsor policy experiments. It should make state-by-state comparisons, either all at once or over time, to determine the success of different policies. With some luck, new policy experiments wouldn't require fresh legwork: we could learn lessons from relevantly similar European countries. We could, for example, track natural experiments in countries comparable to the United States that had nationalized health care, strict gun control, and a social-protection program.[59]

What would happen if we took seriously the state-of-nature view romanticized by critics of social-protection programs? Imagine the unregulated state, one without an FDA, FCC, SEC, EEOC, or NHSTA. It is a dark and foreboding world, a world of food poisoning, drug fatalities, rampant crime, deceptive marketing, chaotic highways, unaccountable sexism and racism in the market, financial ruin caused by unscrupulous entrepreneurs, and constant fear in response to it all. In order to loosen the grip of this fiction of the unregulated state, we have to strengthen the relationship between legislation and science. A decent society takes every opportunity it can, many of them supplied by science, to better serve citizens in their personal pursuits.

Whenever we embrace the virtues of a compassionate society, we should also acknowledge that it is our human biases that cripple our compassion. Psychological discounting causes us to neglect our future selves and the lives of those remote from us. The status quo bias leads us to thoughtlessly reproduce costly decisions, and to ignore more valuable courses of action. Legislation anchored by solid science can disable these biases, or turn them into opportunities. These enhancements improve effective opportunities, and needn't interfere with our autonomy, or our sense of ourselves as free actors. Not all utopian visions keep one foot on the ground, but ours can manage to if we raise the floor of well-being.

Conclusion

Empathy's Future and a New American Demos

THERE ARE MANY VARIATIONS ON THE STORY OF AMERI-can freedom, stories of rags to riches, of immigration and the search for prosperity, and of refuge from persecution. Loftier versions begin with stories of American freedom as well, rooted in an airy vision of the state of nature, or in an idealization of the economic actor as supremely rational. These stories provide a familiar or persuasive format to begin scholarly discussion or to silence political critics. But their influence far exceeds their warrant.

This book presents an alternative story grounded not in the abstractions of political theory or economics, but in the moisture and grit of human psychology. This earthy story, about how real people make their choices and the real psychological resources they can wisely spend on that task, is far more likely to yield practical advice to improve human well-being. But such a realistic view also can be hopeful, especially when we make good use of the truths uncovered. A scientific psychology both recommends and helps us to adopt an outside perspective on ourselves.

Empathy is typically reactive, but it can also be preventive. Smart empathy can beat back danger's crest. We are intuitively aware of our empathic powers, but insensitive to the way distance in time, geography, and culture makes our empathy falter. We have seen the biases that have gone unnoticed by policymakers. We mispredict what we need to be happy; as we've seen in chapter 1, we "miswant."[1] People recklessly ignore their future well-being and imperiled strangers' dire needs, and cannot bring themselves to abandon inferior but entrenched options. For many people, the only thing preventing them from helping others is the belief that doing so would make them worse off. And although there are literally thousands of policies that could improve citizens' lives without making anyone else significantly worse off, people do not call for such empathic policies.[2]

One of the most charming, even magical, features of people is their tendency to make the best of their situations. We adapt to a less-than-perfect state. This tendency, like the biases that are a centerpiece of this book, is an unconscious process. We adapt to the familiar menu of choices in our society in much the same way that, à la the status quo bias, we resign ourselves to existing options and don't pursue better alternatives.

I have tried to suggest the potential role of science in making those options more effective and available to everyone. While the average U.S. worker today who neglects the risks of a lean retirement will still live perhaps two decades longer, in generally better health, than a citizen of ancient Athens, workers in some industries still have life expectancies and health risks similar to those of a citizen of classical Greece in 350 B.C.

Policy by intuition and impressionistic judgment has had its run. With the newfound power of scientifically informed policy comes a new question: Should policy bodies attempt to provide goods that are known to make people happier or improve their well-being even when these goods are neither requested nor valued once provided? At first, this question seems absurd. If citizens want something, they can just ask for it. But this naïve expectation ignores the preference reversal lesson of chapter 3's tutorial on bias: preference reversals indicate that many of our preferences are constructed rather than merely exposed. But more generally, knowing that—or anything else about biases—doesn't make them go away.

As part of a grand outside strategy, my chief recommendation has been to pass many of the law-making functions of the legislature through the House Committee on Science and Technology, and to begin discussing the need for a Committee on Social Science. But there are two related and hopeful reactions to the newfound promise of science-based policy. Both are authentic and positive projects, not utopian constructions. The first policy movement anticipates a human tendency, sometimes noble and often useful, to adapt to circumstances that fall short of our hopes and even threaten to erode our well-being. The second outlines an opportunity for the public to consider their personal, social, and political priorities without filtering those values and priorities through a two-party system in a politicized campaign. Both movements correct for a number of systematic frailties related to the status quo bias and our unquestioning acceptance of default options.

Government well-being programs will press these psychological tools hard in the service of policy. Before the inauguration of the much-maligned gross domestic product measure, politicians, economists, and policy planners found it difficult to track the steps government could take to strengthen the private economy and make our lives better. But now the National Accounts System (NAS) records these activities. Daniel Kahneman, Alan Krueger, and other psychologists and economists have proposed a system of National Time Accounting (NTA). If the GDP tracks money, the NTA would track the way Americans spent their time, and thus would provide an alternative to narrowly economic ways of measuring a society's well-being. This approach would follow people's actual evaluations of their emotional experiences in the use of their time.

National Accounts originally tracked narrowly economic activity by using the crude measure of prices. With so slim a focus, a few peculiar consequences should not be surprising. In the calculation of GDP, for example, diamonds are more valuable than water. In fact, there are many valuable experiences and goods that don't show up in these measures, such as so-called non-market values. Also absent is a person's psychological resilience, which can be strained to work longer hours, to brace that person under physical pressure, and to ignore social costs such as reduced status and indignity.

A National Time Account, then, allows us to develop further the analogy between mining human resources and natural ones. If, as development economist Partha Dasgupta says, GNP is no more than a measure of current economic activity, then wages, too, are just a measure of current labor activity.[3] And if it is possible that a country can showcase a high GNP by blowing its natural resources on a consumption binge, it is also possible for a country to boost its GNP by squeezing from its workers unwholesome amounts of resilience and stamina while on a productivity binge. What shows up, then, is a high per capita GNP. But in light of how we got it, a high per capita GNP is a poor measure of at least non-market well-being.

Many of the activities that make our lives better—activities and creations we dearly value—cannot be directly measured by such accounts. The beauty of poetry and painting, the love of friends and family, relaxation and leisure, sport and exercise, reading, working, learning—these features of life all contribute to our well-being. Using contemporaneous ratings of these activities while we do them, early efforts to perform time accounting register the extent to which people enjoy these activities. For example, when people rate how enjoyable their present activities are,[4] the lowest rated are the morning and evening commutes, along with working itself. On the other hand, activities such as "intimate relations" and "socializing after work," ranked first and second, followed by dinner, relaxing, lunch, and exercise. In fact, a good night's rest is among the best predictors of a person's enjoyment of activities the following day.[5] It is easy to dismiss talk of measuring such delicate and subjective joys, but researchers have done their job well, crafting measurement procedures worthy of government policy. With this data now in hand, it is eye-opening that we always make time for the most unpleasant activities of the day, such as working and commuting, and allow them to crowd out the top six. We could therefore achieve lasting elevation of well-being by substituting low-ranking with higher-ranking activities. The National Time Accounting proposal, if put into service, could bring about such a durable improvement. It would allow us to test, and then implement, opportunities for improved well-being, and greater happiness, by identifying more satisfying substitutes for less enjoyable activities, time asleep for a longer commute, time with friends for overtime. With the time accounting research now brewing, we may soon see National Accounts that track non-market goods that contribute to human well-being. What's more, research in psychology and behavioral finance will spearhead this movement through government offices.

These are common sources of individual well-being, but sources that we cannot create as individuals. It takes a government either to permit or institutionalize time and incentives to exercise these enjoyable capabilities. A decent government is always on the lookout for ways to improve its service to citizens. It *bridges* empathy gaps, yes. But a vigilant government also *searches* for empathy gaps, because people aren't always aware of the many forces that separate them from others, such as acting on ill-formed preferences or irrationally discounting our futures. This vigilance is necessary because the forces that pull at the ordinary citizen are so complex. And when our heads are turned, to smile at our children or drive to work, our individual and social well-being can be mined.

In order to recover our trust in government, we need to see public officials constantly proposing enterprising ways to make our lives better, and to correct blameless imbalances: proposals to make us healthier, provide more leisure and vacation, more time for socializing with friends, more health protection, and in general, more real or effective opportunities, rather than mere freedom from the interference of others. In an affluent America, the American politician instead responds with a familiar slogan, "Just give 'em more freedoms." But it turns out that freedoms are only as useful as the quality of your options, and aggressively humane service improves these options.

The main goal of a vigilant government—a government that creates opportunities for people to do what they enjoy most—is not to prevent people from working many hours, under stressful conditions, if they so desire, but to inform citizens that doing so may have effects they might not want, effects that are difficult to recognize and track.

But we can improve our lives in other ways. If we shift from the question of what activities we most enjoy to the question of what people most care about, minipublics or citizen panels provide a way for sciences to have a humane impact on policy. A minipublic is a small cross-section of a population, and it is empanelled to consider, and deliver a report on, policy issues facing the residents of anything from a community to a country. Minipublics are designed to be small enough to engage in genuine deliberation, and representative enough to be truly democratic.

Minipublics may be used to clarify our values—values that are subject to bias. We may know what we enjoy but not how to order the things we most care about. Modern liberal democracy has been touted as the final stage of political development, or certainly the highest yet attained.[6] The United States is the wealthiest nation, and is among the happiest.[7] But we still don't know at what cost. There isn't much call even to ask that question. In a nation whose average household income so far exceeds basic needs, it would be a wonder if we weren't among the happiest of nations. But that should make us ask both why more than 60 percent of the U.S. population—mostly the poor and middle class—struggle to secure some of the most basic achievements of modern democracy, and why other liberal democracies are happier with far lower mean household incomes.

There is a lot more to well-being than equality and living standards. There is also the desire for security, the eradication of terrorism, and the control of violence. A minipublic can ask people how they order their priorities.

If a government and its leaders want to know what its citizens think and value, it needs to ask them, and do so correctly. The single-question poll doesn't have the depth to tap any shared vision. For that, citizens will need to deliberate, take time to reconsider, and where appropriate, consult with experts. And the government will need to listen to the products of citizen deliberation.

Deliberative polls, citizen panels, consensus conferences, or minipublics—whatever you call them—are simple, reliable, direct, and inexpensive ways to tap into a consensus, or source of disagreement, among citizens.[8] Citizen panels could determine citizen preferences, both long term and short term, so that the government could make laws that reflect those preferences. They could register people's interests and priorities, either at the state or the national level. They could also be used to follow the accuracy (or the nature of the inaccuracy) of affective forecasting. For example, just how mistaken are people about their "getting used" to commuting, and so on. Finally, citizen panels are cheap—a lot cheaper than, for example, making a bad policy decision.

Minipublics could fill in those gaps between ordinary citizens and the politicians isolated from them. Americans long to feel that they are actually represented. Yet, accurate representation is hard to get. Democracy in the United States allows wealthy individuals and organizations to hire lobbyists, who exert influence over lawmakers. And with its wealth in the hands of so few, this system of advantage makes it impossible for the views of ordinary citizens to be heard or, more important, honored.

A citizen panel is a great equalizer. For as much influence as an extremely wealthy individual might have over other citizens, on a panel, each person's view receives equal weight. Wealthy panelists cannot, for example, hire lobbyists to influence other members. As a result, panels promise to accurately represent citizen preferences, and serve as a center for open, truthful, and autonomous deliberation.

Unfortunately, partisan mischief in the past has led the American public to distrust government-sponsored panel reports. Many can recall the so-called Meese Commission on Pornography, President Reagan's blue-ribbon panel, which traveled across the country to uncover unseemly behavior at every truck stop, massage parlor, and porn house. Pulling back the curtain on many twenty-five-cent video booths, the panel concluded that they were disgusted by it every time they had to do it in the name of their study. The commission was given only a year to complete a study on the complicated role of pornography in our society, a budget of $400,000 and a staff of nine. With so few resources, it is perhaps not surprising that the eleven-member committee commissioned no empirical studies. But this neglect was disappointing, because many of the issues could have been resolved only empirically. This disappointment should stimulate a further lesson: The best science of the time must be used in the evaluation of the results, but also in the design of the study.

Not surprisingly, the panel had no credibility with the American public. It was evident to them that the commission was rigged, not impartial. Six of the commissioners had already openly called for government action against pornography. As a prosecutor, the commission chair, Henry Hudson, had successfully crusaded against a number of adult theaters and bookstores. In the end, the Meese Commission Report was seen for what it was: bad social science in the service of a political agenda.[9]

My proposal has a more pristine pedigree; a deliberative poll is no blue-ribbon panel. Members are not handpicked by political administrators. The panelists are instead ordinary folks, selected randomly within different social categories, who have no direct stake in the topic. Homemakers, electricians, teachers, accountants, the unemployed, doctors, and cab drivers, once selected, could be asked to address issues ranging from the minimum wage and sin taxes to drug enforcement and health coverage. As everyday citizens, their only stake would be that they pay taxes for various state and federal programs, and live with the results. Once together, the panelists would study the target issue in a way that was informed and reflective. They would meet more than once to talk, share information, consult with experts, and listen to their testimony. Panelists would also listen to people who had a more direct stake in policy outcomes, thereby giving the panelists a direct empathic connection to the issue. After full deliberation, the panelists would assemble a report on the consensus issues among them. The purpose would be not to create a consensus, but to record one after everyday folks had deliberated on the issue at hand. The report would be designed to fully represent sources of the panel's agreement and disagreement. Finally, the panel would make the report easily available, so that it could be discussed by the wider public.

Americans have not had much experience with citizen panels, but such panels are highly regarded in Europe and Canada, and they could be so in the United States. All citizens must be able to see that the panel is not a technocratic snow job, and that it represents the attitudes and policy preferences of ordinary citizens, and directly represents the diversity of citizen views in the United States.

There is no shortage of real-life models. As I've pointed out, citizen panels are used in Europe and Canada, chiefly to discuss and make policy. In 2004, a Citizens' Assembly in British Columbia gathered 160 randomly selected citizens, held 50 public hearings, and spent more than 10 months charged with proposing a new referendum system for the province. The provincial government guaranteed that the recommendation of the Citizens' Assembly would appear on the ballot as a referendum proposal, and the vote on it would be binding on the current political institutions. It was the first time a representative subset of ordinary citizens had been empowered to propose basic changes to a democratic country's political institutions, to be decided upon in a general or local election.[10]

More often there is no guarantee in the United States that a panel's recommendations will be pursued, but rather an expectation that its decisions will be taken up in the policy process. Panel members are urged to clarify their values, explain their priorities, and describe their implementation plans for a chosen policy or solution. When compared to the voting process, minipublics provide real breathing room. When voting, Americans are used to squeezing a trip to the polls in between political sound bites, keeping their boss happy, making dinner, and taking care of their children. That is no way to make policy decisions about utilities, hospitals, schools, insurance coverage, pollution, food standards, and health care. Panel members can deliberate and weigh the evidence at their own pace.

Deliberation is a critical ingredient of this modern agora. A panel's decision is not reducible to the demographics of its members, because a person's demographic is not his destiny. A poor Mexican immigrant could be an atheist, even though he belongs to a group that is overwhelmingly Catholic. A wealthy black woman might be pro-choice and hawkish. These combinations come as no surprise to the experts who draw up panels. A government study could use U.S. Census information to locate and contact individuals who would complete a representative sample. Like jurors, panelists would be paid for their participation, though it might cost more to secure the purely voluntary participation of a panelist. Citizens would then be empanelled to represent a fair cross-section of the target population, be it a single province of rural Canada or a large chunk of the United States.[11]

Demographic gaps are spanned when we empathize. We are more likely to help people and plan for their well-being when we focus on our attachment or similarity to others, as with kinship and friendship. These similarities help us to "merge our identities" with others, and so feel more concern for our neighbors, taking action on their behalf. But it is awfully risky to tie the fate of those worse off to our fragile exercises in sentimentality, or to our voyeuristic attempts to understand strangers very different from us, which are performed at our discretion, and can be pushed aside as a matter of caprice or mood.

We can use minipublics to clarify our values and set priorities. We can use forecasting customs to trim our expenses and improve our accuracy. We can use choice structures to shake people free from costly defaults. We can, once again, use government to promote a common vision of well-being.

In short, citizen panels can vault the empathy gaps to which constitutional bodies are prone. After all, even if a representative or senator is the sole source of income in his family, all congresspersons are in the top 5 percent of annual income and are, therefore, unlikely to empathize fully with the ordinary citizens for whom the measures are needed.[12] The panels, however, *are* those citizens.

Minipublics can accurately uncover citizen values in the small

and on the cheap. It may seem awkward to graft a directly representative structure onto a majoritarian political arrangement in the United
States. Majoritarian governments, by definition, need not offer proportional representation. But most novel surgeries are both awkward
and necessary.

The American settlements that founded the United States had a
shared vision based on the desire for religious freedom, genuine political representation, and economic prosperity. The rapid rate at
which well-being improved for the settlers is perhaps not surprising.
Starvation and illness were so widespread that any successes in agriculture or industry produced dramatic improvements in well-being.
And of course, slavery and appropriation of occupied lands fueled
American prosperity. Once the majority of citizens had been delivered from the anxieties of subsistence, however, gains in well-being
were harder to come by. And that is why our efforts today to improve
well-being further must be more deliberate, more surgical, and more
fully informed by the subtleties of scientific findings.

But there is another reason why the best route to improvement is
deliberate: the administrative obstacles to constructing a good society are greater than ever before. There is a big difference between democracy in an early American village and democracy in a multicultural,
technologically sophisticated country of three hundred million people. With a population so large and the distance between citizen and
elected official so great, only wisely planned policies—education
programs, career retraining, health coverage, retirement funding,
environmental protection, and foreign aid—can make improved
well-being a specific goal of life in our modern democracy.

There is no risk that we will lose our ability to empathize; humans are wired to respond to the immediate suffering of others. But
in the age of megademocracy, as the psychological distance imposed
by population size, cultural diversity, and geographic boundaries
makes the concerns of our remote human family seem vanishingly
small, there is a real risk that we will lose hold of our humanity.
We can close that distance, that empathy gap. But it will take work,
ingenuity, and an openness to experiencing the pain of others.

The idea of a new demos, and a modern agora, may seem idealistic. But there is nothing pie in the sky about pools of citizens deliberating with the advice of scientists; such groups already exist. There is nothing exotic about a government Committee on Science and Technology; the House of Representatives already uses one to make law. And there is nothing utopian about a government that is aggressively humane, constantly searching for ways to make our lives more satisfying and comfortable. Whatever the fate of these positive proposals, they are not grounded in the foolish optimism that our society will improve whenever we recognize the need. Well-being programs designed for the common good must give the greatest number of people a fighting chance to be happy. A humane government steps in with social plans when our individual judgment fails us. A new twenty-first-century Enlightenment of the head and heart, of rationality and empathy, can help us build and implement those social plans so that we don't fail others.

Acknowledgments

C OGNITIVE SCIENTISTS SPEND THEIR CAREERS STATIONED
at the borders of several intellectual territories—in my case,
philosophy, psychology, neuroscience, behavioral economics, and social policy. And I have been fortunate to rely on many
other specialists when I was not already in command of the geography. When your research relates fresh, technical details spanning vast
domains, solitary scholarship is not an option. Gratefully, the need to
connect otherwise discrete issues like judgment and decision making, the good life and societal well-being, put me in contact with the
world beyond my laptop.

I want to thank the many universities and centers that invited me
to present this ongoing work: University of Illinois at Chicago, New
York University Law School, Northern Illinois University, University
of Pennsylvania, California State University–Long Beach, Northwest-
ern University, University of Cincinnati, University of Washington,
University of Chicago, and the Max Planck Institute in Berlin.

This project was pleasantly interrupted by another and, in the fall
of 2004, Mike Bishop and I completed a book, *Epistemology and the
Psychology of Human Judgment*, in which we presented a deliberate,
though irreverent, alternative to the theory of knowledge as it is con-
ceived and practiced in the English-speaking world. I am grateful to

Loyola for granting me a leave immediately following the appearance of that book, in the fall of 2005. This schedule allowed me to return to *The Empathy Gap* while visiting the Philosophy Department and the Center for Decision Research in the Graduate School of Business at the University of Chicago. While there, I presented material from chapters 3 and 4 of this book at the University of Chicago Graduate School of Business in October 2005, and benefited from questions and comments at that session from Ann McGill and Richard Thaler. I was especially flattered when Professor Thaler, director of the center, e-mailed me requesting a copy of my PowerPoint slides, which contained the examples of the "fly in the urinal," chevron road pattern, and casino self-ejection. Two of these featured cases, behavior-shaping and choice-shaping, appeared in earlier work of mine, and they have since stimulated much discussion. I revisit those examples in this book. Elsewhere at the center, Nick Epley, Uri Gneezy, Tanya Menon, and George Wu were all generous conversationalists and great lunch companions, managing to turn an ordinary meal into an intellectual feast. I especially want to thank Reid Hastie, for sponsoring my visiting appointments there in the spring and fall of 2005. Some of the material in this book even made its way into a philosophy of social science course I taught as a visiting professor in the Philosophy Department at the University of Chicago to a lively group of graduate and advanced undergraduate students.

Writing is fun, but testing and talking about ideas is why I got into the business. I have been very fortunate to have friends like Paul Abela, Mike Bishop, Joe Mendola, and Abe Schwab, who are always ready to talk. So was my friend Danny Shivakumar. I miss him and I hope this is a book he would have liked.

In writing this book I benefited from the sure advice of Wendy Wolf, my editor at Viking/Penguin, along with Noirin Lucas and Elizabeth Parker. My research assistants Matt Butcher and Matt Kelsey at Loyola ran down voluminous factual details, and I am grateful for their thorough work. And Rafe Sagalyn was a wise steward. Along the way, I also enjoyed a great gumbo of other knowledge and talent, owing to economists, psychologists, historians, philosophers, political scientists, lawyers, legal scholars, business school faculty, and foundation managers. These colleagues, friends, and acquaintances have stepped in with references, arguments, advice, and questions. I am lucky they were ready with answers, and even luckier that I fish with a few of them. So thanks to Brad Barber, Mike Bishop, John Boatright, Mark Brown, David Buller, Tom Carson, Joe Cesario, Stuart Comstock-Gay, Bob Cooter, Ed Diener, Richard Easterlin, Nick Epley, Richard Farr, Heide Fehrenbach, Baruch Fischhoff, Adam Galinsky, Howard Garb, Philip Gasper, Simon Gervais, Gerd Gigerenzer, William Grove, Jon Haidt, Reid Hastie, Andy Koppelman, Alan Krueger, Rich Lucas, Richard McAdams, Heidi Malm, Maya Mathur, Vandana Mathur, Paul Moser, Dominic Murphy, Shaun Nichols, Jide Nzelibe, Mary Beth Oliver, Thomas Pogge, Claire Priest, Dave Reichling, Robert Remez, Norma Reichling, Max Schanzenbach, Josef Stern, Ken Tupy, Tom Ulen, Diane Whitmore-Schanzenbach, Bill Wimsatt, and Wendy Wood. And a special thanks to Steve Pinker for seeing the value in this project from the start.

Special efforts deserve special mention. Sometimes within minutes, Vince Mahler at my home institution of Loyola University in Chicago answered my questions about European welfare measures. Kathleen Adams mobilized her friends and colleagues over far-ranging questions in anthropology, and Peter Sanchez filled some necessary gaps in my political science education. Also at Loyola, the Parmly Sensory Sciences Institute has supported my research on spoken language processing, and for decades was a vital center for serious, comparative experimental research and theoretical discussion about sensory systems. Parmly is now at its end, and it is fitting to register my gratitude to the scientists and staff there.

When you get to live your life teaching young people and thinking about things that are difficult and wonderful, it is important to acknowledge your rare fortune. And in my case the fortune has reached embarrassing proportions. My wife, Janice Nadler, shares her life with me. Our kids, Jack and Jessie, are happy and full of excitement and questions. Andrea Madsen makes their lives (and ours) even more fun. And Pat and Don Nadler are at once ideal grand-parents and in-laws. Everyone should be so lucky.

Evanston, IL
March 2008

Notes

INTRODUCTION: DECENCY TO SPARE

1. The data both here and below are to be found at King, Parrish, and Tanik, 2006. Efforts to limit the interest charged on payday loans are discussed at http://www.npr.org/templates/story/story.php?storyId=14853904&ft=1&f=1001.

2. A fee of $15 per $100 borrowed amounts to a stunning annual percentage rate (or APR) of about 390 percent, the effective interest rate for a meager loan term of 14 days. The national average APR for a payday loan is around 500 percent, with a corresponding average fee of $19.23 to borrow $100 for 2 weeks.

3. Graves and Peterson, 2005. Their analysis showed that, in nearly every state, military towns were among the highest in number of payday lenders per capita. For more general coverage of the breaking tide against these lenders, see Henriques, 2004.

4. Skiba and Tobacman, 2008.

5. King, Parrish, and Tanik, 2006, pp. 9 and 11.

6. Brooks, 2006.

7. Of course, the losses to a long-term investor from overconfidence are easy to calculate. Assume an index investor earns 10 percent per year and saves ten thousand per year. Assume another investor saves the same amount, but earns only 9 percent per year. After thirty years of savings, the investor with the 10 percent return has a portfolio worth $1.64 million, while the investor with a 9 percent return has a portfolio worth $1.36 million—a two hundred and eighty thousand dollar difference. In light of the research done by

Barber and Odean, 2000, the difference is likely to be a bit larger, because
the 1 percent "overconfidence penalty" assumed here is a bit conservative.

8. Kumar, 2007.

9. The federal bill in question is the Payday Lending Provision of the 2007
Defense Authorization Bill, sponsored by Sen. Jim Talent (R-Missouri), H.R.
5122, the John Warner National Defense Authorization Act for Fiscal Year
2007. The relevant provision is Subtitle F, Section 670, which imposes a
new scheme of rate regulation and disclosure for consumer credit offered to
members of the armed services and their dependents.

10. Carr, 2007.

11. Morton, 2007.

12. Garcia, 2007.

13. For a nice exposé of personal responsibility rhetoric in financial settings,
see Hacker, 2006.

14. Jonathan Haidt's work has been important in putting the emotions on the
map in the cognitive sciences. See especially Haidt, 2006, and his earlier
work referenced there.

15. Glover, 1999, presents a deep and thoughtfully rendered discussion of
humanity.

16. We can move out to what philosopher Peter Singer, 1997, calls the "expanding circle."

17. Peterson, 2005.

18. Condorcet, 1955 [1792], chap. 24.

19. See Bucks et al., 2005, for the Federal Reserve survey for 2004, and the new
triennial Federal Reserve survey for 2007.

20. According to the Investment Company Institute, this includes equity and
mutual fund holdings in employee-sponsored retirement plans. See http://
www.ici.org/statements/res/rpt_05_equity_owners.pdf.

21. See American Gaming Association, http://www.americangaming.org/; for
2006 figures, see http://www.igwb.com/pdf/2006grossgambling.pdf.

22. Schroeder, 2007.

23. Brooks, 2006.

24. Lee, 2002.

25. Advisory Committee on Student Financial Assistance, 2001; http://www.
ed.gov/about/bdscomm/list/acsfa/StaffBriefing3.ppt.

26. Kaiser, 2006.

27. It is equally revealing to compare the actual rates of salary increase for CEOs
and ordinary workers; from 1990 to 2005, pay for CEOs increased almost
300.0 percent (adjusted for inflation), while production workers gained
only 4.3 percent. When inflation is taken into account, the purchasing
power of the federal minimum wage actually *declined* by 9.3 percent. Anderson, S., J. Cavanagh, S. Klinger, and L. Stanton, 2005.

28. Frank, 2007.

29. See, for example, work by Robert Nozick, 1974; Phillip Pettit, 1997; Gerald Cohen, 2000; Rawls, 1971; T. M. Scanlon, 1998; Thomas Pogge, 2002; Richard Arneson, 1997; and Peter Singer, 2002. Gerald Cohen puts one modern theme about egalitarian forms of liberalism more succinctly: *If You Are an Egalitarian, Why Are You So Rich?*
30. For a clear and jarring profile of the influence of socioeconomic status on college experiences and outcomes, see Walpole, 2003.
31. Kressel, Chapman, and Leventhal, 2007.

CHAPTER 1: BRIDGING THE EMPATHY GAP

1. Aquinas, 1917 [1270].
2. Adam Smith, 1853.
3. Stotland, 1969.
4. Krebs, 1975.
5. McClure, Laibson, Loewenstein, and Cohen, 2004.
6. This appears to be an assumption of some psychologists studying empathy, such as Batson, 1991.
7. These numbers are from the Food and Agriculture Organization of the United Nations; see http://www.fao.org/docrep/004/y3557e/y3557e06.htm.
8. For a close look at how the British spend their aid, see Wright, 2001, especially pp. 404–405.
9. Shimizu, 2000.
10. Hostetler, 1968, pp. 145–46.
11. Iacoboni, et al., 2005.
12. Jackson, Brunet, Meltzoff, and Decety, 2006.
13. Ramachandran, 2006.
14. Harris and Fiske, 2006. Also see Fiske, Cuddy, Glick, and Xu, 2002; for some theoretical background and further experimental findings, see Cuddy, Fiske, and Glick, 2007.
15. For one such provisional verdict, see Hauser, 2000, p. 224; a competing view can be found in Preston and de Waal, 2002. In another book, Hauser, 2006, includes illuminating discussions of empathy and moral psychology generally.
16. Slovic, 2007.
17. Van Boven and Loewenstein, 2003.
18. Hastie, 2002, pp. 25–26; Sunstein et al., 2002, pp. 29–30.
19. Van Boven, Loewenstein, and Dunning, 2005.
20. Trope and Liberman, 1998.
21. Ariely and Loewenstein, 2005.
22. Ibid., p. 11.
23. Ibid.
24. Naughton and Clymer, 2006.

25. Buss, 2004, p. 15.
26. Small and Simonsohn, in press.
27. Social distance is one measure of Trope and Liberman's (2003) influential "construal level" theory of psychological distance, which includes spatial and temporal distance as well as hypotheticality.
28. Putnam, 2000.
29. Kahan and Nussbaum, 1996.
30. Washington, D.C., NBER Working Paper Number 11924.
31. Greenhouse, 2003.
32. Hoffman, 2000, p. 199.
33. Williams, 1989.
34. Nisbett and Ross, 1980. But when explaining *one's own* failures, the pattern shifts; the person attributes his or her failure to features of the situation, and explains the failures of others in terms of their dispositions ("I'm unlucky, you're a loser," in the case of actor-observer failures).
35. Hewstone, 1990.
36. Forgas, Furnham, and Frey, 1990.
37. Nisbett, 2003, pp. 123–27.
38. Campbell, Carr, and MacLachlan, 2001.
39. Godwin, 1994.
40. Neumayer, 2005; also see Langevin-Falcon, 2002.
41. Estroff-Marano, 1999.
42. Schelling, 1968.
43. Small and Loewenstein, 2003.
44. Fetherstonhaugh, Slovic, and Johnson, 1997, p. 283.
45. Nisbett and Ross, 1980, p. 43.
46. Small, Loewenstein, and Slovic, 2007.
47. Small and Loewenstein, 2005.
48. Sunstein, 2005, pp. 537–38.
49. Nadler, 2005.
50. There is some evidence that people use the emotional stress of affected parties as a proxy for harm. See Nadler and Rose, 2003.
51. All of this information, and that in the following paragraph, can be gleaned from Gruber, 2005, and National Immunization Survey, 2004a and 2004b.
52. http://www.cdc.gov/MMWR/preview/mmwrhtml/mm5231a3.htm.
53. Ordering priorities is a complicated matter. Kitcher, 2001, contains a very nice discussion of prioritizing schemes in the case of science.
54. All figures below come from the following sites, unless otherwise indicated: European Union, Eurostat, 2005, http://europa.eu.int/comm/eurostat/. U.S. domestic aid figure from U.S. Office of Management and Budget, 2006. GDP figure from Government Printing Office Access, 2006. U.S. population figure from FedStats, 2006; http://www.fedstats.gov/.
55. These figures come from Shah, 2006 (which cites the OECD).

56. Miller, Bersoff, and Harwood, 1990.
57. Nelson and Baumgarte, 2004.
58. Triandis, 1994, p. 225.
59. UNICEF, 2005.
60. Rose, 2008, at http://www.chicagotribune.com/business/chi-sun_health_0210 feb10,0,1758041.story; also see McGregor, 2007 at http://www.business week.com/bwdaily/dnflash/content/aug2007/db2007081_804238.htm? chan=search.
61. For a very useful discussion of the psychology of deferred gratification in the context of saving, see Shafir and Thaler, 2006.
62. UNICEF, 2005.
63. Slovic, 2007, p. 14.

CHAPTER 2: THE TRAPPINGS OF FREEDOM

1. Freedomhouse.org.
2. Tocqueville, 1945, Vol. 2, p. 99.
3. Lefcourt, 1976, p. 31.
4. This literature is vast. For a way into the topic, see Botti and Iyengar, 2004.
5. Schweder et al., 1990, p. 199.
6. Of course, there are many pre-scientific discussions of free will, such as T. S. Eliot's "The Hollow Men" or Francis Bacon's "Idols," but these don't detail causal mechanisms. Instead, they are poetic and philosophical speculations.
7. National Public Radio, 2001.
8. But an important scientific movement within philosophy makes the psychological study of traditional philosophical concepts such as free will, empathy, moral sentiments, semantics, consciousness, introspection, and knowledge constitutive of philosophical theses. This continues one legacy of naturalism in philosophy. Some of this work is experimental. For a flavor of work targeting free will in particular, see Nichols and Knobe, 2007. Stephen Stich is one significant force propelling this naturalistic movement forward. Appiah, 2007, is a clear and lively, though not entirely enthusiastic, discussion of experimental philosophy in ethics.
9. And here, I am afraid, most traditional philosophers who study free will have not helped us to understand the real importance of experiments that expose as overblown our sense that we are the source of our behavior. Instead, most professional philosophical publication continues a lifetime of orthodox work on the topic, or a legacy leading back to the Constitution and beyond. It argues that the experiments don't show that free will is *impossible*, or that the "feeling" of free will is *thoroughly counterfeit*. But even if we grant those philosophers that the concept of free will is not literally incoherent, that its existence is physically possible, and that our introspective

evidence for it is not completely corrupt, we are still in the dark. Free will isn't an impossible concept, but its true exercise is rarer than we think. And the seductive feeling of free will is not completely corrupt, but it is a pretty lousy indicator of real choice. For the gripping psychological evidence, see Wegner, 2002.

10. Aristotle, 1985, Book III.
11. Descartes, 1641, *Meditation IV.*
12. Descartes, 1649, *Passions of the Soul, I,* art. 41.
13. Hume, 1977 [1748], sect. viii, part 1.
14. Nietzsche, 1998 [1889], "The Four Great Errors," sec. 7.
15. Quinn and Wood, 2005; Wood, Quinn, and Kashy, 2002.
16. Stirman and Pennebaker, 2001.
17. See, e.g., Thompson, 1999.
18. Libet, 1985.
19. Bargh, Chen, and Burrows, 1996.
20. Ibid.
21. Aarts and Dijksterhuis, 2002.
22. Dijksterhuis, Bargh, and Miedema, 2000.
23. It is enough that he knows who he is. And while I am confident that I am wonderful to work with, I am equally certain that he didn't actually love me. Instead, the "end-of-phone-conversation" cadence primed his "talking-to-my-spouse" script—apparently more than it did mine.
24. Dijksterhuis and Van Kippenberg, 1998.
25. Macrae and Johnston, 1998.
26. Zhong and Lillienquist, 2006.
27. Wegner and Erber, 1992.
28. Rizzolatti, Fogassi, and Gallese, 2000, p. 550.
29. Dijksterhuis and Bargh, 2001.
30. Hitt, 1996.
31. Smith and Curnow, 1966.
32. Its 2006 Web site statement explained why it is important to place branded products right inside popular media formats: In a world of multitasking, and with viewing options like on-demand and TIVO, the thirty-second commercial spot is less powerful as a means for "delivering the brand" to an audience. Of course, these efforts not only shape, but create, preferences. According to the company, Alloy Entertainment "develops and produces original books, television, series, and feature films." (http://www.alloy entertainment.com/) But that is a bit underdescribed. Teens are the chief target of this entertainment, and its specialty is "integrating" the consumer and luxury products of paying clients into the books and movies that Alloy creates as advertising vehicles.
33. As Rawls puts the point: "It is fitting . . . that the fair terms of social cooperation between citizens as free and equal should meet the requirements of full

publicity . . . [P]ublicity ensures, so far as practial measures allow, that citizens are in a position to know and accept the pervasive influences of the basic structure that shapes their conception of themselves, their character and ends. . . . It means that in their public political life nothing need be hidden." (1993, p. 68)

34. Thaler and Sunstein, 2003, represents one approach to improving judgment that proposes isolated and selective intrusions into particular decisions that people make. This version of paternalism—"libertarian paternalism"—more or less accepts the existing norms of happiness, health, and the good life as we find them in the contemporary United States.
35. Wilson, 2002.
36. Nisbett and Wilson, 1977.
37. Maier, 1931, pp. 189.
38. Ibid., pp. 188–89.
39. Todorov et al., 2005.
40. Ballew and Todorov, 2007.
41. Rasinski, 1989.
42. Ibid., p. 391.
43. Alesina et al., 2001, p. 211.
44. Small and Lerner, 2006.
45. Rector, 1992. This lecture is taken from his testimony to the U.S. Congress Joint Economic Committee, given on September 3, 1992, p. 10.
46. Tocqueville, 1945, p. 64.
47. Diderot, 1972, p. 237.
48. Kant, 1983, p. 41.
49. Dahl, 1985, p. 283.
50. Ibid., p. 58, commenting on this presumption.
51. Berger, Meredith, and Wheeler, February 2006.
52. Mumford and Whitehouse, 1991; Mumford and Whitehouse, 1992.
53. Wansink, 2006, pp. 47–53.
54. Harris, 1995.
55. Harris, 1998, pp. 212–13.
56. World Values Survey, calculated in Alesina, et al., 2001.
57. See Dennett, 2003, who speaks of "bootstrapping ourselves free," p. 259.

CHAPTER 3: CAN WE REBUILD THIS MIND? A TOOL KIT FOR SPOTTING BIASES

1. See Bishop and Trout, 2005, for a systematic response to the empirical literature on judgment and decision making, and a positive theory for evaluating the quality of reasoning.
2. Adam Smith, 1776, Book I, chap. 10, paragraphs 29 and 32.
3. For another illustration of base-rate neglect, here is a class exercise. Ask students to flip a coin fifty times, recording the sequence. Pick one student

and ask him to write out a sequence that he imagines would result from flipping a coin fifty times. Put all of these sequences in a hat. Promise the students that you will pick out the one that was generated by imagination. Then do a statistical analysis of the sequence that will identify significant departures from randomness. A person's sequence will include non-random patterns. In particular, people try to make the sequence "more random" by devising sequences that look more like what they imagine is a stereotypically random series, with lots of "independent" heads or tails standing alone.

4. Neufville, 1999, pp. 230–31.
5. Gibbs, 1994, p. 86.
6. Neufville, 1999. Also see Neufville, 1994, pp. 239–46.
7. In fact, the problems extend beyond construction projects. The same problems dog nearly every new company. Consider the high base rate of planning errors in software development itself, such as that used for Denver's baggage delivery: "To veteran software developers, the Denver debacle is notable only for its visibility. Studies have shown that for every six new large-scale software systems that are put into operation, two others are canceled. The average software development project overshoots its schedule by half; larger projects generally do worse. And some three quarters of all large systems are 'operating failures' that either do not function as intended or are not used at all" (Gibbs, 1994, p. 86).
8. Duflo, Kremer, and Robinson, 2005.
9. In the balance of Kahneman and Tversky, 1979, they offer a five-step corrective procedure that recognizes that "[t]he prevalent tendency to underweigh or ignore distributional information is perhaps the major error of intuitive prediction" (p. 416). This five-step exercise is as follows:

(1) Selection of a reference class. Identify the class to which this case belongs, a class for which there is known distributional information.
(2) Assessment of the distribution of the reference class. Determine the relative frequency of these kinds of cases for this class.
(3) Intuitive estimation. Based on specific information about the particular case of interest, ask how this case differs from other members of this class. This exercise should allow you to assess how well this case can serve as a basis for accurate prediction of outcomes.
(4) Assessment of predictability. Without the product-moment correlation between predictions and outcomes, one must rely on subjective estimates of prediction-outcome correlation.
(5) Correction of the intuitive estimate. Use frequency information to correct any incorrect subjective estimates that might misrepresent base-rate information. The biggest threats here are the hindsight bias and overconfidence bias. The goal is to reduce the distance between the intuitive estimate and the average.

Adapting this scheme to a recognizable academic example: (1) look at your CV; (2) select the reference class (if the solicitation is for an article, then articles are your reference class); (3) count the number of articles you were able to complete over a representative period of time (perhaps five years or so); (4) ask whether there is anything unusual about the article that would make it unrepresentative of those on your CV. Is it longer or shorter? Would it be more or less closely related to the topics you have been working on?; and (5) predict the likelihood of completing the project by the deadline.

10. Fischhoff, Slovic, and Lichtenstein, 1977, pp. 552–64.
11. What about scientists? Surely scientists' training and experience deliver them from the overconfidence bias in their areas of expertise. Alas, no—or at least, not always. Physicists, economists, and demographers have all been observed as suffering from the overconfidence bias, even when reasoning about the content of their special discipline. See Henrion and Fischhoff, 1986. It would appear that scientists, too, place more faith in the subjective trappings of judgment than is warranted.
12. Henrion and Fischhoff, 1986
13. Gervais, Heaton, and Odean, 2007.
14. But our understanding of an event is affected by how it is cast, and the patterns of connection are suggested by the cast. In one famous experiment, Loftus and Palmer, 1974, asked forty-five students to view seven different film clips of a car accident. The students were divided into five groups. One group was asked, "About how fast were the cars going when they contacted each other?" For each of the other groups, the word *contacted* was replaced respectively with *hit, bumped, collided,* or *smashed.* The group that received the word *smashed* assigned a speed that was nine miles per hour faster than that receiving the word *contacted,* leading Loftus and Palmer to conclude that even small differences in the specific form of the question can guide the reconstruction of the event. In a second experiment, Loftus and Palmer found that the question "About how fast were the cars going when they smashed into each other?" yielded the highest proportion of answers that the accident included broken glass, even though the film clips involved none.
15. Kahneman, Knetsch, and Thaler, 1986, p. 731.
16. Schneider, et al., 2001.
17. Salovey and Williams-Piehota, 2004; Apanovitch, McCarthy, and Salovey, 2003. See, more generally, Rothman and Salovey, 1997; and Cialdini, 2003.
18. Tversky, Sattath, and Slovic, 1988; also see Slovic and Lichtenstein, 1968.
19. Ritov and Baron, 1992; Baron and Ritov, 1994.
20. Ritov and Baron, 1990.

21. Iademarco and Castro, 2003.
22. Kahneman, Knetsch, and Thaler, 1991. Also see Samuelson and Zeck-hauser, 1988.
23. Allen, 2004.
24. Johnson and Goldstein, 2003.
25. For a discussion of the status quo bias in the context of organ donation, as well as auto insurance coverage, see ibid.
26. The minimum wage will be raised, in accordance with the Fair Minimum Wage Act of 2007. Minimum wage will reach $7.25 per hour by the twenty-sixth month after the act takes effect.
27. Tversky and Kahneman, 1974, p. 1127.
28. Gilens, 1996; also see Gilens, 1999.
29. Many excellent sources, such as http://www.schoolsafety.us/pubfiles/savd.pdf, include suicides in their counts of "violent deaths" or "school shootings." But they are separately coded as "suicides" so that you may draw the necessary distinctions; for a compilation of some of these data, also see http://youthviolence.edschool.virginia.edu/violence-in-schools/school-shootings.html and Curran and Holle, 1997. The social importance of an event is not mitigated by its low frequency, of course. So there are other reasons that school shootings may be psychologically prominent or memorable despite their low relative frequency (when compared to, say, fatal lightning strikes). For example, we assign a higher cost to the death of a young person than an older person, and school shooting fatalities are typically young, while lightning strikes do not select for age. In addition, lightning strikes seem uncontrollable, so the resulting fatalities appear practically unavoidable, whereas school shootings seem avoidable when appropriate precautions are taken. But availability can certainly be one reason an event is seen as higher in frequency than it actually is.
30. Fischhoff and Beyth, 1975.
31. Central Intelligence Agency, 1978.
32. For an excellent study of the hindsight bias in a legal context, see Rachlinski, 1998. For a thorough post-mortem on this era of neglect, see Sunstein, Hastie, Payne, Schkade, and Viscusi, 2002, especially chap. 6.
33. Berlin, 2000.
34. Tversky and Kahneman, 1974.
35. Northcraft and Neale, 1987.
36. Englich and Mussweiler, 2001.
37. Gilovich, 1991, p. 77.
38. Bloom and Brundage, 1947; DeVaul et al., 1957; Oskamp, 1965; Milstein et al., 1981.
39. DeVaul et al., 1957.
40. Khatri et al., 2003.

41. Judge and Higgins, 2000.
42. Campion, Pursell, and Brown, 1988, p. 36.
43. Gilovich, 1991.
44. Eliot, 1871, chap. 79.
45. Kahneman and Lovallo, 1993. The designations of "inside" and "outside" strategies can be found there.
46. Lord, Lepper, and Preston, 1984.
47. Plous, 1993, p. 228.
48. Koriat, Lichtenstein, and Fischhoff, 1980.
49. Piatelli-Palmarini, 1994, p. 15. "We will begin to improve ourselves precisely when we can deal with these very abstractions" (ibid., p. 14).
50. Arkes, 1991; Arkes, Christensen, Lai, and Blumer, 1987.
51. Reeves, 2002 (citing research by Don Moore, Max Baxerman, and George Loewenstein).

The relevant passage of Sarbanes-Oxley is Section 203(j), quoted below:

SEC. 203. AUDIT PARTNER ROTATION. Section 10A of the Securities Exchange Act of 1934 (15 U.S.C. 78j-1), as amended by this act, is amended by adding at the end the following:

(j) AUDIT PARTNER ROTATION—It shall be unlawful for a registered public accounting firm to provide audit services to an issuer if the lead (or coordinating) audit partner (having primary responsibility for the audit), or the audit partner responsible for reviewing the audit, has performed audit services for that issuer in each of the 5 previous fiscal years of that issuer. URL for above: http://thomas.loc.gov/cgi-bin/query/ F?c107:1:./temp/~c107LuUxAJ:e92687:

For the full text of the bill, see: http://thomas.loc.gov/cgi-bin/ query/z?c107:H.R.3763.ENR:%20

52. Cain, Loewenstein, and Moore, 2005.
53. Bazerman, 2005.
54. I presented this example in October 2005 at a talk I delivered while visiting at the Center for Decision Research, The Graduate School of Business, University of Chicago. It also appears in Trout, 2005, where I develop the theme of self-binding for the purposes of greater autonomy.
55. Schneider, 2002.
56. Heller, 2005.
57. Sunstein, 1993, p. 33.
58. U.S. Food and Drug Administration, 2005.

CHAPTER 4: OUTSIDE THE MIND

1. Kahan, 1996.
2. Schwartz, 2004. In a legal context of negotiation, see Guthrie, 2003.
3. Wood, Tam, and Guerrero-Witt, 2005.
4. Verplanken and Wood, 2006.
5. U.S. Office of National Drug Control Policy, 2004.
6. Finkelstein, Fiebelkorn, and Wang, 2003. Further breakdown in cost: Centers for Disease Control and Prevention, 2006.
7. Centers for Disease Control and Prevention, 2002a.
8. This was the last year in which a serious analysis was done; Colditz, 1999.
9. Samuelson and Zeckhauser, 1988.
10. Fevrier and Gay, 2004.
11. Reductions in tooth decay by water fluoridation: 40–49 percent for primary teeth or baby teeth; and 50–59 percent for permanent teeth or adult teeth (American Dental Association, "Fluoridation Facts," pp. 13–14). Also of interest is American Dental Association, 2008, the press kit on fluoridation.
12. Centers for Disease Control and Prevention, 2005, 2007a, and 2007b.
13. Kahane, 2000.
14. Centers for Disease Control and Prevention, 2002b, p. 21.
15. Ibid.
16. Alhakami and Slovic, 1994.
17. Though the Starbucks card and Purell soap handouts did improve handwashing performance. Dubner and Levitt, 2006.
18. Zhong and Liljenquist, 2006.
19. I presented this urinal example in October 2005 at a talk I delivered while visiting at the Center for Decision Research, The Graduate School of Business, University of Chicago; see Newman, 1997.
20. Available for purchase on the Web; Urinal Fly, 2008.
21. I presented this chevron example in October 2005 at a talk I delivered as a visitor at the Center for Decision Research, The Graduate School of Business, University of Chicago. It also appears in Trout, 2005, where I use this as an example of the acceptance of a perceptual trick to enhance our autonomy and advance our long-term interests.
22. Lynn, 1997.
23. Van der Horst and Hoekstra, 1994, pp. 63–68.
24. Trout, 2005.
25. All locations retrieved from Google (Google Earth computer program). Google Inc.; Ver. 4.2.0198.2451/2007.9.12. http://earth.google.com/ Accessed October 16, 2007.
26. Lambert, Lin, Chang, Gandhi, 1999; Lambert, Chang, and Lin, 2001; Staub, 1993.
27. Phillips, Jarvinen, and Phillips, 2005, pp. 1–9.
28. Luce and Pisoni, 1998.

29. The research behind the computer program can be found in Lambert et al. (1999, 2001, 2002). The list is posted at Institute for Safe Medication Practices, 2005.
30. Baker, 2005.
31. Studdert, et al., 2006.
32. See the recent case of Miracle Gro, which fired an employee who did not comply with this regulation. It has led to a court battle. Cf. National Public Radio, 2007.
33. This finding is so widely accepted now it no longer engenders controversy. One way into this literature is Simon, VonKorff, Piccinelli, Fullerton, and Ormel, 1999.
34. Kravitz et al., 2005.
35. Greene and Winters, 2005.
36. National Science Foundation, Division of Science Resources Statistics, 2005b. For an even more detailed table of the above, see ibid., 2006a; note that NIH is a department within HHS. See this table for a breakdown of each agency: National Science Foundation, Division of Science Resources Statistics, 2005a. Historical information on government-wide spending by area (social science included) can be found at: 1984–1994: National Science Foundation, Division of Science Resources Statistics, 2006b; 1995–2005: National Science Foundation, Division of Science Resources Statistics, 2006c.
37. Wells et al., 2006.
38. Loftus, 1991.

CHAPTER 5: STAT VERSUS GUT

1. Papile, 2001.
2. Baron, Bazerman, Shonk, 2002. Also see Bazerman and Malhorta, 2006.
3. Matthew 26:11.
4. Hourwich, 1894; Gordon, 1922.
5. Sen 1981a, 1981b.
6. Gladwell, 2005.
7. Hogarth and Schoemaker, 2005, p. 307.
8. Dawes, 1982, p. 393.
9. Howard and Dawes, 1976, p. 478.
10. Trout, 2002.
11. Dawes, Faust, and Meehl, 1989, p. 1670.
12. Meehl, 1957, p. 273.
13. Schorow, 2007, quoting William Wheaton, p. 7.
14. Interview with commissioner of the Maryland Board of Parole, National Public Radio, *All Things Considered*, January 5, 2004.
15. On the 1998 version of the instrument, the VRAG predicts violence by

putting together the values of twelve predictor variables (Quinsey, Harris, Rice, and Cormier, 1998), such as whether the person is married. For most of these variables, there is no well-confirmed theory that explains their incremental validity, even if we feel we can tell a good story about why each variable contributes to the accuracy of prediction.

16. See Section V, subsection C, "Exclusion of Sex Offenders," Parole Decision-Making, The Policy of the Massachusetts Parole Board, Maureen E. Walsh, chairperson, Massachusetts Parole Board, December 2006; working version.

17. Aegisdottir, et al., 2006.

18. Carroll, Wiener, Coates, Galegher, and Alibrio, 1982, p. 225.

19. Personal e-mail correspondence with Ken Tupy, General Council for Illinois's Prisoner Review Board, July 5, 2007.

20. Illinois Administrative Code, Section 1610.50, The Parole Release Decision:

a) The Exercise of Discretion. The Board will make the parole release decision on the basis of all available relevant information. The Board grants parole as an exercise of grace and executive discretion as limited or defined by the Illinois General Assembly in duly adopted legislation. The Board shall not parole a person eligible for parole, if it determines that:

1) There is a substantial risk that he will not conform to reasonable conditions of parole; or

2) His release at that time would depreciate the seriousness of his offense or promote disrespect for the law; or

3) His release would have a substantially adverse effect on institutional discipline.

b) Factors Affecting the Parole Release Decision. The parole release decision is a subjective determination based on available relevant information. In determining whether to grant or deny parole, the Board looks primarily to the following factors evident from the inmate's prior history, committing offense, institutional adjustment and parole plan, although the decision is not limited to these factors when other relevant compelling information is presented.

21. California Department of Corrections and Rehabilitation, 2006. This documents the charge of the Board of Parole Hearings: "BPH considers parole release and establishes the terms and conditions of parole for all persons sentenced in California under the Indeterminate Sentencing Law, persons sentenced to a term of less than life under Penal Code Section 1168 (b), and for persons serving a sentence of life with possibility of parole."

22. Grove et al., 2000; Aegisdottir et al., 2006.

23. New Jersey Parole Board, Annual Report at the N.J. Parole Board Web site,

http://www.state.nj.us/parole/. The 2005 Annual Report Document is at http://www.state.nj.us/parole/docs/reports/AnnualReport05.pdf. See especially p. 27.

24. Texas Board of Pardons, 2006.

25. For a nice overview by the founding author, see Thaler, 1999.

26. Epley, Mak, and Idson, 2006; Epley and Gneezy, 2007; Epley, 2008.

27. The standard profile of Congress—CRS Report for Congress—lists no senator with a Ph.D.

28. As of July 2006, 91 percent of House members had bachelor's degrees (396 out of 435) and 97 percent of senators (97 out of 100) did; 28 percent of House members had master's degrees (120 out of 435) and 19 percent of senators (19 out of 100) did; 39 percent of House members (170 out of 435) had law degrees, and 58 percent of senators (58 out of 100) did (Amer, 2006).

29. And in a sense it has already been addressed. There is a two-hundred-page book on how to appoint experts to government committees. See National Academy of Sciences, 2005.

30. Personal e-mail correspondence, October 17, 2007.

31. Despite these weighty responsibilities, congressional rules allow members to make decisions as though they have a limo to catch. The U.S. Senate does not require actual reading of a bill, only that the bill's title be read, albeit on three different legislative days. In the U.S. House of Representatives, though, if you are really pressed for time, the second title-reading may be skipped. Although Rule XVIII, clause 5(a), requires a full reading of a bill (which may be demanded by any member) before general debate, in practice, verbatim readings are usually dispensed with by unanimous consent, by suspension of the rules, or by special rule. Deschler and Johnson, chap. 24, sec. 11; Deschler and Johnson, chap. 27, sec. 7.1; Manual Sec. 942. "Dispensing with the reading is common practice" (House Practice, 108th Edition, chap. 44 §§2–5). In the House, the bill is read entirely during the Committee of the Whole, whose membership includes all representatives. The committee is used as a forum for debate on a bill and proposed amendments. It can decide whether to include amendments or send legislation back to a working committee, or it can recommend that a bill be killed. But it does not have authority to pass legislation. One hundred attendees constitute a quorum (less than half of what constitutes a quorum in the full House).

32. HHS Press Office, 1998.

33. Ibid.

34. Ibid.

35. Also see NIH Consensus Development Statement on Interventions: National Institutes of Health, 1997.

36. Goodlatte, 1999. Also see page E356 of the Congressional Record.

37. Here is a sample of the economic and moral arguments:

    What we are talking about here is lowering costs of risky behavior. We are saying that we will pay for the needles to perform this risky behavior. But there is another much larger element that has not been discussed so far, and that has to do with the concept that all risky behavior be socialized; that is, through the medical system, it is assumed that those who do not participate in risky behavior must pay for the costs of the risky behavior, whether it has to do with cigarettes or whether it has to do with drugs or whether it has to do with any kind of safety.

    So, therefore, the argument is that we have to save money in medical care costs by providing free needles. But there is another position, and that is that we might suggest that we do not pay for free needles and we might even challenge the concept that we should not be paying people and taking care of them for risky behavior, whether it is risky sexual behavior or risky behavior with drugs.

    I think this is very clearly the problem, and I do not believe we should be socializing this behavior because, if we do, we actually increase it. If we lower the cost of anything, we increase the incidence of its use. So if the responsibility does not fall on the individual performing dangerous behavior, they are more likely to, and this is just part of it, the idea that we would give them a free needle.

    But there is a moral argument against this as well. Why should people who do not use drugs or do not participate in dangerous sexual procedures and activities have to pay for those who do? And this is really the question, and there is no correct moral argument for this. And the economic argument is very powerful. It says that if we lower the cost, we will increase this behavior (R. Paul, 1998).
38. Fossella, 1998.
39. For a more pessimistic assessment of forecasting customs based on related concerns, see Harcourt, 2007.
40. Nisbett, 1993.

CHAPTER 6: THE NEW REPUBLIC

1. National Center for Health Statistics, 2006.
2. Myers, 2000.
3. Roese, 2005.
4. In a wealthy nation such as the United States, the overall correlation between money and happiness is low. In the slums of Calcutta, the correlation is much higher. Diener and Seligman, 2004, p. 8. The correlations were, respectively, .13 and .45.
5. Briggs, 2006.
6. Kahneman, Krueger, Schkade, Schwarz, and Stone, 2004a.

7. Biodiversity Partnership, 2006.
8. National Park Service, 2007. As the program states: "Prior to the program, the U.S. tax code favored the demolition of older buildings over saving and using them. Starting in 1976, the Federal tax code became aligned with national historic preservation policy to encourage voluntary, private sector investment in preserving historic buildings."
9. Rosenwald, 2007; also see Finkelstein, Linnan, Tate, and Birken, 2007.
10. Baker, 2007.
11. For a further description of the difference, see Plambeck, 1996a and 1996b.
12. Oster and Jensen, 2007.
13. Nearly thirty thousand people in 2004 alone.
14. National Academy of Sciences, 2005.
15. Engelhardt and Gruber, Working Paper 10466.
16. Office of Tax Analysis, Department of the U.S. Treasury, July 25, 2006.
17. Levitt and Donohue, 2001.
18. Wilson, R., 2002.
19. McDonald, 1997.
20. Seiden, 1978.
21. www.suicidology.org.
22. National Center for Health Statistics, 2007.
23. Kellermann et al., 1992.
24. Wintemute, Parham, et al., 1999.
25. See Freud's 1895 "Project for a Scientific Psychology."
26. Katyal, 2002, p. 1043.
27. Newman, 1972, pp. 47–48.
28. Cisneros, 1995, p. 10.
29. Hesseling, 1994.
30. Clarke, 1997.
31. Eichel, 2006.
32. Ibid.
33. National Highway Traffic Safety Administration, National Center for Statistics and Analysis, 2004.
34. National Highway Traffic Safety Administration, 2004.
35. Texas Department of Public Safety, 1999.
36. Another, more controversial, approach picks two demographically similar states, one with a helmet law and one without, and then compares their death rates for motorcyclists. Looking at the same state before and after the imposition of a law is in some ways a preferable method, because the same state can act as its own (virtually perfect) demographic control, whereas there are always potentially vitiating demographic differences between two or more states.
37. Hargrove, 2006.

38. Kahane, 2000.
39. Cohen and Einav, 2003.
40. Levitt and Porter, 2001, p. 614.
41. Cohen and Einav, 2003, p. 841.
42. Ibid., p. 828.
43. Sass and Zimmerman, 2000. According to footnote 2: "[I]t has been found that safety helmets reduce peripheral vision by less than 3% and that riders compensate for this reduction by increasing their head movements before lane changes. In addition, helmets do not substantially reduce a driver's hearing beyond that already caused by noise generated from the cycle's engine" (see Insurance Institute for Highway Safety, 1999, p. 196).
44. Trout and Buttar, 2000.
45. The most thorough defense of the existence of cognitive hazards can be found in Klick and Mitchell, 2006.
46. Rawls, 1971/1999, revised edition, p.480.
47. For a lovely rehearsal of the government's role in producing an administrative state to safeguard entitlements of the wealthy, see Holmes and Sunstein, 1999.
48. Rainbolt, 1989, provides an excellent discussion of the rationale for paternalism in these cases.
49. Sapolsky, 1998, p. 308.
50. Sigh, Jr., 2004.
51. Hume, 1739–40, p. xxiii.
52. For one plausible account of how close the United States once came to FDR-style social protection for all citizens, see Sunstein, 2004.
53. Bartels, M., 2005, pp. 15–31.
54. Bartels, L., 2004.
55. Ministry of Social Affairs and Health, Finland, 2006.
56. U.S. Census, 2007.
57. Government of Denmark, 1953.
58. The data are available at U.S. Office of Management and Budget, 2005; for one useful and graphic interpretation, see McGoury, 2007.
59. Alesina and Glaeser, 2004, offers an excellent comparative overview and analysis of redistributive and antipoverty policies in European countries and the United States.

CONCLUSION: EMPATHY'S FUTURE AND A NEW AMERICAN DEMOS

1. Gilbert and Wilson, 2000.
2. This goes for all domains of economic exchange, such as employment. One might think, following orthodox principles, that the market rewards with higher wages those employees whose jobs carry an elevated threat to well-being. It appears that hotel and restaurant workers, along with cab and limo

drivers, are targeted for murder at higher rates than those in other occupations. Is this increased risk of murder a consideration made by applicants? Is there a "murder premium" in these wages, compared to occupations of similar skill level and demand? Is the behavior of job seekers sensitive to this increased risk, even if they are not aware of it? (Khan, 2003) In research that isolates gender as a factor in the choice of risky versus less risky jobs, gender explains only about a quarter of the worker sorting (DeLeire and Levy, 2004).

3. "The problem is that, as it doesn't include the depreciation of capital assets, GNP isn't capable of reflecting the future prospects of a nation. It would be wrong to regard a country as rich simply because its GNP per head is high: it could be blowing its capital assets on a consumption binge. As regards future prospects, GNP is a measure of current economic activity, nothing more. It may, in fact, correlate well with current well-being, but that would be an empirical fact, not an analytic truth" (Dasgupta, 2001, p. 29).

4. Kahneman, et al., 2004a.

5. Kahneman, et al., 2004b, p. 1778.

6. That may be. It remains to be seen just how much of its affluence rests on its control over the resources of other countries. See Pogge, 2002.

7. See Layard, 2005.

8. For two very different but equally valuable discussions of the purpose of minipublics, see Ackerman and Fishkin, 2004, and Goodin and Dryzek, 2006.

9. Wilcox, 1987, p. 941.

10. Citizens' Assembly on Electoral Reform, 2004.

11. See, for example, http://www.americaspeaks.org/, for a description of "national discussions" and other projects designed to engage citizens in democratic decision making.

12. 2005 Economic Data from the U.S. Census Bureau.

Bibliography

Aarts, H., and A. Dijksterhuis. 2002. "Category activation effects in judgment and behavior: The moderating role of perceived comparability." *British Journal of Social Psychology* 41: 123–38.

Ackerman, B., and J. Fishkin. 2004. *Deliberation Day*. New Haven, Conn.: Yale University Press.

Advisory Committee on Student Financial Assistance. 2001. "Access for low SES students," September 21. Retrieved April 3, 2008, from the U.S. Department of Education Web site: www.ed.gov/about/bdscomm/list/acsfa/StaffBriefing3.ppt.

Aegisdottir, S., M. White, P. Spengler, A. Maugherman, L. Anderson, R. Cook, C. Nichols, G. Lampropoulos, B. Walker, G. Cohen, and J. Rush. 2006. "The meta-analysis of clinical judgment project: Fifty-six years of accumulated research on clinical versus statistical prediction." *The Counselling Psychologist* 34, no. 3 (May): 341–82.

Alesina, A., E. Glaeser, and B. Sacerdote. 2001. "Why doesn't the United States have a European-style welfare state?" *Brookings Papers on Economic Activity* 2: 187–277.

Alhakami, A. S., and P. Slovic. 1994. "A psychologic study of the inverse relationship between perceived risk and perceived benefit." *Risk Analysis* 14: 1085–96.

Allen, S. 2004. "When love isn't enough." *Boston Globe*, September 7.

Alloy, Inc. Branded Entertainment. 2006. Branded Entertainment mission statement, July 5. Retrieved February 26, from the Alloy Marketing Web site: http://www.alloymarketing.com/entertainment/branded_entertainment.html.

Amer, M. 2006. "109th Congress: A Profile." CRS Report for Congress. Kindly provided to me by Office of the Clerk, U.S. House of Representatives. Retrieved February 26, 2008, from the U.S. Senate Web site: http://www. senate.gov/reference/resources/pdf/RS22007.pdf.

American Dental Association. 2005. Fluoridation facts, June 29. Retrieved February 26, 2008, from the American Dental Association Web site: http://www.ada.org/public/topics/fluoride/facts/fluoridation_facts.pdf.

————. 2008. Media press kits: Fluoride and fluoridation. Retrieved February 26, 2008, from the American Dental Association Web site: http://www.ada.org/public/media/presskits/fluoridation/index.asp.

Anderson, S., J. Cavanagh, S. Klinger, and L. Stanton. 2005. *Executive Excess 2005: Defense Contractors Get More Bucks for the Bang*. Washington, D.C.: Institute for Policy Studies/United for a Fair Economy.

Apanovitch, A. M., D. McCarthy, and P. Salovey. 2003. "Using message framing to motivate HIV testing among low-income, ethnic minority women." *Health Psychology* 22, no. 1: 60–67.

Appiah, K. A. 2008. *Experiments in Ethics*. Cambridge, Mass.: Harvard University Press.

Aquinas, T. 1917 [1270]. *The Summa Theologica*. Vol 2, Part II. New York: Benziger Brothers.

Ariely, D., and G. Loewenstein. 2005. "The heat of the moment: The effect of sexual arousal on sexual decision-making." *Journal of Behavioral Decision-Making* 18: 1–12.

Aristotle. 1985. *Nichomachean Ethics*. Trans. Terence Irwin. Indianapolis: Hackett Publishing.

Arkes, H. 1991. "Costs and benefits of judgment errors: Implications for debiasing." *Psychological Bulletin* 110: 486–98.

Arkes, H., C. Christensen, C. Lai, and C. Blumer. 1987. "Two methods of reducing overconfidence." *Organizational Behavior and Human Decision Processes* 39: 133–44.

Arneson, R. 1997. "Paternalism, utility, and fairness." In G. Dworkin (ed.) *Mill's On Liberty: Critical Essays*. Lanham, Md.: Rowman and Littlefield, pp. 83–114.

Baker, D. 2007. "New helmet law for under-18 cyclists, skateboarders." *Albuquerque Journal,* June 18. Retrieved February 26, 2008, from the *Albuquerque Journal* online edition Web site: http://www.abqjournal.com/news/state/aphelmetlaw06-18-07.htm.

Baker, T. 2005. *The Medical Malpractice Myth*. Chicago: University of Chicago Press.

Ballew II, C., and A. Todorov. 2008. "Predicting political elections from rapid and unreflective face judgments." *Proceedings of the National Academy of Sciences*. Early edition PNAS online: Ballew and Todorov, 10.1073/pnas.0705435104.

Barber, B., and T. Odean. 2000. "Trading is hazardous to your wealth: The common stock investment performance of individual investors." *The Journal of Finance* 55: 773–806.

Bargh, J., M. Chen, and L. Burrows. 1996. "Automaticity of social behavior: Direct effects of trait construct and stereotype activation on action." *Journal of Personality and Social Psychology* 71: 230–44.

Baron, J., and I. Ritov. 1994. "Reference points and omission bias." *Organizational Behavior and Human Decision Processes* 59: 475–98.

Baron, J., M. H. Bazerman, and K. Shonk. 2006. "Enlarging the societal pie through wise legislation." *Perspectives on Psychological Science* 1, no. 2: 123–32.

Bartels, L. 2004. "Partisan politics and the U.S. income distribution." Working paper. Retrieved February 26, 2008, from the Russell Sage Foundation Web site: https://www.russellsage.org/publications/workingpapers/politics incdist/document.

Bartels, M. 2005. "Homer gets a tax cut: Inequality and public policy in the American mind." *Perspectives on Politics* 3, no. 1 (March): 15–31.

Batson, C. D. 1991. *The Altruism Question: Toward a Social-Psychological Answer*. Hillsdale, N.J.: Lawrence Erlbaum Associates.

Bazerman, M. 2005. *Judgment in Managerial Decision-Making* (6th edition). New York: John Wiley and Sons.

Bazerman, M., and D. Malhorta. 2006. "Economics wins, psychology loses, and society pays." In D. De Cremer, M. Zeelenberg, and J. Keith Murnighan, eds., *Social Psychology and Economics*. Mahwah, N.J.: Lawrence Erlbaum Associates, pp. 263–80.

Berger, J., M. Meredith, and S. C. Wheeler. 2006. "Can where people vote influence how they vote? The influence of polling location type on voting behavior," GSB Research Paper No. 1926, February.

Berlin, L. 2000. "Malpractice issues in radiology: Hindsight bias." *American Journal of Roentgenology* 175: 597–601. Retrieved February 26, 2008, from the American Journal of Roentgenology Web site: http://www.ajronline. org/cgi/content/full/175/3/597

Biodiversity Partnership. 2006. "Federal programs: Federal conservation incentive programs," June 29. Retrieved November 15, 2007, from the Biodiversity Partnership Web site: http://www.biodiversitypartners.org/incentives/pdf/incentives.pdf.

Bishop, M., and J. D. Trout. 2005. *Epistemology and the Psychology of Human Judgment*. New York: Oxford University Press.

Bloom, R. F., and E. G. Brundage. 1947. "Predictions of success in elementary school for enlisted personnel." In D. B. Stuit, ed., *Personnel Research and Test Development in the Naval Bureau of Personnel*. Princeton, N.J.: Princeton University Press, pp. 233–61.

Blumenthal, J. A. Forthcoming. "Law and the emotions: The problems of affective

forecasting." Retrieved February 26, 2008, from the Social Science Research
   Network Web site: http://ssrn.com/abstract=497842.

Botti, S., and S. Iyengar. 2004. "The psychological pleasure and pain of choosing: When people prefer choosing at the cost of subsequent outcome satisfaction." *Journal of Personality and Social Psychology* 87, no. 3: 312–26.

Briggs, J. E. 2006, July 18. "In 'food deserts' of city, healthy eating a mirage."
   Chicago Tribune, p. 1, section 1, continued on p. 14.

Brooks, R. 2006. "Credit past due." *Columbia Law Review* 106: 994–1028.

Bucks, B., A. Kenwickell, K. Moore. 2005. "Recent changes in U.S. family finances: Evidence from the 2001 and 2004 Survey of Consumer Finances."
   Federal Reserve Board's Survey of Consumer Finances for 2004. Retrieved
   February 26, 2008, from the Federal Reserve Web site: http://www.federal
   reserve.gov/pubs/oss/oss2/2004/bull0206.pdf.

Buss, D. 2004. "The bungling apprentice." In J. Brockman, ed., *Curious Minds:
   How a Child Becomes a Scientist*. New York: Pantheon, pp. 13–18.

Cain, D. M., G. Loewenstein, D. A. Moore. 2005. "The dirt on coming clean:
   Perverse effects of disclosing conflicts of interest." *Journal of Legal Studies* 34:
   1–25.

California Department of Corrections and Rehabilitation. 2006. "Divisions
   boards: The board of parole hearings." Retrieved February 26, 2008, from
   the California Department of Corrections and Rehabilitation Web site:
   http://www.cdcr.ca.gov/Divisions_Boards/BOPH/index.html.

Campbell, D., S. Carr, and M. MacLachlan. 2001. "Attributing 'third world poverty' in Australia and Malawi: A case of donor bias?" *Journal of Applied Social
   Psychology* 31, no. 2: 409–30.

Campion, M. A., E. D. Pursell, and B. K. Brown. 1988. "Structured interviewing: Raising the psychometric properties of the employment interview." *Personnel Psychology* 41: 25–42.

Carr, K. 2007. "Foggy fortunes: Payday lenders' futures unclear as efforts persist
   to cap interest rates, limit number of locations." *Crain's Cleveland Business*,
   December 17, 2007, Finance; p. 9.

Carroll, J., R. Winer, D. Coates, J. Galegher, and J. Alibrio. 1982. "Evaluation,
   diagnosis, and prediction in parole decision-making." *Law and Society Review*
   17: 199–228.

Centers for Disease Control and Prevention. 2002a. "Highlights: Annual smok-
   ing-attributable mortality, years of potential life lost, and economic costs—
   United States, 1995–1999," April 12. *Morbidity and Mortality Weekly Report
   (MMWR)*.

———. 2002b. "Guidelines for hand hygiene in health-care settings," October
   25. *Morbidity and Mortality Weekly Report (MMWR)* 51, no. RR-16, p. 21.

———. 2005. "Rubella no longer major public health threat in the United
   States," October. Retrieved February 26, 2008, from the Centers for Disease

Control and Prevention Web site: http://www.cdc.gov/od/oc/media/pressrel /r050321.htm.

————. 2006. "Overweight and obesity: Economic consequences," October 3. Retrieved from the Centers for Disease Control and Prevention Web site: http://www.cdc.gov/nccdphp/dnpa/obesity/economic_consequences.htm.

————. 2007a. "Pertussis," February 14. Retrieved February 26, 2008, from the Centers for Disease Control and Prevention Web site: http://www .cdc.gov/vaccines/pubs/pinkbook/downloads/pert.pdf.

————. 2007b. "Measles: Q&A about disease and vaccine," June 1. Retrieved from the Centers for Disease Control and Prevention Web site: http://www.cdc.gov/vaccines/vpd-vac/measles/faqs-dis-vac-risks.htm.

Central Intelligence Agency (CIA). 1978. "Hindsight biases in evaluation of intelligence reporting." Retrieved February 26, 2008, from the Central Intelligence Agency Web site: https://www.cia.gov/library/center-for-the-study-of-intelligence/csi-publications/books-and-monographs/psychology-of-intelligence-analysis/art16.html#rft149.

Cialdini, R. B. 2003. "Crafting normative messages to protect the environment." *Current Directions in Psychological Science* 12: 105–109.

Cisneros, H. G. 1995. *Defensible Space: Deterring Crime and Building Community*. Rockville, Md.: U.S. Department of Housing and Urban Development.

Citizens' Assembly on Electoral Reform, British Columbia. 2004. "Improving democracy in B.C.: The final report," December 10. Retrieved February 26, 2008, from the Citizens' Assembly on Electoral Reform Web site: http:// www.citizensassembly.bc.ca/public.

Clarke, Ronald V., ed. 1997. *Situational crime prevention* (2nd edition). Albany, N.Y.: Harrow and Heston.

Cohen, A., and L. Einav. 2003. "The effects of mandatory seat belt laws on driving behavior and traffic fatalities." *Journal of Economics and Statistics* 85, no. 4 (November): 828–43.

Cohen, G. 2000. *If You're an Egalitarian, How Come You're So Rich?* Cambridge, Mass.: Harvard University Press.

Colditz, G. A. 1999. "Economic costs of obesity and inactivity: Roundtable consensus statement." *Medicine and Science in Sports Excercise* 31, no. 11, suppl. 1 (December).

Condorcet, J. de. 1955 [1792]. *Sketch for a Historical Picture of the Progress of the Human Mind*. London: Weidenfeld and Nicolson.

Cuddy, A., S. Fiske, and P. Glick. 2007. "The BIAS Map: Behaviors from intergroup affect and stereotypes." *Journal of Personality and Social Psychology* 92: 631–48.

Curran, E. B., and R. L. Holle. 1997. "Lightning fatalities, injuries, and damage reports in the United States from 1959–1994." NOAA Technical Memorandum NWS SR-193, October. Retrieved February 26, 2008, from the NOAA

National Severe Storms Laboratory Web site: http://www.nssl.noaa.gov/
papers/techmemos/NWS-SR-193/techmemo-sr193.html.

Dahl, R. A. 1985. *A Preface to Economic Democracy*. Berkeley: University of California Press.

Dasgupta, P. 2001. *Human Well-Being and the Natural Environment*. Oxford: Oxford University Press.

Dawes, R. 1982. "The robust beauty of improper linear models in decision-making." In D. Kahneman, P. Slovic, and A. Tversky, eds., *Judgment Under Uncertainty: Heuristics and Biases*. Cambridge: Cambridge University Press, pp. 391–407. First appeared in (1979) *American Psychologist* 34: 571–82.

Dawes, R., D. Faust, and P. Meehl. 1989. "Clinical versus actuarial judgment." *Science* 243: 1668–674.

DeLeire, T., and Levy, H. 2004. Worker sorting and risk of death on the job. *Journal of Labor Economics* 22(4): 925–53.

Dennett, D. 2003. *Freedom Evolves*. New York: Viking.

Descartes, R. 1996 [1641]. *Meditations on First Philosophy*. Trans. J. Cottingham. Cambridge: Cambridge University Press.

Descartes, R. 1989 [1649]. *Passions of the Soul*. Trans. S. H. Voss. Indianapolis: Hackett.

Deschler, L. and C. W. Johnson. 1997. "Deschler's precedents, including references to provisions of the constitution and laws, and to decisions of the courts." U.S. GPO, HD94-661.

DeVaul, R. A., F. Jervey, J. A. Chappell, P. Carver, B. Short, and S. O'Keefe. 1957. "Medical school performance of initially rejected students." *Journal of the American Medical Association* 257: 47–51.

Diderot, D. 1972. "Eclecticism." In *Encyclopaedia*. Cited from Arthur M. Wilson. *Diderot*. Oxford: Oxford University Press.

Diener, E., and M. E. P. Seligman. 1994. "Beyond money: Toward an economy of well-being." *Psychological Science in the Public Interest* 5, no. 1: 1–31. Retrieved February 26, 2008, from the Association for Psychological Science Web site: http://www.psychologicalscience.org/pdf/pspi/pspi5_1.pdf.

Dijksterhuis, A., J. Bargh, and J. Miedema. 2000. "Of men and mackerels: Attention and automatic social behavior." In H. Bless and J. Forgas, eds., *The Message Within: The Role of Subjective Experience in Social Cognition and Behavior*. Philadelphia: Psychology Press, pp. 37–51.

Dijksterhuis, A., and J. Bargh. 2001. "The perception-behavior expressway: Automatic effects of social perception on social behavior." *Advances in Experimental Social Psychology* 33: 1–40.

Dijksterhuis, A., and A. van Kippenberg. 1998. "The relation between perception and behavior, or how to win a game of Trivial Pursuit." *Journal of Personality and Social Psychology* 74: 865–77.

Dubner, S. and S. D. Levitt. 2006. "Selling soap." *New York Times* (Freakonomics column), September 24.

Duflo, E., M. Kremer, and J. Robinson. 2005. "Understanding technology adoption: Fertilizer in Western Kenya, preliminary results from field experiments." Working Paper, MIT.

Eichel, L. 2006. "In the City, any day can be a killing day." *Philadelphia Inquirer,* July 16.

Eliot, G. 1871. *Middlemarch.* New York: Penguin Classics.

Engelhardt, G., and J. Gruber. "Social security and the evolution of elderly poverty." Working Paper No. 10466. Retrieved February 26, 2008, from the National Bureau of Economic Research Web site: http://www.nber.org/papers/w10466.

Englich, B., and T. Mussweiler. 2001. "Sentencing under uncertainty: Anchoring effects in the courtroom." *Journal of Applied Social Psychology* 31, no. 7: 1535–51.

Epley, N. 2008. "Rebate psychology." *New York Times,* January 31, A27. Retrieved February 26, 2008 from the New York Times Web site: http://www.nytimes.com/2008/01/31/opinion/31epley.html?_r=1&n=Top/Opinion/Editorials%20and%20Op-Ed/Op-Ed/Contributors&oref=slogin.

Epley, N., and A. Gneezy. 2007. "The framing of financial windfalls and implications for public policy." *Journal of Socio-economics* 36: 36–47.

Epley, N., D. Mak, and L. Idson. 2006. "Bonus or rebate? The impact of income framing on spending and saving." *Journal of Behavioral Decision Making* 19: 213–27.

Estroff-Marano, H. 1999. "Depression: Beyond serotonin." *Psychology Today,* Mar/Apr. Retrieved February 26, 2008, from the *Psychology Today* Web site: http://www.psychologytoday.com/articles/pto-19990301-000031.html.

Eurostat. 2008. Eurostat home page. Retrieved February 26, 2008, from the European Commission Web site: http://europa.eu.int/comm/eurostat/.

FedStats. 2006. FedStats home page. Retrieved April 2, 2008, from the FedStats Web site: http://www.fedstats.gov/.

Fetherstonhaugh, D., P. Slovic, J. Johnson, and J. Friedrich. 1997. "Insensitivity to the value of human life: A study of psychophysical numbing." *Journal of Risk and Uncertainty* 14: 283–300.

Fevrier, P., and S. Gay. 2004. "Informed consent versus presumed consent: The role of the family in organ donations," June. Retrieved February 26, 2008, from the Archive of the former site www.EconWPA.wustl.edu: http://129.3.20.41/eps/hew/papers/0509/0509007.pdf.

Finkelstein, E. A., I. C. Fiebelkorn, and G. Wang. 2003. "National medical spending attributable to overweight and obesity: How much, and who's paying?" *Health Affairs,* May 14. Retrieved February 26, 2008, from the *Health Affairs: The Policy Journal of the Health Sphere* Web site: http://content.healthaffairs.org/cgi/content/full/hlthaff.w3.219v1/DC1.

Finkelstein, E. A., L. A. Linnan, D. F. Tate, and B. E. Birken. 2007. "A pilot study testing the effect of different levels of financial incentives on weight loss among overweight employees." *Journal of Occupational and Environmental Medicine* 49, no. 9: 981–89.

Fischhoff, B. and R. Beyth. 1975. "'I knew it would happen': Remembered probabilities of once-future things." *Organizational Behavior and Human Decision Processes* 31, no. 1 (February): 1–16.

Fischhoff, B., P. Slovic, and S. Lichtenstein. 1977. "Knowing with certainty: The appropriateness of extreme confidence." *Journal of Experimental Psychology: Human Perception and Performance* 3: 552–64.

Fiske, S. T., A. J. C. Cuddy, P. Glick, and J. Xu. 2002. "A model of (often mixed) stereotype content: Competence and warmth respectively follow from status and competition." *Journal of Personality and Social Psychology* 82: 878–902.

Food and Agriculture Organization of the United Nations. 2002. "Long-term perspectives: The outlook for agriculture." From the report World agriculture: Towards 2015/2030. Retrieved February 26, 2008, from the Food and Agriculture Organization Web site: http://www.fao.org/docrep/004/y3557e/y3557e06.htm.

Forgas, J., A. Furnham, and D. Frey. 1990. "Cross-national differences in attributions of wealth and economic success." *Journal of Social Psychology* 129: 643–57.

Forster, E. M. 1910. *Howards End*. London: Edward Arnold.

Fossella, V. J. 1998. "Prohibiting the expenditure of federal funds for distribution of needles or syringes for hypodermic injection of illegal drugs." Delivered before Congress, April 29, Congressional Record.

Frank, R. 2007. *Falling Behind*. Berkeley: University of California Press.

Freedom House. Ongoing. Freedom house home page. Retrieved February 26, 2008, from the Freedom House Web site: www.freedomhouse.org.

Freud, S. 1985. "Project for a scientific psychology." In J. M. Masson, ed. and trans., *The Complete Letters of Sigmund Freud to Wilhelm Fliess, 1887–1904*. Cambridge, Mass., and London: Belknap Press/Harvard University Press.

Garcia, K. 2007. "The fat fight: The risks and consequences of the federal government's failing public health campaign." Yale Law School Faculty Scholarship Series.

Gervais, S., J. Heaton, and T. Odean. 2007. "Overconfidence, Investment Policy, and Manager Welfare." Working Paper. Duke University.

Gibbs, W. W. 1994. "Software's chronic crisis." *Scientific American*, September: 86–95. Retrieved February 28, 2008, from the *Scientific American* Web site: http://www.cis.gsu.edu/~mmoore/CIS3300/handouts/SciAmSept1994.html.

Gilbert, D., and T. Wilson. 2000. "Miswanting: Some problems in the forecasting of future affective states." In J. P. Forgas, ed., *Feeling and Thinking: The Role of Affect in Social Cognition*. New York: Cambridge University Press, pp. 178–97.

Gilens, M. 1996. "Race and poverty in America: Public misperceptions and the American news media." *Public Opinion Quarterly* 60, no. 4: 513–35.

_____. 1999. *Why Americans Hate Welfare: Race, Media, and the Politics of Anti-Poverty Policy*. Chicago: University of Chicago Press.

Gilovich, T. 1991. *How We Know What Isn't So*. New York: The Free Press.

Gladwell, M. 2005. *Blink: The Power of Thinking Without Thinking*. New York: Little, Brown and Company.

Glover, J. 1999. *Humanity: A Moral History of the Twentieth Century*. London: Cape.

Godwin, D. D. 1994. "Antecedents and consequences of newlyweds' cash flow management." *Financial Counseling and Planning* 5: 161–90.

Goodin, R., and J. Dryzek. 2006. "Deliberative impacts: The macro-political uptake of mini-publics." *Politics and Society* 34, no. 2 (June): 219–44.

Goodlatte, B. 1999. "Introduction of legislation to prohibit federal funds from being used to develop needle exchange programs—Hon. Bob Goodlatte." Congressional Record, Extensions of Remarks, March 4.

Google Earth. 2007. Satellite images, October 16. Google (*Google Earth*) computer program. Google Inc.; Ver. 4.2.0198.2451/2007.9.12. Retrieved October 15, 2007, from Google Earth Web site: http://earth.google.com/.

Gordon, M. 1922. "Russian famine in 1923: Grounds for prediction that another year of food shortage is inevitable." *New York Times*, August 27.

Government of Denmark. 1953. The Constitutional Act of Denmark and the Act of Succession. Retrieved February 26, 2008, from the Folketing (National Parliament) of Denmark Web site: http://www.folketinget.dk/pdf/constitution.pdf.

Graves, S., and C. Peterson. 2005. "Predatory lending and the military: The law and geography of 'payday' loans in military towns." *Ohio State Law Journal* 66, no. 4: 653–832. Retrieved February 26, 2008, from the University of Florida Levin College of Law Web site: http://www.law.ufl.edu/faculty/peterson/pdf/66%20Ohio%20State%20L%20J%20653.pdf.

Greene, J., and M. Winters. 2005. "Public high school graduation and college-readiness rates: 1991–2002." Center for Civic Innovation at the Manhattan Institute: Education Working Paper, No. 8, February. Retrieved February 26, 2008, from the Bill and Melinda Gates Foundation Web site: http://www.gatesfoundation.org/nr/downloads/ed/Researchevaluation/GradRates ManhattanInstitute.pdf.

Greenhouse, L. 2003. Week in Review Desk, *New York Times*, July 6. p. 3, sec. 4, col. 1.

Grove, W. G., D. H. Zald, B. Lebow, B. Snitz, and C. Nelson. 2000. "Clinical versus statistical prediction: A meta-analysis." *Psychological Assessment* 12: 19–30.

Gruber, S. 2005. "USAID: Assistance for Iraq: Health," August 11. Retrieved February 26, 2008, from the USAID Web site: http://www.usaid.gov/iraq/accomplishments/health.html.

Guthrie, C. 2003. "Panacea or Pandora's box? The costs of options in negotiation." *Iowa Law Review* 88: 601–653.

Hacker, J. 2006. *The Great Risk Shift*. New York: Oxford University Press.

Haidt, J. 2006. *The Happiness Hypothesis: Finding Modern Truth in Ancient Wisdom*. New York: Basic.

Harcourt, B. 2007. *Against Prediction*. Chicago: University of Chicago Press.

Hargrove, T. 2006. "A fatal freedom: Deaths in motorcycle accidents on rise." Scripps Howard News Service, May 25. Retrieved February 26, 2008, from Scripps Howard News Service Web site: http://www.shns.com/shns/g_index2.cfm?action=detail&pk=FATALFREEDOM-05-25-06.

Harris, J. R. 1995. "Where is the child's environment? A group socialization theory of development." *Psychological Review* 102: 458–89.

———. 1998. *The Nurture Assumption: Why Children Turn Out the Way They Do*. New York: Free Press.

Harris, L., and S. Fiske. 2006. "Dehumanizing the lowest of the low: Neuroimaging responses to extreme outgroups." *Psychological Science* 17: 847–53.

Hastie, R. 2002. "Overview: What we did and what we found." In C. Sunstein, R. Hastie, J. Payne, D. Schkade, and W. Kip Viscusi. *Punitive Damages: How Juries Decide*. Chicago: University of Chicago Press, pp. 17–28.

Hauser, M. 2000. *Wild Minds*. New York: Henry Holt and Company.

———. 2006. *Moral Minds*. New York: Ecco/HarperCollins.

Heller, J. 2005. "Payment protection systems uses an on time alarm." *St. Petersburg Times,* July 23.

Henrion, M., and B. Fischhoff. 1986. "Assessing uncertainty in physical constants." *American Journal of Physics* 54: 791–98.

Henriques, D. 2004. "Seeking quick loans, soldiers race into high-interest traps." *New York Times*, December 7. Tuesday Correction Appended, sect. A, col. 1; Business/Financial Desk, "Lenders at the Gate: Debtors in the Barracks," p. 1.

Hesseling, R. 1994. "Displacement: A review of the empirical literature." In R. V. Clarke, ed., *Crime Prevention Studies, Vol. 3*. Monsey, N.Y.: Criminal Justice Press.

Hewstone, M. 1990. "The 'ultimate attribution error'? A review of the literature on intergroup causal attribution." *European Journal of Social Psychology* 20: 311–35.

HHS Press Office. 1998. "Research shows needle exchange programs reduce HIV infections without increasing drug use," April 20. Retrieved February 26, 2008, from the U.S. Department of Health and Human Services Web site: http://www.hhs.gov/news/press/1998pres/980420a.html.

Hitt, J. 1996. "The theory of supermarkets." *New York Times Magazine,* March 10, p. 58.

Hoffman, M. 2000. *Empathy and Moral Development*. New York: Cambridge University Press.

Hogarth, R., and P. Schoemaker. 2005. "Beyond blink: A challenge to behavioral decision-making." *Journal of Behavioral Decision-Making* 18: 305–309.

Holmes, S., and C. Sunstein. 1999. *The Cost of Rights*. New York: W. W. Norton.

Hostetler, J. A. 1968. *Amish Society (rev. ed.)*. Baltimore, Md.: Johns Hopkins University Press.

Hourwich, I. 1894. "Russia in the international market." *The Journal of Political Economy* 2, no. 2: 284–90.

House Practice. 2006. 108th Edition, ch. 44 §§2–5. Retrieved February 26, 2008, from the Government Printing Office Access Web site: http://www. gpoaccess.gov/hpractice/browse_108.html.

Howard, J. W., and R. Dawes. 1976. "Linear prediction of marital happiness." *Personality and Social Psychology Bulletin* 2, no. 4 (Fall): 478–80.

Hume, D. 2000 [1739–1740]. *A Treatise of Human Nature*. Oxford: Oxford University Press.

———. 1977 [1748]. *An Enquiry Concerning Human Understanding*. Indianapolis: Hackett Publishing.

Iacoboni, M., I. Molnar-Szakacs, V. Gallese, G. Buccino, J. C. Mazziotta, and G. Rizzolatti. 2005. "Grasping the intentions of others with one's own mirror neuron system." *Public Library of Science Biology* 3, no. 3. Retrieved February 26, 2008, from the *Public Library of Science* Web site: http://0-biology. plosjournals.org.ilsprod.lib.neu.edu/perlserv/?SESSID=c2bc3b59cbb0b6e 389cc7387ac724e3&request=get-document&doi=10.1371/journal. pbio.0030079.

Iademarco, M. F., and K. G. Castro. 2003. "Epidemiology of tuberculosis." *Seminars in Respiratory Infections* 18, no. 4: 225–40.

Institute for Safe Medication Practices. 2005. "ISMP's list of confused drug names," July 25. Retrieved February 26, 2008, from the Institute for Safe Medication Practices Web site: http://www.ismp.org/Tools/confuseddrugnames.pdf.

International Gaming and Wagering Business. 2007. "2006 gross gambling revenues by industry and change from 2005 (in millions)," October 29. Retrieved February 28, 2008, from the International Gaming and Wagering Business Web site: http://www.igwb.com/pdf/2006grossgambling.pdf.

Investment Company Institute. 2005. "Equity ownership in America, 2005," November 14. Retrieved February 28, 2008, from the Investment Company Institute Web site: http://www.ici.org/statements/res/rpt_05_equity_ owners.pdf.

Jackson, P., E. Brunet, A. Meltzoff, and J. Decety. 2006. "Empathy examined through the neural mechanisms involved in imagining how I feel versus how you feel pain: An event-related fMRI study." *Neuropsychologica* 44: 752–61.

Johnson, E. J., and D. G. Goldstein. 2003. "Do defaults save lives?" *Science* 302: 1338–39.

Judge, T. A., and C. A. Higgins. 2000. "The employment interview: A review of recent research and recommendations for future research." *Human Resource Management Review* 10, no. 4: 383–406.

Kahan, D. 1996. "Gentle nudges and hard shoves: Solving the sticky norms problem." *University of Chicago Law Review* 67: 607–45.

Kahan, D., and M. Nussbaum. 1996. "Two conceptions of emotion in criminal law." *Columbia Law Review* 96, no. 2: 269–374.

Kahane, C. J. 2000. "Fatality reduction by safety belts for front-seat occupants of cars and light trucks: Updated and expanded estimates based on 1986–99 FARS Data." NHTSA Report Number DOT HS 809 199, December. Retrieved February 26, 2008, from the National Highway Traffic Safety Administration Web site: http://www.nhtsa.dot.gov/cars/rules/regrev/evaluate/809199. html.

Kahneman, D., A. Krueger, D. Schkade, N. Schwarz, and A. Stone. 2004a. "Toward national well-being accounts." *Memos to the Council of Behavioral-Economic Advisors* 94, no. 2 (May): 429–34.

Kahneman, D., A. Krueger, D. Schkade, N. Schwarz, and A. Stone. 2004b. "A survey method for characterizing daily life experience: The day reconstruction method." *Science* 306, December 3: 1776–80.

Kahneman, D., and A. Tversky. 1979. "Intuitive prediction: Biases and corrective procedures." In D. Kahneman, P. Slovic, and A. Tversky, eds., *Judgment Under Uncertainty: Heuristics and Biases*. New York: Cambridge University Press.

Kahneman, D., and D. Lovallo. 1993. "Timid choices and bold forecasts: A cognitive perspective on risk taking." *Management Science* 39: 17–31.

Kahneman, D., J. L. Knetsch, and R. Thaler. 1986. "Fairness as a constraint on profit seeking: Entitlements in the market." *American Economic Review* 76, no. 4 (September): 728–41.

Kahneman, D., J. L. Knetsch, and R. Thaler. 1991. "Anomalies: The endowment effect, loss aversion, and status quo bias." *Journal of Economic Perspectives* 5, no. 1: 193–206.

Kaiser Family Foundation and the Health Research and Educational Trust. 2006. Employer Health Benefits Survey, retrieved February 26, 2008, from the Kaiser Family Foundation Web site: http://www.kff.org/insurance/ehbs archives.cfm.

Kant, I. 1795 (1923). "Zum ewigen Frieden," in *Kants Werke*, Berlin: Prussische Akademie Ausgabe, vol. VIII, 341–86. Trans. H. Nisbet, "Perpetual Peace," in *Kant: Political Writings*, Cambridge: Cambridge University Press, H. Reiss (ed.), 1991, pp. 93–130. All page references are to the German original. Quotations in English are from the English translation on the web: Perpetual Peace: A Philosophical Sketch.

———. 1983. *Perpetual Peace and Other Essays*. Trans. Ted Humphrey. Indianapolis and Cambridge: Hackett Publishing Company.

Katyal, N. 2002. "Architecture as crime control." *Yale Law Journal* 111: 1039–1139.

Kellermann, A. L., et al. 1992. "Suicide in the home in relation to gun ownership." *The New England Journal of Medicine* 327, August 13: 467–72.

Khan, K. 2003. "The 10 most dangerous jobs in America. Extra for MSN Money," October 24. Retrieved February 26, 2008, from the MSN Money Web site: http://moneycentral.msn.com/content/invest/extra/P63405.asp?Printer.

Khatri, S., J. Erwin, C. Kahl, and Y. Steubinger. 2003. "Effect of communication media on judgments in job interviews." *Small Business Advancement National Center*, University of Central Arkansas.

King, U., L. Parrish, and O. Tanik. 2006. "Financial quicksand: Payday lending sinks borrowers in debt with $4.2 billion in predatory fees every year," November 30. Retrieved February 26, 2008, from the Center for Responsible Lending Web site: http://www.responsiblelending.org/pdfs/rr012-Financial_Quicksand-1106.pdf.

Kitcher, Philip. 2001. *Science, Truth, and Democracy*. New York: Oxford University Press.

Klick, J., and G. Mitchell. 2006. "Government regulation of rationality: Moral and cognitive hazards." *Minnesota Law Review* 90: 1620–63.

Koriat, A., S. Lichtenstein, and B. Fischhoff. 1980. "Reasons for confidence." *Journal of Experimental Psychology: Human Learning and Memory* 6: 107–18.

Kravitz, R. L., R. M. Epstein, M. D. Feldman, C. E. Franz, R. Azari, M. S. Wilkes, L. Hinton, and P. Franks. 2005. "Influence of patients' requests for direct-to-consumer advertised antidepressants: A randomized controlled trial." *Journal of the American Medical Association* 293: 1995–2002.

Krebs, D. 1975. "Empathy and altruism." *Journal of Personality and Social Psychology* 32: 1134–46.

Kressel, L., G. Chapman, and E. Leventhal. 2007. "The influence of default options on the expression of end-of-life treatment preferences in advance directives." *General Internal Medicine* 22: 1007–10.

Kumar, A. 2007. "Pressure mounts on Va. payday lenders; Coalition plans to push legislature for limits." *The Washington Post*, Monday, December 3, Metro sec., p. B01. Quoting Del. Harvey B. Morgan (R-Gloucester).

Lambert, B. L., D. Donderi, and J. W. Senders. 2002. "Similarity of drug names: Comparison of objective and subjective measures." *Psychology and Marketing* 19, no. 7–8: 641–61.

Lambert, B. L., K-Y. Chang, and S-J. Lin. 2001. "Effect of orthographic and phonological similarity on false recognition of drug names." *Social Science and Medicine* 52, no. 12: 1843–57.

Lambert, B. L., S-J. Lin, K-Y. Chang, and S. K. Gandhi. 1999. "Similarity as a risk factor in drug-name confusion errors: The look-alike (orthographic) and sound-alike (phonetic) model." *Medical Care* 37, no. 12: 1214–25.

Langevin-Falcon, C. 2002. "Donor bias," December 14. Retrieved February 26,

2008, from the Department of Journalism at New York University Web site: http://journalism.nyu.edu/pubzone/race_class/donor.htm.

Layard, R. 2005. *Happiness: Lessons of a New Science*. London: Penguin.

Lefcourt, H. 1976. *Locus of Control: Current Trends in Theory and Research*. Hillsdale, N.J.: Erlbaum/Wiley.

Levitt, S., and J. Donohue. 2001. "The impact of legalized abortion on crime." *Quarterly Journal of Economics* 116, no. 2: 379–420.

Levitt, S., and J. Porter. 2001. "Sample selection in the estimation of air bags and seat belt effectiveness." *The Review of Economics and Statistics* 83 (November): 603–15.

Liberman, N., and Y. Trope. 1998. "The role of feasibility and desirability considerations in near and distant future decisions: A test of temporal construal theory." *Journal of Personality and Social Psychology* 75: 5–18.

Libet, B. 1985. "Unconscious cerebral initiative and the role of conscious will in voluntary action." *The Behavioral and Brain Sciences* 8: 529–66.

Loftus, E. 1991. *Witness for the Defense: The Accused, the Eyewitnesses, and the Expert Who Puts Memory on Trial*. New York: St. Martin's Press.

Loftus, E., and J. Palmer. 1974. "Reconstruction of automobile destruction: An example of the interaction between language and memory." *Journal of Verbal Learning and Verbal Behavior* 13: 585–89.

Lord, C., M. Lepper, and E. Preston. 1984. "Considering the opposite: A corrective strategy for social judgment." *Journal of Personality and Social Psychology* 47: 1231–43.

Luce, P. A., and D. B. Pisoni. 1998. "Recognizing spoken words: The neighborhood activation model." *Ear and Hearing* 19: 1–36.

Lynn, C. 1997. "Psychedelic chevrons slow drivers." *Transportation Alternatives*, May/June 1997. Retrieved February 26, 2008, from the *Transportation Alternatives* Web site: http://www.transalt.org/files/newsroom/magazine/972Mar Apr/04-5reclaiming.html#p.

McClure, S. M., D. I. Laibson, G. Loewenstein, and J. D. Cohen. 2004. "Separate neural systems value immediate and delayed monetary rewards." *Science* 306: 503–7.

McDonald, M. 1997. "ASU considers science tower safety options." General News, *State Press*, February 11.

McGoury, S. 2007. "United States national debt (1938 to present): An analysis of the presidents who are responsible for the borrowing," May 6. Retrieved February 26, 2008, from Steve McGoury's personal Web site: http://www.cedarcomm.com/~stevelm1/usdebt.htm.

McGregor, J. 2007. "Being unhealthy could cost you—money." *BusinessWeek*, August 2. Retrieved February 26, 2008, from the *BusinessWeek* Web site: http://www.businessweek.com/bwdaily/dnflash/content/aug2007/db 2007081_804238.htm?chan=search.

Macrae, C. N., and L. Johnston. 1998. "Help, I need somebody: Automatic action and inaction." *Social Cognition* 16: 400–417.

Maier, N. R. F. 1931. "Reasoning in humans II: The solution of a problem and its appearance in consciousness." *Journal of Comparative Psychology* 12: 181–94.

Meehl, P. 1957. "When should we use our heads instead of the formula?" *Journal of Counselling Psychology* 4: 268–73.

Miller, J. G., D. M. Bersoff, and R. L. Harwood. 1990. "Perceptions of social responsibilities in India and the United States: Moral imperatives or personal decisions." *Journal of Personality and Social Psychology* 58: 33–47.

Milstein, R. M., L. Wilkinson, G. N. Burrow, and W. Kessen. 1981. "Admission decisions and performance during medical school." *Journal of Medical Education* 56: 77–82.

Ministry of Social Affairs and Health, Finland. 2006, October 16. "Finland's family policy." Brochures of the Ministry of Social Affairs and Health 2006:12eng. Helsinki, Finland, October 16. Retrieved February 26, 2008, from the Ministry of Social Affairs and Health Web site: http://www.stm.fi/Resource.phx/publishing/store/2006/10/hm1161607115538/passthru.pdf.

Morton, P. 2007. "Subprime credit-card offers soar; Home equity drained; Offers to sub-prime clients up 41% in U.S. in first six months." *National Post's Financial Post & FP Investing* (Canada), October 10. National Edition, p. FP3.

Mumford, D. B., and A. M. Whitehouse. 1991. "Sociocultural correlates of eating disorders among Asian school girls in Bradford." *British Journal of Psychiatry* 158: 222–28. And in *The International Journal of Eating Disorders* 1992: 173–84.

Myers, David. 2000. "The funds, friends, and faith of happy people." *American Psychologist* 55: 56–67.

Nadler, J. 2005. "Flouting the law." *Texas Law Review* 83: 1399–441.

Nadler, J., and M. Rose. 2003. "Victim impact testimony and the psychology of punishment." *Cornell Law Review* 88: 419–56.

National Academy of Sciences. 2005. *Science and Technology in the National Interest: Ensuring the Best Presidential and Federal Advisory Committee Science and Technology Appointments.* Washington, D.C.: National Academies Press.

National Center for Health Statistics. 2006. "Life expectancy at birth, at 65 years of age, and at 75 years of age, by race and sex: United States, selected years 1900–2004," November. Retrieved February 26, 2008, from the Centers for Disease Control and Prevention Web site: http://www.cdc.gov/nchs/data/hus/hus06.pdf#027.

———. 2007. "Deaths, percent of total deaths, and death rates for the 15 leading causes of death: US and each state, 2004," April 11. Retrieved February 26, 2008, from the Centers for Disease Control and Prevention Web site: http://www.cdc.gov/nchs/data/dvs/LCWK9__2004.pdf.

National Highway Traffic Safety Administration. 2004. "Traffic safety facts: Motorcycle helmet use laws," April. Retrieved February 26, 2008, from the NHTSA
Web site: http://www.nhtsa.dot.gov/people/injury/new-fact-sheet03/Motor
cycleHelmet.pdf.

————. National Center for Statistics and Analysis. 2005. "Traffic safety facts:
2004 data," December 7. Retrieved February 26, 2008, from the NHTSA
Web site: http://www-nrd.nhtsa.dot.gov/Pubs/809908.pdf.

National Immunization Survey. 2004a. "Estimated vaccination coverage with
individual vaccines and selected vaccination series among children 19–35
months of age by state and Immunization Action Plan area—US, National
Immunization Survey, 2004." Retrieved February 26, 2008 from the Centers for Disease Control and Prevention Web site: http://www2a.cdc.gov/
nip/coverage/nis/nis_iap.asp?fmt=v&rpt=tab02_antigen_iap&qtr=Q1/
2004-Q4/2004.

————. 2004b. "Estimated vaccination coverage with individual vaccines and
selected vaccination series among children 19–35 months of age living below the poverty level by state and Immunization Action Plan area—US, National Immunization Survey, 2004." Retrieved February 26, 2008, from the
Centers for Disease Control and Prevention Web site: http://www2a.cdc.
gov/nip/coverage/nis/nis_iap.asp?fmt=v&rpt=tab14_pov_iap&qtr=Q1/
2004-Q4/2004.

National Institutes of Health. 1997. "Interventions to prevent HIV risk behaviors,"
February 11–13. Retrieved February 26, 2008, from the National Institutes of
Health Web site: http://consensus.nih.gov/1997/1997PreventHIVRisk104html.
htm.

National Park Service. 2007. "Historic preservation tax incentives," October 26.
Retrieved November 15, 2007, from the U.S. Department of the Interior
National Park Service Web site: http://www.nps.gov/history/hps/tps/tax/.

National Public Radio. 2001. "Poverty in America." Kaiser Family Foundation,
and Kennedy School of Government. Retrieved February 26, 2008, from the
National Public Radio Web site: http://www.npr.org/programs/specials/poll/
poverty/.

————. 2004. "Interview with Commissioner of the Maryland Board of Parole,"
January 5. All Things Considered.

————. 2007. "Interview with Jim King, Scotts Vice President of Corporate
Communications," March 4. Weekend Edition Sunday. Retrieved February
26, 2008, from the National Public Radio Web site: http://www.npr.org/
templates/story/story.php?storyId=7706152.

National School Safety Center. "Report on School Associated Violent Death."
In-House Report of the National School Safety Center, Westlake Village, Calif.
Retrieved February 27, 2008, from http://www.schoolsafety.us/pubfiles
/savd.pdf.

National Science Foundation, Division of Science Resources Statistics. 2005a.

"Federal obligations for research, by top agency funders: FY 2003-2005," November 16. Retrieved February 26, 2008, from the National Science Foundation Web site: http://www.nsf.gov/statistics/infbrief/nsf06300/table 3.gif.

———. 2005b. "Federal support for R&D and R&D plant projected at $110 Billion in FY 2005," November 16. Retrieved February 26, 2008, from the National Science Foundation Web site: http://www.nsf.gov/statistics/infbrief/nsf06300/nsf06300.pdf.

———. 2006. "Preliminary federal obligations for research, by agency and field of science and engineering: FY 2005," May 10. Retrieved February 26, 2008, from the National Science Foundation Web site: http://www.nsf.gov/statistics/nsf06313/pdf/tab22.pdf.

———. 2006b, May 10. Federal obligations for applied research, by detailed field of science and engineering: FY 1984–94. Retrieved February 26, 2008, from the National Science Foundation Web site: http://www.nsf.gov/statistics/nsf06313/pdf/tab126.pdf.

———. 2006c. "Federal obligations for applied research, by detailed field of science and engineering: FY 1995–2005," May 10. Retrieved February 26, 2008, from the National Science Foundation Web site: http://www.nsf.gov/statistics/nsf06313/pdf/tab127.pdf.

Naughton, J. M., and A. Clymer. 2006. "Gerald Ford, 38th President, Dies at 93." *New York Times,* December 27, p. 1. Retrieved February 26, 2008, from: http://www.nytimes.com/2006/12/27/washington/27webford.html?pagewanted=1&_r=1&adxnnl=1&adxnnlx=1204016667-x7krvVCdi0AaHSzr3Xlqsw.

Nelson, D., and R. Baumgarte, 2004. "Cross-cultural misunderstandings reduce empathic responding. *Journal of Applied Social Psychology* 34(2): 391–401.

Neufville, R. de. 1994. "The baggage system at Denver: Prospects and lessons." *Journal of Air Transport Management* 1, no. 4 (December 1994): 239–46.

———. 1999. "Airport privatization: Issues for the United States." *Safety, Economic, Environmental, and Technical Issues in Air Transportation.* Transportation Research Record 1662, Paper 99.0218, pp. 24–31.

Neumayer, E. 2005. "Unequal access to foreign spaces: How states use visa restrictions to regulate mobility in a globalised world." *Labor and Demography*.

New Jersey State Parole Board. 2005. Annual Report. Chairman J. D'Amico. Retrieved February 26, 2008 at http://www.state.nj.us/parole/docs/reports/AnnualReport05.pdf.

Newman, B. 1997. "Apple turnover: Dutch are invading JFK arrivals building and none too soon—U.S.'s best-known airport has been a lousy place to land, walk or stand—Using flies to help fliers." *Wall Street Journal,* May 13.

Newman, O. 1972. *Defensible Space: Crime Prevention Through Urban Design.* New York: Macmillan.

Nichols, S., and J. Knobe. 2007. "Moral responsibility and determinism: The cognitive science of folk intuitions. *Nous* 41: 663–85.

Nietzsche, F. 1998 [1889]. *Twilight of the Idols, or How to Philosophize with a Hammer*. New York: Oxford University Press.

Nisbett, R. 2003. *The Geography of Thought*. New York: Free Press.

Nisbett, R., ed. 1993. *Rules for Reasoning*. Hillsdale, N.J.: Erlbaum.

Nisbett, R., and L. Ross. 1980. *Human Inference: Strategies and Shortcomings of Social Judgment*. Englewood Cliffs, N.J.: Prentice-Hall.

Nisbett, R., and T. Wilson. 1977. Telling more than we can know: Verbal reports on mental processes. *Psychological Review* 84, no. 3: 231–59.

Northcraft, G., and M. Neale. 1987. "Experts, amateurs, and real estate: An anchoring-and-adjustment perspective on property pricing decisions." *Organizational Behavior and Human Decision Processes* 39, no. 1 (February): 84–97.

Nozick, R. 1974. *Anarchy, State, and Utopia*. New York: Basic Books.

Oskamp, S. 1965. Overconfidence in case study judgments. *Journal of Consulting Psychology* 63: 81–97.

Oster, E. F., and R. T. Jensen. 2007. "The power of TV: Cable television and women's status in India," August. NBER Working Paper No. W13305. Retrieved February 26, 2008, from the Social Science Research Network: http://ssrn.com/abstract=1005907.

Papile, L. 2001. "The Apgar score in the 21st century." *New England Journal of Medicine* 344, no. 7 (February 15): 519–20.

Paul, R. 1998. "Prohibiting the expenditure of federal funds for distribution of needles or syringes for hypodermic injection of illegal drugs." Delivered before Congress on April 29. Congressional Record. Retrieved February 26, 2008, from the U.S. House of Representatives Web site: http://www.house.gov/paul/congrec/congrec98/cr042998a.htm.

Peterson, R. 2005. "The neuroscience of investing: fMRI of the reward system." *Brain Research Bulletin* 67: 391–97.

Pettit, P. 1997. *Republicanism: A Theory of Freedom and Government*. Oxford: Oxford University Press.

Phillips, D. P., J. R. Jarvinen, and R. R. Phillips. 2005. "A spike in fatal medication errors at the beginning of each month." *Pharmacotherapy* 25, no. 1: 1–9.

Piattelli-Palmarini, M. 1994. *Inevitable Illusions: How Mistakes of Reason Rule Our Minds*. New York: John Wiley and Sons.

Plambeck, J. A. 1996a. "The fuel industry: Natural gas and petroleum." *Intute Sciences,* July 15. Retrieved February 26, 2008, from the *Intute Sciences* Web site: http://www.intute.ac.uk/sciences/reference/plambeck/chem1/p01264a.htm.

———. 1996b. "The fuel industry: Wood, coal, and domestic gas." *Intute Sciences,* July 15. Retrieved February 26, 2008, from the *Intute Sciences* Web site: http://www.intute.ac.uk/sciences/reference/plambeck/chem1/p01264a. htm.

Plous, S. 1993. *The Psychology of Judgment and Decision-Making*. New York: McGraw-Hill.

Pogge, T. 2002. *World Poverty and Human Rights*. Cambridge: Polity.

Preston, S., and F. de Waal. 2002. "Empathy: Its ultimate and proximate bases." *Behavioral and Brain Sciences* 25: 1–72.

Putnam, R. 2000. *Bowling Alone: The Collapse and Revival of American Community*. New York: Simon and Schuster.

Quinn, J. M., and W. Wood. 2005. *Habits Across the Lifespan*. Unpublished manuscript, Duke University.

Quinsey, V. L., G. T. Harris, M. E. Rice, and C. A. Cormier. 1998. *Violent Offenders: Appraising and Managing Risk*. Washington, D.C.: American Psychological Association.

Rachlinski, J. 1998. "A positive psychological theory of judging in hindsight." *University of Chicago Law Review* 65: 571–625.

Rainbolt, G. 1989. "Prescription drug laws: Justified hard paternalism." *Bioethics* 3: 45–58.

Ramachandran, V. S. 2006. "Mirror neurons and the brain in the vat." *Edge: The Third Culture,* June 19. Retrieved February 26, 2008, from the *Edge: The Third Culture* Web site: http://www.edge.org/3rd_culture/ramachandran06/ramachandran06_index.html.

Rasinski, K. 1989. "The effect of question-wording on public support for government spending." *Public Opinion Quarterly* 53: 388–94.

Rawls, J. 1971. *A Theory of Justice*. Cambridge, Mass.: Harvard/Belknap.

———. 1993. *Political Liberalism*. New York: Columbia University Press.

———. 1971/1999. *A Theory of Justice. Revised Edition*, Oxford/New York: Oxford University Press.

Rector, R. 1992. "The paradox of poverty: How we spent $3.5 trillion without changing the poverty rate." The Heritage Foundation. Retrieved February 26, 2008, from the Heritage Foundation Web site: http://www.heritage.org/Research/Welfare/upload/100202_1.pdf.

Reeves, F. 2002. "The psychology of accounting fraud." *Pittsburgh Post-Gazette* (citing research by Don Moore, Max Baxerman, and George Loewenstein), December 11. Retrieved February 26, 2008, from the *Pittsburgh Post-Gazette* Web site: http://www.post-gazette.com/businessnews/20021211moorep2.asp.

Ritov, I., and J. Baron. 1990. "Reluctance to vaccinate: Omission bias and ambiguity." *Journal of Behavioral Decision-Making* 3: 263–77.

———. 1992. "Status-quo and omission bias." *Journal of Risk and Uncertainty* 5: 49–61.

Rizzolatti, G., L. Fogassi, and V. Gallese. 2000. "Cortical mechanisms subserving object grasping and action recognition: A new view on the cortical motor functions." In M. Gazzaniga, ed., *The New Cognitive Neurosciences* (2nd edition). Cambridge, Mass.: MIT Press, pp. 539–52.

Roese, N. 2005. *If Only: How to Turn Regret into Opportunity*. New York: Broadway Books/Random House.

Rose, B. 2008. "Employers experiment with tough get-healthy regimes." *Chicago Tribune*, February 10. Retrieved February 26, 2008, from the *Chicago Tribune* Web site: http://www.chicagotribune.com/business/chi-sun_health_0210feb10,0,1758041.story.

Rosenwald, M. S. 2007. "An economy of scales: Paying people to lose weight helps drop pounds and health-care costs," *Washington Post*, November 11. Retrieved November 15, 2007, from the *Washington Post* Web site: http://www.washingtonpost.com/wp-dyn/content/article/2007/11/10/AR2007111000074.html.

Rothman, A. J., and P. Salovey. 1997. "Shaping perceptions to motivate healthy behavior: The role of message framing." *Psychological Bulletin* 121, no. 1: 3–19.

St. John, A. 2007. "Payday loan interest rates capped at 36 percent," October 1. Retrieved February 26, 2008, from the National Public Radio Web site: http://www.npr.org/templates/story/story.php?storyId=14853904&ft=1&f=1001.

Salovey, P., and P. Williams-Piehota. 2004. "Field experiments in social psychology: Message framing and the promotion of health protective behaviors." *American Behavioral Scientist* 47: 488–505.

Samuelson, W., and R. Zeckhauser. 1988. "Status quo bias in decision-making." *Journal of Risk and Uncertainty* 1: 7–59.

Sapolsky, R. 1998. *Why Zebras Don't Get Ulcers*. San Francisco: W. H. Freeman.

Sass, T. R., and P. R. Zimmerman. 2000. "Motorcycle helmet laws and motorcyclist fatalities." *Journal of Regulatory Economics* 18, no. 3 (November): 195–215.

Scanlon, T. 1998. *What We Owe to Each Other*. Cambridge, Mass.: Belknap/Harvard.

Schelling, T. C. 1968. "The life you save may be your own." In S. B. Chase, Jr., ed., *Problems in Public Expenditure Analysis*, pp. 127–62. Washington, D.C.: Brookings Institution.

Schneider, G. 2002. "Some request voluntary bans: Process easier in other states." *Louisville Kentucky Courier-Journal*, December 24.

Schneider, T., P. Salovey, A. Apanovitch, J. Pizarro, D. McCarthy, J. Zullo, and A. J. Rothman. 2001. "The effects of message framing and ethnic targeting on mammography use among low-income women." *Health Psychology* 20: 256–66.

Schorow, S. 2007. "Economist critiques housing price predictions." *Techtalks* 51, no. 17 (February 14). Retrieved February 26, 2008, from the Massachusetts Institute of Technology Web site: http://web.mit.edu/newsoffice/2007/techtalk51-17.pdf.

Schroeder, S. 2007. "We can do better: Improving the health of the American people." *New England Journal of Medicine* 357: 1221–28.

Schwartz, B. 2004. *The Paradox of Choice: Why More Is Less.* New York: HarperCollins.

Schweder, R., M. Mahapatra, and J. Miller. 1990. "Culture and moral development." In J. Stigler, R. Schweder, and G. Herdt, eds., *Cultural Psychology: Essays on Comparative Human Development.* New York: Cambridge University Press, pp. 130–204.

Seiden, R. H. 1978. "Where are they now? A follow-up study of suicide attempters from the Golden Gate Bridge." *Suicide and Life-Threatening Behavior* 8, no. 4: 203–16.

Sen, A. 1981a. "Ingredients of famine analysis: Availability and entitlements." *Quarterly Journal of Economics* 95: 433–64. Reprinted in *Resources, Values, and Development.* Cambridge, Mass.: Harvard University Press, 1984, pp. 452–84.

———. 1981b. *Poverty and Famines: An Essay on Entitlement and Depression.* Oxford: Oxford. University Press.

Shafir, E., and R. Thaler. 2006. "Invest now, drink later, spend never: On the mental accounting of delayed consumption." *Journal of Economic Psychology* 27: 694–712.

Shah, A. 2006. "Poverty facts and stats." Retrieved February 26, 2008, from the Global Issues Web site: http://www.globalissues.org/TradeRelated/Facts.asp.

Shimizu, H. 2000. "Japanese cultural psychology and empathic understanding: Implications for academic and cultural psychology." *Ethos* 28, no. 2: 224–47.

Sigh Jr., J. W. 2004. "NASA spinoffs: Bringing space down to earth," February 2. Retrieved February 26, 2008, from the Space Place Web site: http://www.thespaceplace.com/nasa/spinoffs.html.

Simon, G. E., M. VonKorff, M. Piccinelli, C. Fullerton, and J. Ormel. 1999. "An international study of the relation between somatic symptoms and depression." *The New England Journal of Medicine* 341, no. 18: 1329–35.

Singer, P. 1997. "The drowning child and the expanding circle." *New Internationalist*, April 28–30.

———. 2002. *One World.* New Haven, Conn.: Yale University Press.

Skiba, P., and J. Tobacman. 2008. "Do Payday Loans Cause Bankruptcy?" Working paper, February.

Slovic, P. 2007. "'If I look at the mass I will never act': Psychic numbing and genocide." *Judgment and Decision Making* 2, no. 2: 79–95.

Slovic, P., and S. Lichtenstein. 1968. "The relative importance of probabilities and payoffs in risk-taking." *Journal of Experimental Psychology* 78: 1–18.

Small, D., and G. Loewenstein, 2003. Helping a victim or helping the victim: Altruism and identifiability. *The Journal of Risk and Uncertainty* 26, no. 1: 5–16.

Small, D., and G. Loewenstein. 2005. "The devil you know: The effects of identifiability on punitiveness." *Journal of Behavioral Decision Making* 18, no. 5: 311–18.

Small, D., G. Loewenstein, and P. Slovic. 2007. "Sympathy and callousness: The impact of deliberative thought on donations to identifiable and statistical victims." *Organizational Behavior and Human Decision Processes* 102, no. 2: 143–53.

Small, D., and J. S. Lerner. 2006. "Emotional policy: Personal sadness and anger shape policy judgements." *Political Psychology (Special Issue on Emotion in Politics)*.

Small, D., and U. Simonsohn. Forthcoming. "Friends of victims: Personal experience and prosocial behavior." *Journal of Consumer Research*.

Smith, A. 1776. *An Enquiry into the Nature and Causes of the Wealth of Nations*. London: Strahan and Cadell.

———. 1853. *The Theory of Moral Sentiments*. London: Henry G. Bohn.

Smith, P., and R. Curnow. 1966. "'Arousal hypothesis' and the effects of music on purchasing behavior." *Journal of Applied Psychology* 50, no. 3: 255–56.

Staub, P. K. 1993. "Avoiding medication errors in brand name selection," September 19. Retrieved February 26, 2008, from the U.S. Food and Drug Administration Web site: www.fda.gov/ohrms/dockets/AC/03/slides/4007 OPH1_01_Staub.ppt.

Stirman, S. W., and J. W. Pennebaker. 2001. "Word use in the poetry of suicidal and nonsuidcidal poets." *Psychosomatic Medicine* 63: 517–22.

Stotland, E. 1969. "Exploratory studies of empathy." In L. Berkowitz (ed.), *Advances in Experimental Social Psychology, Vol. 4*. New York: Academic Press, pp. 271–314.

Studdert, D. M., M. M. Mello, A. A. Gawande, T. K. Gandhi, A. Kachalia, C. Yoon, A. L. Puopolo, and T. A. Brennan. 2006. "Claims, errors, and compensation payments in medical malpractice litigation." *New England Journal of Medicine* 354, no. 19 (May 11): 2024–33.

Sunstein, C. 1993. *Democracy and the Problem of Free Speech*. New York: The Free Press.

———. 2004. *The Second Bill of Rights: FDR's Unfinished Revolution and Why We Need It More Than Ever*. New York: Basic Books.

———. 2005. "Moral heuristics." *Behavioral and Brain Sciences* 28: 531–42.

Sunstein, C., R. Hastie, R. Payne, D. Schkade, and W. Viscusi. 2002. *Punitive Damages: How Juries Decide*. Chicago: University of Chicago Press.

Texas Board of Pardons and Paroles. 2006. Owens, N. (Chair). Annual report 2005. May 30. Texas Department of Criminal Justice. Retrieved February 26, 2008, from the Texas Department of Criminal Justice Web site: http:// www.tdcj.state.tx.us/bpp/publications/AR%202005.pdf.

Texas Department of Public Safety. 1999. "Final 1998 motor vehicle traffic accident data." Retrieved February 26, 2008, from Texas Department of

Public Safety Web site: http://www.txdps.state.tx.us/director_staff/Public_information/final98.htm.

———. 2004. "Final 2001 motor vehicle traffic accident data." Retrieved April 5, 2008, from Texas Department of Public Safety Web site: http://www.txdps.state.tx.us/director_staff/public_information/pr020204.htm.

Thaler, R. 1999. "Mental accounting matters." *Journal of Behavioral Decision Making* 12: 183–206.

Thaler, R., and C. Sunstein. 2003. "Libertarian paternalism." *American Economic Review* 93, no. 2: 175–79

Thompson, S. 1999. "Illusions of control: How we overestimate our personal influence." *Current Directions in Psychological Science* 8, no. 6: 187–90.

Tocqueville, A. 1945 [1845 French edition]. *Democracy in America*. Philips Bradley, ed. New York: Knopf.

Todorov, A., A. Mandisodza, A. Goren, and C. Hall. 2005. "Inferences of competence from faces predict election outcomes." *Science*, June 10, 308, no. 5728: 1623–26.

Triandis, H. C. 1994. *Culture and Social Behavior*. New York: McGraw-Hill.

Trope, Y., and N. Liberman. 2003. "Temporal construal." *Psychological Review* 110: 403–21.

Trout, J. D. 1998. *Measuring the Intentional World: Realism, Naturalism, and Quantitative Methods in the Behavioral Sciences*. New York: Oxford University Press.

———. 2002. "Scientific explanation and the sense of understanding." *Philosophy of Science* 69, no. 2: 212–33.

———. 2005. "Paternalism and cognitive bias." *Law and Philosophy* 24, no. 4 (July): 393–434.

Trout, J. D. and S. Buttar. 2000. "Resurrecting 'death taxes': Inheritance, redistribution, and the science of happiness." *Journal of Law and Politics* 16, no. 4: 765–847.

Tversky, A., and D. Kahneman. 1974. "Judgment under uncertainty: Heuristics and biases." *Science* 185 (September): 1124–31.

Tversky, A., S. Sattath, and P. Slovic. 1988. "Contingent weighting in judgment and choice." *Psychological Review* 95, no. 3: 371–84.

UNICEF. 2005. "Child poverty in rich countries," Innocenti Report Card No. 6. UNICEF Innocenti Research Center, Florence, Italy.

Urinal Fly. Urinal Fly products page. 2008, February 11. Retrieved February 26, 2008 from the Urinal Fly Web site: http://www.urinalfly.com/category.cfm?category=1.

U.S. Census Bureau. 2007. "Statistical abstract of the United States," December 20. Retrieved February 26, 2008, from the U.S. Census Bureau Web site: http://www.census.gov/prod/www/statistical-abstract.html.

U.S. Food and Drug Administration. 2005. "Sec. 585.500 Mushrooms, canned or dried (freeze-dried or dehydrated)—Adulteration involving maggots, mites, decomposition (CPG 7114.13)," November 29. Retrieved February

26, 2008, from the U.S. Food and Drug Administration Web site: http://
www.fda.gov/ora/compliance_ref/cpg/cpgfod/cpg585-500.htm.

U.S. Office of Management and Budget. 2005. "Budget of the United States government for fiscal year 2006: Historical tables," February 23. Washington,
D.C.: U.S. Government Printing Office. Retrieved February 26, 2008, from
the White House Web site: http://www.whitehouse.gov/omb/budget/fy2006
/pdf/hist.pdf.

_____. 2006. "Outlays by function and subfunction 1940–2009." Re-
trieved February 26, 2008, from the White House Web site: http://www
.whitehouse.gov/omb/budget/fy2006/hist.html.

U.S. Office of National Drug Control Policy. 2004. "The economic costs of drug
abuse in the United States: 1992–2002," December. Retrieved February 26,
2008, from the White House Web site: http://whitehousedrugpolicy.gov/
publications/economic_costs.

U.S. Office of Tax Analysis. 2006. "A dynamic analysis of permanent extension
of the President's tax relief," July 25. Retrieved February 26, 2008, from the
U.S. Department of the Treasury Web site: http://www.treasury.gov/press/
releases/reports/treasurydynamicanalysisreporjjuly252006.pdf.

Van Boven, L. and G. Loewenstein. 2003. "Social projection of transient drive
states." *Personality and Social Psychology Bulletin* 29, no. 9: 1159–68.

Van Boven, L., G. Loewenstein, and D. Dunning. 2005. "The illusion of courage
in social predictions: Underestimating the impact of fear of embarrassment
on other people." *Organizational Behavior and Human Decision Processes* 96:
130–41.

Van der Horst, R., and W. Hoekstra. 1994. "Testing speed reduction designs for
80 kilometre per hour roads with simulator." *Transportation Research Record*
1464: 63–68.

Verplanken, B., and W. Wood. 2006. "Interventions to break and create consumer habits." *Journal of Public Policy and Marketing. Special Issue: Helping
Consumers Help Themselves: Improving the Quality of Judgments and Choices*
25, no. 1: 90–103.

Virginia Youth Violence Project, School of Education, University of Virginia. Retrieved February 26, 2008 at http://youthviolence.edschool.virginia.edu/vi-
olence-in-schools/school-shootings.html.

Walpole, M. 2003. "Socioeconomic status and college: How SES affects college
experiences and outcomes." *The Review of Higher Education* 27, no. 1:
45–73.

Walsh, M. E. et al. 2006. "Exclusion of sex offenders," Policy of the Massachusetts Parole Board, section V, subsection C, parole decision-making, working version.

Wansink, B. 2006. *Mindless Eating: Why We Eat More Than We Think.* New York:
Bantam-Dell.

Washington, E. "Female socialization: How daughters affect their legislator fathers' voting on women's issues." NBER Working Paper Number 11924.

Wegner, D. 2002. *The Illusion of Conscious Will*. Cambridge, Mass.: MIT Press.

Wegner, D., and R. Erber. 1992. "The hyperaccessibility of suppressed thoughts." *Journal of Personality and Social Psychology* 63, no. 6: 903–12.

Wells, G., A. Memon, and S. Penrod. 2006. "Eyewitness evidence: Improving its probative value." *Psychological Science in the Public Interest* 7, no. 2: 45–75.

Wilcox, B. 1987. "Pornography, social science, and politics: When research and ideology collide." *American Psychologist* 42, no. 10: 941–43.

Williams, C. 1989. "Empathy and burnout in male and female helping professionals." *Research in Nursing and Health* 12: 169–78.

Wilson, R. 2002. "Personal Exemptions and Individual Income Tax Rates, 1913–2002," June 26. Internal Revenue Service, Statistical Data Section. Retrieved February 26, 2008, from the Internal Revenue Service Web site: http://www.irs.gov/pub/irs-soi/02inpetr.pdf.

Wilson, T. 2002. *Strangers to Ourselves*. Cambridge, Mass.: Harvard University Press.

Wintemute, G. J., C. A. Parham, J. J. Beaumont, M. Wright, and C. Drake. 1999. "Mortality among recent purchasers of handguns." *New England Journal of Medicine* 341, no. 21 (November 18): 1583–89.

Wood, W., L. Tam, and M. Guerrero-Witt. 2005. "Changing circumstances, disrupting habits." *Journal of Personality and Social Psychology: Attitudes and Social Cognition* 88: 918–33.

Wood, W., J. M. Quinn, and D. A. Kashy. 2002. "Habits in everyday life: Thought, emotion, and action." *Journal of Personality and Social Psychology* 83, no. 6: 1281–97.

Wright, K. 2001. "Generosity vs. altruism: Philanthropy and charity in the United States and United Kingdom." *Voluntas: International Journal of Voluntary and Nonprofit Organizations* 12 (December 4): 399–416.

Zhong, C. B., and K. Lilienquist. 2006. "Washing away your sins: Threatened morality and physical cleansing." *Science* 313 (September 8): 1451–52.

Index